MW01247907

DISCOVERING LIFE'S PURPOSE

Discovering
LIFE'S PURPOSE
RE-EXAMINING *THE CLUB*

DEL H. SMITH
XULON PRESS

Xulon Press
2301 Lucien Way #415
Maitland, FL 32751
407.339.4217
www.xulonpress.com

© 2018 by Del H. Smith

© 2022 Second Edition

All rights reserved solely by the author. The author guarantees all contents are original and do not infringe upon the legal rights of any other person or work. No part of this book may be reproduced in any form without the permission of the author. The views expressed in this book are not necessarily those of the publisher.

Scripture quotations taken from the Holy Bible, English Standard Version (ESV®).Copyright © 2001 by Crossway Bibles, a publishing ministry of Good News Publishers. Used by permission.

Printed in the United States of America.

Paperback ISBN-13: 9781545612040
Ebook ISBN-13: 9781545639382

APPRAISALS

I s life's purpose pre-determined? This book takes the position it is. If so, we must *discover* it rather than develop our own purpose. But how? A process called *Experiential Learning* led the author to *his* discovery of life's purpose. Whatever your own conclusions, I'm confident you will find what you read about *Experiential Learning* thought-provoking.

Dr. Robert E. Johnson, Professor, Royal Military College
Kingston, Ontario, Canada

I am sure nothing is more important for each of us than discovering life's purpose. For me, life's purpose is pretty clearly stated by Jesus Christ. However, I find most people need more than religious teachings. The author is one of these people. He discovered life's purpose by applying *Experiential Learning*. This book illustrates *Experiential Learning*, provides you a template to use in applying it and gives you an example of how you might apply it by tracing the author's personal adventure. It's an adventure I highly recommend to you.

Fr. Dan Kubala, Pastor, St. Matthew Parish
Aventura, Florida, USA

Many Christians of all denominations are troubled by their inability to prove the existence of God, the Bible is God's Word, the divinity of Jesus and other articles of their faith. Lacking the time and background to research such questions, their doubts persist. This book provides a fresh approach to answering these critical questions of faith. The author's personal journey can be a guide to yours. His research, logic, compelling evidence and excellent step by step building of the case for his own passionate beliefs are inspiring. His engaging writing style and colloquial language make this book an enjoyable and easy read.

Jim Johnson, Founder, Farmington Leasing Limited
Agincourt, Ontario, Canada

Studies show about 2% of Church members are fervent and committed to achieving deeper intimacy with their God. What are the rest of us missing? Is there a hole in our hearts – a longing for "something more"? As I started to mend that hole I felt God's acceptance and unconditional love. As a *cradle* Roman Catholic, I found this book addressed the accountability and rewards I encountered on my journey towards becoming a *fervent* Catholic. I recommend it as a source of the connection and peace I find as I continue that journey.

Wayne Rays, Founder, Marble Renewal of Toronto
Richmond Hill, Ontario, Canada

DEDICATION

To my wife, Marcelle Carmen Kipp-Smith, and my late wife, Margaret Jean (Peggy) Gillis, both of whose patient listening, discipline, example, counsel and support have immensely enriched my *Experiential Learning* to date.

To my children, Sean Anthony, Robert Alan and Tracy Anne, whose lives and thinking inspired this book and whose pieces of glass will, one day, enrich my ongoing *Experiential Learning*.

ACKNOWLEDGEMENTS

I am deeply indebted to many of my friends and family whose thoughtful commentary on earlier drafts of this book's Prologue, Introduction and back cover content has enriched the book's appeal.

I am most indebted to those dedicated friends who comprehensively edited pre-publication manuscripts. These include Fr. Ricardo Davis, Simon Irving, Jim Johnson, Robert Johnson, Fr. Dan Kubala, David Male, Wayne Rays, Laura Smith and Don Spearin. Their many suggestions have immeasurably helped organize, clarify and simplify my thinking.

Cover Art: Tracy Anne Smith

Author Photo: JoAnne Robbins-Smith

Contents

PROLOGUE

This is the story of what became the most important journey of my life. I was raised in a loving home – the first born of a non-believing mother and an agnostic father. My mother's non-belief plagued her and led her to send her children to Church.

There, I quickly learned what was expected of me. I was to be quiet and not fidget. As I grew, I met other children and some of them became good friends. Church had become a social outlet. When my family moved, I left my friends and the Church behind.

As a young adult, I began to learn more about the Church. Most of what I learned didn't make sense to me. I looked for reasons to accept Church teaching and found none. I decided there *were* none. I realized I had become an atheist. I became puzzled as to why people I liked and respected appeared to go along with the Church. They could give me no satisfying answers. My resistance hardened. I was thankful I had avoided being duped.

In my 20's, I met two Roman Catholics. One became my best friend and the other, my late wife. Neither could substantiate their faith but both were still strongly committed to it. Faith without substantiation intrigued me. I respected both highly and enjoyed discussing religion with them but came to no conclusions that satisfied me.

However, my respect for them caused me to question my rejection of religion. I realized if I were right and they were wrong, there were no bad consequences for any of us. However, if they were right and I was wrong, I was on thin ice. I decided I had better explore religion more seriously.

I was wary of dogma unsupported by reason. I sought reason and found it very difficult to find. My dogged persistence finally uncovered sufficient reason to lead to my acceptance. I came to the conclusion Christianity was more likely than not to be true. I converted to Roman Catholicism.

I was a dedicated, but unfulfilled Roman Catholic. Although my conversion was sound, I remained dissatisfied. The more I thought about my faith, the more I realized I didn't *know* any of it. I participated "religiously" but realized I was merely going through the motions. As I became more involved in my marriage and raising our family, I put religion and life's purpose out of my mind. I remained a lukewarm Roman Catholic.

As an empty-nester, my skepticism led me to pursue how I could *know* what I claimed to believe. I discovered a way independent of religious teaching. I was able to develop sound and supported knowledge that the fundamental Christian teachings are true. This changed everything. I began to take my pursuit of life's purpose very seriously.

However, as I re-examined religion, my skepticism led me to question everything. I questioned the validity of the Bible. I questioned whether Christ was the Son of God. I questioned whether the New Testament accurately presented His teachings. I questioned much of the Roman Catholic Catechism. I questioned how one could actually *love* God. I questioned why I should love bad people. I questioned Christ's miracles and, especially, the Eucharist.

Pursuit of these questions directed my journey. Their answers led me to my *knowledge* of life's purpose and a better understanding of it. It has been the most important journey of my life. I share it with you in the hope that your reflection on it will enrich your journey and *your* knowledge of life's purpose.

INTRODUCTION

Discovering our purpose may just be life's most important quest. Despite this, few have the necessary time and resources to devote to its pursuit. We are so busy putting one foot in front of the other that we forget to look up and see where we are going. This book presents to you, in a few evenings read, the results of a decade and a half of research into the discovery of life's purpose.

What is *The Club* and what does it have to do with discovering life's purpose?

The Club is, of course, the (multi-denominational) Christian Church. Its founder, Jesus Christ, established its tenets and guidelines but never wrote them down. He taught them but left the interpretation of His teachings up to fallible humans. As a result, *The Club* charter, known as the Bible, contains gems of wisdom alongside obvious contradictions. After His death, *The Club* was formed and an (unavoidably fallible) human leader was appointed. It grew, slowly at first but at an increasing pace. Its problems came with its growth. Groups of its members disagreed with its leader and formed separate denominations or religions. Each denomination leader fallibly interpreted *The Club* charter differently. Each denomination established a growing number of clubhouses throughout the world. Again, problems came with growth. Fallible local leaders in one community interpreted their denomination's religion differently than their peers.

To its credit, *The Club*, unlike many others, is non-exclusive. It welcomes non-members to its meetings. It encourages them to participate in as many or as few of its activities, and as often or as seldom, as they like. Its activities provide food for thought and a nourishing sense of community. However, the question remains, why accept the welcome of an institution whose human failings are so evident?

No single institution on Earth has more thoroughly studied life's purpose than *The Club*. Consequently, it is a most valuable resource for discovering life's purpose. One does not need to accept its teachings to benefit from them. One need only re-examine (or, for a growing number of people, examine) them. Questioning them is far more beneficial than ignoring them. This book provides a way to re-examine its teachings independent of *The Club*. This way is *Experiential Learning*[1].

Experiential Learning is simply learning from life experience. You use *your* life experiences as a means to re-examine and evaluate assertions, ideas and beliefs. This book shows you how to get the most out of *Experiential Learning*. It will give you a better understanding of it by tracing my experience with it.

You need not be a member of *The Club* to benefit from my experience. A growing number of you know next to nothing about it. For the first third of my life I was, like you, a non-member. My upbringing provided me no connection with it. I shared many of your objections.

If you are a past member of *The Club* you may still benefit from my experience. Like you, my early examination of it turned me away. I found nothing to support its claim that our creator loves us. Lacking evidence, I concluded it was as likely as not that our creation was a diversion abandoned by our creator, or simply its source of the type of amusement we experience watching Survivor. I became an atheist.

Whether you are a non- or past member, if you follow my journey, you will likely discover things you hadn't thought about. Even if you still have doubts at the end, I think you'll find the journey was worthwhile.

You may be a loyal (or a lapsed) member who finds *The Club* leaves you wanting. You may realize you are merely going through the motions (or have stopped going through them altogether). You may wish it could deliver what it promises. PARTS THREE through SEVEN may deliver much of what you are wanting. They may lead you to a more intimate relationship with your creator. PARTS ONE and TWO will help you understand why some (or in many cases all) of your loved ones have rejected *The Club*.

You may be familiar with Pascal's Wager[2]. Pascal posited we all bet our eternal lives on our acceptance or rejection of Christian teaching in

---

[1]   My adaptation of *Experiential Learning* is based on the model developed by Dr. David A. Kolb. He describes his model in a book of the same name – Kolb, David A. *Experiential Learning*. Upper Saddle River, NJ: Prentice Hall Inc., 1984

[2]   Blaise Pascal (1623–62) was a French mathematician, physicist, inventor, writer and philosopher.

that, if we live as if it were true and it turns out to have been false, we lose little and benefit from having lived a good life. Conversely, if we reject it and it turns out to have been true, we lose the unimaginable good our creator wants for us. Hence, Pascal concluded we should all live our lives as if Christianity were correct that our *creator's* purpose – that we choose to become like Him – is life's purpose.

Would you agree with Pascal that, by considering (and even acting on) this possibility, you wouldn't really be losing anything, even if your consideration eventually leads you to a rejection of Christian teaching?

Joining me in this, you will explore some very interesting questions and new ways of thinking about them.

- Are *any* of atheism's arguments that no God exists sound?
- Can we *know* our creator loves us and offers us an eternity of love?
- Is there any support for the Church's position the Bible is the Word of God?
- Is there any support for the Church's position Jesus Christ is the Son of God?
- What did Christ mean by loving God with *all* your heart, mind, soul and strength?
- Does Christ's insistence that we love our enemies make any sense?
- Is there any support for the Bible's claim that Jesus' miracles were real?

One last thought before we begin. My daughter recently shared with me a quote from Rumi.

> The truth was a mirror in the hands of God. It fell and broke into pieces. Everybody took a piece of it and they looked at it and thought they had the truth.

As I ruminated (pun intended) on this quote, I couldn't help thinking how great it would be if we each shared our piece of glass with one another. We could work together to fit the pieces back together. The more progress we made, the more truth would emerge. Given enough time, we might eventually finish and *all* know life's purpose.

What follows is my piece of glass. I'll begin with what *led* to my active pursuit of *Experiential Learning*.

PART ONE

EARLY EXPERIENTIAL LEARNING

CHAPTER 1

CHILDHOOD EXPERIENCES

One of my early memories is of walking on Sunday mornings with my brother about a dozen city blocks to Trinity United Church in my childhood home of Peterborough, Ontario. We didn't think much about the fact our parents did not accompany us. Like most kids, we just did what we were told. Well, we actually did a few things we weren't told as well.

Our mother always prepared an offering envelope for us. The envelope had two separate pockets, one for the church itself and one for the missions. Each pocket contained a bit of small change. As the older brother, I was in charge of the envelope. Each Sunday, as we walked along, I opened both pockets of the envelope to see how much money they contained. I told my brother we would take about half of it and visit the candy store on the way back from church. He accepted his older brother's authority. If either pocket contained a quarter, we had to stop at the candy store on the way *to* church in order to exchange it for smaller coins to split between the church and the candy store. I don't believe I ever told my mother we did this.

After a couple of years of success with this initiative, I became aware of two reasons why our parents did not accompany us to church. The reason I first discovered was that our father had returned from five years in the army during WWII. Sunday mornings, alone without us, were opportunities for some intimacy, which fate had long denied them. Over the years, I discovered a more profound reason. Neither my mother nor my father were believers. From time to time my mother would share with me the fact she wished with all her heart she could believe, but she could

3

not overcome her persistent doubts. At one point my father told me he was an agnostic and how this differed from being an atheist.

As a result of their non-belief, none of us children had any religious training in the home. In fact, there was almost no religious discussion in our home. The exception to this was our Christmas dinner. In preparation my mother would highlight several Bible passages in Matthew and Luke, which describe Christ's birth. Before the meal began, the Bible was passed around the table so each of us could read a part of the story.

It was only later in life I discovered how important the prominence of belief in the home can be to the formation of faith. However, to this day, I am unsure what difference it would have made to *my* belief journey had there been a strong faith foundation. I say this because, despite its importance to those who *have* inherited a strong faith, most of the people I know who were taught faith in their childhood have since rejected it.

At one point, it was time for me to be confirmed. I know I must have been baptized to be a candidate for confirmation, but I don't know when. It is an indication of the importance baptism had had for me that I either never asked about it or forgot the answer.

I don't remember going through much preparation for confirmation in the United Church of Canada. I remember having to learn the Apostle's Creed and realizing I would have to state my belief in it. I can remember having no problem with this. I'm pretty sure I looked at it as somewhat similar to being taught the pledge of allegiance to the King of England in Grade School. The King of England was about as remote as was Jesus Christ. Although I pledged allegiance like all my classmates, I never took it seriously. It never occurred to me I would ever have to do anything about what I pledged. Likewise I never took the Apostle's Creed seriously or thought it would make any difference in my life.

In my mid-teens, my family moved to St. Catharines, Ontario and I abandoned my connection with the United Church of Canada. I made new friends, explored new interests and ignored religion. I never thought about life's purpose. I had participated in *Club* activities without learning anything about *The Club*.

CHAPTER 2

ADULT EXPERIENCES

If in our teens we think we know everything, early in a university experience we *know* we have life figured out and how life works. At least, this was the case for me during my years at McMaster University in Hamilton, Ontario.

In my first year of study in Mechanical Engineering I was obliged to select an Arts course to complement my engineering curriculum. Looking at the alternatives, I selected *Comparative Religion* as it involved few if any assignments and the year-end examination promised to be undemanding. Unexpectedly, I found it interesting. It supported my suspicion Christianity wasn't the only route to salvation (whatever that might entail).

It also caused me to re-examine the Apostle's Creed and my confirmation. I soon realized I had no good reason for claiming belief in almost any part of the Apostle's Creed. I had come to accept the validity of the scientific method and the discipline of not accepting any hypothesis as true until it could be proven. I was trained to reject any position arrived at simply by belief, intuition or faith. I decided any position taken without proof was unscientific, unreliable and subject to error. I decided to apply the scientific method to a determination of whether or not what I had claimed as my belief could be proven.

It didn't take long for me to conclude *none* of what I had claimed to be my belief could be proven. A possible exception was there must have been a creator to create everything I and everyone else experience. Until it could be scientifically proven something could create itself, it logically followed everything must have been created by a creator. However, I could find nothing to prove that creator was what we claim to be God.

I could not even find anything to prove that creator still existed, let alone that it retained any interest in us or that it loved us. If I couldn't establish God exists, the rest of the Apostle's Creed was meaningless and could not be taken seriously. The scientific method could not be used to prove any of it. If the scientific method could not establish it, what could?

I realized a lot of people claim the Bible establishes God exists, loves us and wants us to live in eternal intimacy with Him. However, the more I exposed myself to the contents of the Bible, the less faith I had in it as a source of anything credible.

Beginning with its first two pages, it claimed God created the world and everything in it in six days. Meanwhile science had proven the universe was created by the *Big Bang* approximately 13.8 billion years ago and all life descended from an organism, called the last universal ancestor (LUA), which first existed about 3.5 billion years ago.

Equally incredible was its recording of miracles such as the Flood, the Parting of the Red Sea and the Resurrection as well as countless healings. I remain unaware of any scientific proof of a miracle. At that early stage of *Experiential Learning*, I felt the Bible's claim they occurred was unsubstantiated. As a result, equally unsubstantiated was the Christian claim that miracles prove God's existence.

Finally the Bible portrays God as vengeful, wrathful and punishing in the Old Testament and loving, merciful and forgiving in the New Testament. Although the most glaring, this is only one of the many inconsistencies and contradictions of which the Bible is full.[3]

My conclusion was the Bible completely lacked credibility and thus it could not support a belief in God.

I also briefly considered whether Church teaching could support a belief in God. However, time after time, I discovered there was no reasoning behind many Church teachings. The Church simply *claimed* its teachings were true. To support its claims, it relied on the Bible (which I had already discounted) or tradition (which simply meant we've said it was true as long as we can remember so it's still true).

I felt the Church's claim of moral authority was even harder to swallow. Until the 20th century, the Roman Catholic Church colluded with monarchs to maintain serfdom. It instigated the selling of indulgences and sucked up what little money the peasantry had in order to enrich its clergy and feed their egos with castle-like cathedrals and rectories. Well into the 20th century, it strongly discouraged its faithful from reading the

---

[3]   In Chapters 14 and 15 I'll expand on this observation.

Bible and forming their own opinions. Throughout history, religion has been the frequent instigator of wars and atrocities such as the crusades and the inquisition.

My conclusion was the Church could not support a belief in God.

Finally, I turned to believers. What I found was believers in my acquaintance were not even mildly interested in pursuing a reason for their belief in God. Assuming most had no substantiation for their belief, I concluded their belief was groundless. I decided it must be the product of wishful thinking. After all, it is a comfort to be told and to accept God loves you, you will never die and you will live in bliss with Him forever in heaven (the existence of which was equally unsubstantiated).

I adopted atheism and the position life's purpose is earthly fulfillment.

At this point, I did not realize I had begun *Experiential Learning*. I also did not realize I had only *just* begun.

As I said in the *Introduction*, *Experiential Learning* is simply learning from life experience. Its power comes from its three simple stages. The first involves *Perception* – how *well* we see *everything* of substance that we encounter. We need to miss nothing of importance. The second involves *Process* – how well we internalize everything we encounter.

Perception Experiences
Process Learnings
Knowledge of Life's Purpose

We need to learn how to learn. The third involves *Knowledge* of life's purpose. *Process* learnings produce knowledge and, often over time, corrections to that knowledge. Even though *all* knowledge is subject to correction, the knowledge we gain from *Experiential Learning* is the best that is available to us because it is supported by facts and rationale. We must not put off *acting* on this knowledge simply because it might someday be corrected.

How well was I doing at this early stage of *Experiential Learning*? Looking at my template, I believe you can see I was not doing very well at all.

I had refused to accept anything as knowledge that I could not prove. I focused solely on the scientific method. I ignored or discounted any *Perception* experiences that

Perception Experiences	Scientific method
Process Learnings	There is no proof God exists
	Atheism makes sense
Knowledge of Life's Purpose	Earthly fulfillment

didn't pass the test of proof. As a result, my thinking led me to the *Process* learnings there is no proof God exists and atheism makes sense. I became an atheist and accepted my *Knowledge* that life's purpose was earthly fulfillment. I had explored far too few life experiences. I had stubbornly refused to examine *The Club*.

CHAPTER 3

INITIAL EXPERIENTIAL LEARNING

Despite the knowledge of life's purpose to which my *Process* learnings had led me, I couldn't get over the fact that many of my generation claimed to believe in God. I came to question my conclusion their belief was groundless. Could that many people all be wrong? I felt the need to re-examine the position I had settled upon. I decided I would take every opportunity to *challenge* believers to substantiate what they believed. I convinced myself the reason I did this was I honestly wanted to learn what I had been missing. Since then, I've admitted the real reason. I sought the ego satisfaction of proving them wrong and myself right.

In my first year at McMaster University, I discovered I had fallen into the perfect immersion opportunity. My roommate at university was a Roman Catholic. As such, he was a strange animal to me. I had known no Roman Catholics in Peterborough, which at the time of my childhood was a bigoted bastion of religious animosity. As kids, when we saw a priest calling at a Roman Catholic home in our neighbourhood, we *knew* he was pestering them for more money. Fights would break out at football games between the students of the Roman Catholic high school and those of the public high school. Most Protestants did not befriend Roman Catholics.

However, I was no longer in Peterborough. I was in university. This Roman Catholic was different. He quickly became one of my best friends and impressed me as a sound thinker. I did find it strange he would walk to church every Sunday morning and he had joined the Newman (Catholic Student) Society on campus. However, I had discovered an opportunity. I decided to take every chance to exploit this fortuitous development.

On many nights, when we were tired of doing assignments, I would interrupt him to pursue some aspect of his faith. I would get him to describe that aspect to me. I would then ask him to substantiate his belief. He would give me a reason and I would challenge it. When our discussion on that point reached the stage where I was convinced I had refuted his thinking and he had tired of defending it, I would ask him to give me another reason for his belief. This pattern would continue well into the early hours of the morning until I was satisfied I had refuted every reason he could come up with. When I asked him if he had any other arguments to substantiate his belief he simply said, "Because that's what I believe." He ignored my protests that it was unreasonable of him to simply *claim* belief when we had invested so much time in pursuing its substantiation.

I continued to convince myself his faith, like all faith, was groundless. However, I retained a nagging doubt. I was impressed by the fact that so intelligent a person could not be shaken from his belief. I was amazed his belief was so important to him that he would interrupt his Sunday morning preparation for a critical exam to devote a couple of hours to Mass. I was surprised he would devote so much of his scarce time to the Newman Society.

At the end of our third year at McMaster, our positions remained unchanged. He could give me no proof of the soundness of his belief and I could not shake him from his commitment to it. I needed a new opportunity and one fell into my lap. It didn't take long before I became deeply immersed in this new opportunity.

Shortly after I arrived at my summer job at Dow Chemical in Sarnia, I met a couple who invited me to join them for a Sunday picnic and offered to arrange a blind date. My first sight of my blind date was of Peggy descending the staircase in her apartment. This vision has been emblazoned on my mind ever since. I fell madly in love on the spot. I fell deeper and deeper in love that Sunday afternoon as we talked together for hours thanks to the discretion of our hosts. Although I quickly realized my love was unrequited, I pursued her relentlessly throughout the summer. We became good friends but that was not enough for me. Sadly, I had to be satisfied with that for some time.

As she too was a Roman Catholic, I went to Mass with Peggy every Sunday during that summer and we often discussed religion. I realized she was at least as steeped in her faith as was my roommate. She was also a sound and independent thinker. She was an excellent listener and led me to believe she was genuinely interested in my thinking. Our friendship survived the summer and the fearful parting at the start of my final year at McMaster. She accepted a job at St. Joseph's Hospital in Toronto and I accepted a job in Toronto at IBM Canada Ltd. upon graduation. Over the next two years, she would flip back and forth between deciding maybe she loved me and deciding she didn't. In the latter periods I continued to court her and we eventually were married. Early in the preceding two years Peggy once told me, if we ever decided to marry, she would not insist I become a Roman Catholic. This was a generous commitment on her part as "mixed marriages" were strongly discouraged by the Church at that time and her parents would have had a very difficult time accepting her decision. I was impressed with the strength of her will.

CHAPTER 4

STAGE ONE: ACCEPTING THE POSSIBILITY

W hile I struggled with our on again/off again love affair, I began to more aggressively question my rejection of belief in God. There were two reasons for this. The strongest reason was I had met a second person whose intelligence and faith impressed me. Of course she had had an even greater impact on me than had my roommate. The second reason was I had discovered and become greatly influenced by *Pascal's Wager*[4].

As I mentioned in the *Introduction*, Blaise Pascal (1623–62) posited humans all bet with their lives either God exists or not. He concluded, given the possibility God actually does exist and assuming an infinite gain or loss associated with belief or unbelief in said God (as represented by an eternity in heaven or hell), a rational person should live as though God exists and seek to believe in God. If God does not actually exist, such a person will have had only a finite loss (some pleasures, luxury and so on).

This thinking had a profound effect on me. I realized the fact *I* could not find a proof God exists was not a proof He did *not*. I had to *accept the possibility* the God of religion did exist. I was far from believing it but I had to *accept the possibility*.

I found Pascal to be astute. Unless I could be absolutely sure God did not exist there was at least a small chance He did. Even though the likelihood God exists might be small, the risk to me was huge. If an all-powerful, all-knowing God, who could provide me eternal life in heaven, did exist, I risked all by not pursuing that eternal life. I decided to follow Pascal's advice. I decided I should live as though God exists and seek to believe in God. I should seek to believe by whatever means I could find.

---

4   http://www.biography.com/people/blaise-pascal-9434176

As I had begun my re-examination of atheism with two Roman Catholics whom I highly respected, it was natural for me to turn to the Roman Catholic Church to seek to believe in God.

Having moved to Toronto, I learned of the existence of what was then known as the *Catholic Information Centre* located north of Bloor Street, not far from the fraternity house where I boarded. It offered instruction in Roman Catholicism for people interested in determining if they wanted to convert (much as the institutionalized RCIA program does today). It consisted of weekly lectures followed by an opportunity for one-on-one mentoring. I was fortunate enough to have a young seminarian assigned as my mentor.

I retained my skepticism during the lecture sessions, looking for the frequent instances of dogma being pronounced either without supporting rationale or for which the supporting rationale was weak or flawed in my opinion. However, in our one-on-one sessions following the lectures, my mentor patiently heard me out. He listened non-judgementally to my objections and patiently pursued each of them for as long as it took for me to be satisfied. One by one, my objections began to fall away. However, I had so many objections it took the whole length of the course to resolve them.

The toughest objection, and the one I felt could never be resolved, was the doctrine of *Papal Infallibility*. No matter how much of the Roman Catholic Catechism I was able to accept, I could never accept it all. If I had to accept it was infallible in order to be confirmed as a Roman Catholic, my confirmation was never going to happen. My seminarian mentor successfully resolved this last objection as you'll see below.

To my surprise, I was relieved it was resolved. I realized I was impressed with the Roman Catholic Catechism even though I still disagreed with a significant amount of it. I realized I *wanted* to convert. I wanted to become a Roman Catholic. I found the Roman Catholic Church to be much sounder than others to which I had been exposed to this point.

How did the issue of *Papal Infallibility* get resolved? My seminarian mentor explained to me *Papal Infallibility* applies only to the handful of issues where the Pope explicitly states he is speaking *ex-cathedra*. Only on these issues is he claiming to be infallible. The rest of the Roman Catholic Catechism is believed by the Church to be revealed by the Holy Spirit and thus to be absolute truth. Roman Catholics are compelled to reject none of it, especially publicly, but are allowed to question any parts of it in a personal and private way. However, and this was the crucial point for me,

Roman Catholics are *not* required to accept what they are conscientiously questioning.

They *are* required to accept, without qualification, the handful of issues where the Pope claims infallibility. When I explored what these issues were, I was relieved to learn none of them were difficult for me to accept. They were either, in my opinion, *more likely than not* to be true or they did not matter to me one way or the other. Those I found were *more likely than not* to be true were the first five: 1) Christ has both a divine and a human nature; 2) Christ has both a divine and a human will; 3) a person worthy of heaven at the time of death would immediately go there rather than waiting until the final judgement and two others condemning Jansenism as heretical. Jansenism asserts God's role in the infusion of grace is such that it cannot be resisted and does not require human assent. The Catholic doctrine is "God's free initiative demands our free response" – the gift of grace requires human assent. The two that did not matter to me one way or the other were: 1) the doctrine of the Immaculate Conception (that Mary was conceived by normal biological means, but her soul was made immaculate by God at the time of her conception) and 2) the doctrine of the Assumption of Mary into heaven (that the Virgin Mary ". . . having completed the course of her earthly life, was assumed body and soul into heavenly glory.") How did I come to accept these several aspects of *Papal Infallibility*?

CHAPTER 5

STAGE TWO: MORE LIKELY THAN NOT

I had come to the point of accepting it was *more likely than not* Jesus was the Son of God. I realized I could not be *certain* whether or not He was. However, it was the *likelihood* He was that led me to accept the doctrine of *Papal Infallibility*.

As the Son of God, Christ must have had a divine and human nature and will. It made sense to me that a person can reach heaven as soon as they are judged worthy and that God's gift of grace requires human assent. I had no reason to believe or disbelieve Mary was 1) made immaculate at the time of her conception and 2) assumed body and soul into heaven. I decided the absence of my disbelief counted as my belief. Having resolved the issue of *Papal Infallibility*, I was ready to convert to Roman Catholicism and to be confirmed in the Roman Catholic Church.

All that remained for me to do was to revisit the Apostle's Creed and confirm to myself I did completely accept it. I decided my criterion for acceptance of it or any other teaching would be that it was *more likely than not* to be true. To some, this might seem a bit weak, but we're talking about belief here. I could see one could never scientifically *prove* any of the components of the Apostle's Creed. Because it could not be scientifically proven, I felt it would have to be accepted or rejected based solely on likelihood. So this is how I looked at the controversial components of the Apostle's Creed one by one:

"I believe in God the Father, creator of heaven and Earth" – I had already accepted a creator. I now felt the beauty and bounty of His creation made it *more likely than not* He loves us (like a Father).

"... and in Jesus Christ, His only Son, our Lord, who was conceived by the Holy Spirit" – This seemed likely to me for three reasons: 1) I felt our creator would *want* us to voluntarily accept Him; 2) Most of us would remain unable to accept Him until He had come to us in human form; 3) Our creator is unquestionably *capable* of conceiving a human Son.

"On the third day, He arose again" – The apostles' eye witness testimony and sustained conviction under severe persecution made me feel it was *more likely than not* the resurrection was real. As well, I thought our creator *needed* to resurrect His Son in order to show us eternal life.

"I believe in the Holy Spirit" – I decided our creator would give us the "Holy Spirit" to reveal Himself to us after Christ was no longer with us. As well, He would make the existence of the "Holy Spirit" unprovable so our acceptance of Him would be voluntary rather than forced.

"... the Holy Catholic Church" – I had determined the Roman Catholic Church was the best founded of any Church I knew.

"... the communion of saints" – Although I could not be certain of the *existence* of heaven or of purgatory (a place for the deceased to *prepare* themselves for heaven), I felt it *more likely than not* the saints (if they are in heaven) would have the power to communicate with the living and those in purgatory.

"... the forgiveness of sins" – It seemed likely our creator would not deny us forgiveness.

"... the resurrection of the body" – Like the Assumption of Mary, I had no reason not to believe in the resurrection of the body.

"... and in life everlasting" – I thought it likely, having created us, our creator would not abandon us at death. If purgatory exists, we would continue to live there as long as it took for us to prepare ourselves for eternal life in heaven.

I realised I had come to accept it was *more likely than not* the God portrayed by Christianity *did* exist. I felt this qualified as belief. It was certainly a step up from merely *accepting the possibility*.

So, as you can see, I took this confirmation a lot more seriously than I did my teenage confirmation. I had decided I must be able to state my belief without qualification if I were to be confirmed. I was ready.

Looking at my template, you can see my *Experiential Learning* had taken a great leap forward. I had been led to see the folly of ignoring (shaded) *Perception* experiences of substance. My best friend and late wife had led me to consider that life's purpose might be more than earthly

Perception Experiences	Scientific method	My best friend
		My late wife
		Pascal's Wager
		The Catholic Information Centre
		My seminarian mentor
		Bits of the RC Catechism
Process Learnings	There is no proof God exists	I must accept the *possibility* God exists
	Atheism makes sense	The Church establishes a *likelihood* God exists
		The Apostle's Creed is *more likely than not* to be true
Knowledge of Life's Purpose	Earthly fulfillment	Live according to Church teaching

fulfillment. Pascal's Wager added urgency to this consideration. The Catholic Information Centre, my seminarian mentor and my introduction to the Roman Catholic Catechism had enabled my examination of *The Club*'s teachings.

Perception led to new (shaded) *Process* learnings. I realized the lack of proof God exists is not proof He doesn't. I had to *accept the possibility* that God exists. As I pursued this possibility, I came to conclude that Church teaching establishes the *likelihood* God exists. The final crack in my atheism, and my *Knowledge* that life's purpose is earthly fulfillment, was my conclusion the Apostle's Creed was *more likely than not* to be true. Although I felt at this point I had fully examined *The Club*, I would soon discover I had given it far too little examination.

The most valuable part of my *Experiential Learning*, to this point, was that my *Process* learnings had *corrected* my *Knowledge* of life's purpose. I concluded life's purpose is to live according to Church teaching.

Experiential Learning enables us to *correct* our knowledge of life's purpose as well as to *establish* or *confirm* it. Our knowledge at any point in life is the best at which we can then arrive. However, like all human knowledge, it requires correction whenever *Perception* experiences and *Process* learnings lead to that correction, as they had at this point. My examination of *The Club* had already paid dividends. My continuing examination of *The Club* would do so as well.

CHAPTER 6

EARLY FAITH EXPERIENCES

O n the day of my confirmation, my mother and father attended and gave me a rosary. Shortly thereafter I married Peggy, the woman who had insisted I did not need to become a Roman Catholic as a condition of marrying her.

We took seriously the obligation of participating in Mass on Sundays and Holy Days and I especially valued that discipline. I needed discipline and found it lacking in Protestant churches. However, I saw its value as being my gift to God rather than as a source of any benefit to me. My mind wandered regularly during the readings and the homily. I took the sacraments with a grain of salt. I did not feel the body of Christ in the Eucharist. I attended Mass every Sunday and Holy Day willingly, but as a duty rather than as an act of love.

Before long, I began to feel my confirmation had been too easy. Something was missing. Although I had freely and sincerely accepted life's purpose is *more likely than not* to live according to Church teaching, I had to admit to myself that I didn't *know* it was life's purpose. I was uncertain *how* more likely it was – how likely it might be that what I had accepted was *not* the case.

I was aware most Roman Catholics accept their Church's teaching based on faith alone. It doesn't seem to matter to them that they don't (and think they can't) *know* the fundamentals of their faith.

For me, the fact I *didn't* know them made me very uneasy. If what I had accepted was truly life's purpose, I had no choice but to devote my life to fulfilling it. However, I couldn't devote myself fully to a life's purpose that I didn't *know* was the case. Instead, I was simply doing what

I understood to be what I was supposed to do. I was simply going through the motions.

At this point, I had not realized there was anything I could do about this. It took considerably more *Experiential Learning* for me to realize I *could* do something about it. It will take considerably more reading for you to learn *what* I discovered I could do about it. For now, however, I had to accept this troubling situation in which I found myself.

Not long after we were married, we were blessed with the births of two sons and a daughter. Peggy interrupted her nursing career while they were pre-schoolers and we moved every year or two as I pursued my career at IBM Canada Ltd. As the world became more demanding, I took a couple of decades' time out from *Experiential Learning*. This was not a good decision. I now realize if I had made even a little time to continue *Experiential Learning*, I would have experienced additional energy and wisdom to apply to my career and family. That additional energy and wisdom came too late. Naiveté took its place.

Peggy and I naively thought it our duty to give our children the early faith experience, which was ours. She had experienced Roman Catholicism since birth and I was now well into *my* early faith experience. It is commonly held that converts are the most fervent Catholics. So we both had reason to feel it was right to try to instill our faith experience in our children. As well, the Church taught us it was our duty to do so.

We insisted they go to Mass with us each Sunday and Holy Day. For Peggy, it was so they would benefit from the Roman Catholic upbringing that had been hers. For me, it was so they would benefit from the religious upbringing I never had. Despite our best intentions, our insistence hardened their resistance to the teaching and discipline of the Roman Catholic Church.

For Peggy, this was heart-breaking as she felt she had failed in her duty to instill her faith in her children. For me, I thought they, in revolting, were simply going through an experience similar to my own early revolt and it would similarly be only temporary. What I failed to realize was my revolt was *my* choice whereas their revolt was against *our* choice that we had imposed on them as an obligation.

Throughout their adult years, I tried to compensate. I tried to engage my children in religious discussion to no avail. I had missed the opportunity in their formative years. They informed me it is considered rude to bring up the topic of religion in conversation. It is disrespectful of the other's right of privacy. As I approach old age, I still hope to learn what their beliefs are. I feel, by forcing my faith experience on them, I turned them off and led them to mistrust my attempts to engage them in open conversation. My failure to communicate with them about what I believe to be the most important thing in life is my greatest parental failure. Peggy and I had snuffed out what might have been *their* early faith experiences.

Meanwhile, my continuing examination of *The Club* took on a new dimension.

CHAPTER 7

EARLY LOVE EXPERIENCES

At some point in my *Experiential Learning* journey, I was exposed to the concept of agape love. As you may know, agape is selfless, sacrificial, unconditional love, an act of will, the highest type of love. As was my reaction to most foreign concepts, once I thought I understood the definition, I moved on. I pursued it no further. It didn't seem like love to me. The love I had experienced to that point was the love of my parents, triggered by my dependency, the love of my wife, triggered by my attraction to her and the love of my children, triggered by my fatherhood. Everyone else in my life was simply someone I liked, someone I disliked or someone I ignored.

If I had pursued the concept of agape a bit more, several things would have become obvious to me. If the highest type of love is selfless and unconditional, it must be the type of love a perfect being has for us. This conclusion is supported by the realization that, for God to love those of us who reject or ignore Him, His love for us *must* be selfless and unconditional. Might He want us to love Him as He loves us? Might He want us to develop the capacity of selfless and unconditional love?

However, at the time, none of this had occurred to me. I had no idea my failure to explore the concept of agape had been such an important missed opportunity. My next *Perception* experiences corrected this. They led me to several occasions of agape love.

Christ in Others Retreat

One day, when our elder son was in his mid-teens, a school friend dropped by to invite him to participate in a youth retreat called COR (Christ in

Others Retreat). He politely declined but she was more persistent than he. Peggy and I were both surprised and pleased he had agreed to participate. At the same time, we needed to know more about COR before trusting it with our son.

We learned its purpose was to enable teenagers to experience Christ in others and in themselves. Participants would *feel* Christ in others in the love shown them by the COR team, their parents (in absentia) and fellow retreatants. Participants would discover they could *be* Christ for others through both reaching out to the institutionalized and learning to love fellow retreatants. The COR activities focused on both aspects.

We decided we should participate to better understand the experience our son would be going through. The couple running the retreat was introduced as the retreat "mother" and "father". Volunteers, like us, were introduced as "co-parents".

I concluded we had made a big mistake minutes after the retreat started. We learned we would be sleeping on gym mats together with the participants, separated from each other in male and female quarters. During the welcome, co-parents and retreatants sat in a circle on the floor in the dark. After pedantic introductions, participants were encouraged to share their most troubling feelings. This seemed to drag on for hours. When we finally retired, I realized it had only *felt* like hours.

Fortunately, the pace quickened throughout the following day. In small group sessions, retreatants felt more and more comfortable unburdening themselves of their difficult teenage pressures, anxieties and hurts. After reconvening, a sharing helped them realize they were not alone. They felt increasingly accepted. They began to bond and to care for each other.

That afternoon a field trip was organized. Small groups of participants visited nursing homes, hospital wards or assisted-living facilities where they were encouraged to reach out to the residents. After the field trip, they shared how they felt while visiting people who were largely alone in the world. It became clear they had begun to realize others needed love as much as they did. They began to focus more on others and less on themselves.

While all this was going on, the "back office", populated by prior years' retreatants, was working hard behind the scenes. They had devoted their weekend to the new participants. Out of sight, they would prepare and cleanup dining and meeting rooms. In their spare time, they would each write personal letters to as many retreatants as they chose, expressing their agape love for them, their empathy with them and their emotional support. Retreatants' parents were each encouraged to write a love letter to their child as well. A packet of love letters was prepared for each retreatant.

Before dinner, the participants were given their packet and encouraged to go off alone to read their letters. Co-parents sat with anyone who seemed to need emotional support. I saw a young girl in tears and wondered how I would handle an intervention. Despite a lack of confidence in prayer, I still prayed God would help me succeed. I sat down beside her quietly and after a few moments asked her how she felt. She said she had no idea her parents loved her. She said no one had ever told her they loved her.

As I sat with her, I felt a strong love for her even though she was a complete stranger. I felt her need for my presence and love. I thought I felt God's presence, having concluded it was the only thing that could be making me somewhat effective in something so foreign to my experience. I was ashamed of the boredom and impatience I had felt for the first few hours of the retreat and of how I had dismissed all the tentative sharing that first evening. I felt a strong conviction to never again pre-judge others' expressions of their feelings.

I realized how much this girl needed love and to know she was not alone. Dozens of participants had similar feelings. I realized I had experienced an initial small taste of selfless love. I made a commitment to myself to never again be too busy or distracted to spend the time to love another. I was far from loving God, but I had made a start at selflessly loving others. Most importantly for me, I was finally and surprisingly being guided partly by my heart rather than solely by my mind.

Participation House

My next opportunity to selflessly love occurred shortly after the retreat ended. I decided to visit a resident I had met on my COR group's field trip. We had visited *Participation House*, an assisted-living residence. The resident I chose to visit suffered from cerebral palsy.

On my first visit, he was in a wheel chair, which he moved by slapping at a joy stick, having little control over his limbs and none over his fingers. He drooled as he tried to articulate words. Although he was friendly, his limited control over his tongue meant I couldn't understand a word he said. I felt completely incapable of dealing with the situation in which I found myself. I was uncomfortable and looked for the earliest opportunity to extract myself from his room. I finally hit on the idea of leaving with a promise to return. Safely out of the room, I realized I had simply committed myself to the same experience all over again. Looking back at all the "I"s in these last five sentences, I am reminded I had not only been failing in selfless love. I had been completely caught up in how things affected *me*.

Some days later, determined to progress in selflessness, I made a return visit. I learned his name was Alf Saltarelli. I learned he was not only friendly, but also positive. He exhibited absolutely no self-pity. I disciplined myself to do my utmost to understand a bit of what he tried to say to me. He would patiently repeat a single sentence over and over again until I finally understood. In each subsequent visit, I could understand a bit more and became more comfortable with him. He took me on a tour of his residence, unselfconsciously slamming his wheelchair into whatever he could not avoid.

He showed me his IBM Selectric typewriter on which he told me he was writing a book. "As if!" I thought. He demonstrated. Beside the typewriter was a mouthpiece at the end of a stick standing in an empty water glass. The keyboard of the typewriter was covered with clear plastic wrap. He extracted the mouthpiece and, bending over the keyboard, drooled on it as he pressed the keys with the stick. He backspaced frequently to correct and managed a short sentence in a few minutes of effort. A few years later, he gave me a copy of the autobiography he had had published.

Over the weeks and months my feelings went from discomfort with him, to admiration of him, to a love of him. My trepidation in anticipation of each visit faded away once I was with him. The visits themselves were less and less difficult and more and more rewarding. I realized selfless love is an act of will. It does not depend upon attraction. I could will a selfless and unconditional love of this person. I was beginning to suspect my eternal life was dependent upon me learning to selflessly love. I was gradually learning to use my heart as well as my mind. However, I was still not loving God.

Marriage Encounter

My first experience of feeling the glimmers of love for God came unexpectedly. Peggy and I had heard about a couples' retreat called *Marriage Encounter* but had put off participating until we were invited by my sister and her husband to a session they facilitated. My characteristic skepticism was triggered as we spent the first evening sharing introductions and expectations seated on the floor in a circle in a candle-lit room. The highlight of this first evening was my discovery of the double bed that we shared for the weekend.

Next morning we were given a thirty-minute individual assignment to list all the things we loved about our spouses. I was worried my wife's list would be longer than mine. Next, couples shared their lists with each other. I noted a tear as my wife read my list. I felt a deep love for her and felt her love for me. I was as overwhelmed by bringing top of mind the things I loved about Peggy as I was by luxuriating in the realization of the things she loved about me. We felt we had fallen in love all over again.

That afternoon, we were given a second thirty-minute individual assignment to list all the things for which we thanked God. Next we met as a small-group and consolidated our individual lists onto a single flip chart. Finally, the small-group leaders consolidated their group's list with the others' onto a single set of flip charts containing the input of all retreatants. The consolidated list contained fifty-one things for which we thanked God. Peggy and I captured the flip charts on our camera.

As we reflected on the list, we both realized we were experiencing the same thing we had experienced before lunch. Before lunch we had been given the opportunity to think without interruption about everything we loved about each other. It had made us *feel* that love. It had made that feeling of love stronger. Now we were looking at a list of fifty-one things to love about God. As well, that same list was evidence of how much God loved all of us. We had a strong feeling that same process, of thinking without interruption about everything we had to thank God for, could help us *feel* our love for God. It could make that feeling of love stronger. We could fall in love with God.

Following the retreat, we realized our act of sharing our lists with each other had opened lines of communication that had been snuffed out by the distractions of day-to-day living. I began calling my wife from work at least once a day and looking forward to her calls no matter what situations I was dealing with. The more we felt our love for each other, the more we focused our attention on each other. The more we focused our attention on each other, the more we felt our love for each other.

We concluded this same virtuous circle might help us grow a feeling of love for God.

By now my *Perception* set included my best friend, my wife, the Catholic Information Centre, my seminarian mentor, bits of the Roman Catholic Catechism, COR, Participation House and Marriage Encounter. However, my *Perception* set would have to expand further to answer the additional questions that my re-examination of my atheism produced.

Nagging Questions

I had fallen in love with God, but I did not *actively* love God. All Christian churches teach that the first and foremost commandment is to love God with all our heart, with all our soul, with all our mind and with all our strength.

How could I actively love God if I couldn't communicate with God? I did not believe in prayer or in the people who said they felt they were in communication with God when they prayed. I certainly had never heard God speak to me. I thought those who claimed they did were simply kidding themselves.

Why would God even *want* me to actively love Him? It seemed to me an all-powerful, all-knowing God would need nothing from me. What unfulfilled need could He possibly have that would be fulfilled by my love?

Besides *feeling* a love for Him, what could I do to *actively* love Him? How could I actively love a God I couldn't see, hear, feel or touch?

Why would a God that wanted my love keep Himself so remote from me when He was unquestionably capable of allowing me to sense His presence?

Despite all the progress I felt I had made, I was left with more questions than answers. In the absence of an active love of God, I soon lost my *feeling* of being in love with Him. Maybe that was it. Maybe it was simply a feeling. Maybe it wasn't real. I soon largely forgot about it.

Little did I realize then that *Experiential Learning* would one day enable me to *actively* love God by not taking Him for granted, by thanking Him daily for everything I experience, by taking every opportunity to get to know God better and by focusing on God as much of each day as I was able.

However, at this point, none of this could take place. It could not happen until the support for my belief grew beyond being *more likely than not* to be true. It would take a lot more *Experiential Learning* for this growth to occur. Examination of *The Club* is not quickly accomplished.

CHAPTER 8

ACTIVE PURSUIT OF BELIEF

I n my mid 40's, I accepted a position as an IBM Account Manager, sharing responsibility for, what was then, one of the big five Canadian banks. My position gave me the luxury of some flexibility over my daily schedule and the opportunity to delegate much of what needed to be done to the professionals on my sales team.

One day, on the way to my office, as I passed my church I realized I didn't have anything pressing for the first hour of my day. On impulse I turned into the parking lot to attend Daily Mass. This was a first for me. I discovered the weekday Mass was considerably shorter than Masses on Sundays and Holy Days of Obligation. I realized there was no reason why I couldn't make a regular practice of Daily Mass. Although I still had not gotten any benefit out of the Mass and still attended as a duty to God, I thought if I went more frequently than weekly maybe I would be performing my duty even better.

As I sat in the pew during my first Daily Mass, I noticed there were, not unexpectedly, far fewer people in attendance than there were on Sundays. What *was* unexpected was my feeling of being a lot more at peace than on Sundays. There was far less going on around me to distract me and cause my mind to start to wander. I thought about the readings and listened to the short homily. I was surprised to find that one or two points made an impact on me. I realized, for a few minutes, I actually thought about what I was experiencing in the Mass rather than about everything else that was going on at home, at the office and at the bank. However, my attention began to wander as the preparations for the Eucharist began. Almost immediately I started thinking about what I would be doing when the Mass was over.

Later that day, I reflected I had indeed gotten a little bit out of my participation in the Mass. The one or two points that struck me during the readings and homily stayed with me for a short time. I decided it would be worth my while to make a regular practice of Daily Mass whenever I could.

Before long, it was the odd exception when I missed Daily Mass. I felt I got a lot more out of it than the half hour or so I dedicated to it. The benefit I felt was exclusively the result of the readings and the homily. Of course they were not all earth-shattering but most days I continued to notice a point or two that resonated with me. When I reflected on all the time I had spent in business seminars, conferences and symposiums, I was reminded that if I had taken away only a few ideas out of the hours or days each session lasted, I had felt it had been worth my time. Mass was at least equal in benefit per time invested.

However, I continued to get virtually nothing out of the sacraments. I looked for ideas, not repetitive prayers. I thought the Eucharist was a symbolic act and its repetition day after day did nothing for me. I was certain the wafer and wine were not the body and blood of Jesus Christ. I found it strange that what the Church maintained was the climax of the Mass was the least beneficial part of it for me. However, I decided it didn't matter as long as I was able to take away one or two points for reflection most days. That alone was well worth my time.

Sometime later I learned that the daily readings, over a three-year period, cover the *entirety* of the four Gospels. I found this to be quite a revelation. Over the past three years, every passage in all four Gospels had been read to me, and commented upon in the homily, with minimal outside distraction. I began to realize what a rich experience this was.

Much of what I heard in the Gospel readings started to have an impact on my thinking. However, my natural skepticism kept leading me to question whether the Gospels were really the Word of God. Of course, if Jesus were the Son of God and if the Gospels quoted Him correctly, their content was the Word of God and beyond question. However, I couldn't lose two feelings.

Firstly, it seemed to me it was at least *somewhat* likely Jesus was *not* the Son of God. Secondly, it seemed to me it was possible some of the Gospel content had been altered over the centuries (intentionally or not) and thus no longer reports accurately what Jesus said.

Besides the teachings of the Church, what else supported the conviction Jesus was the Son of God and the Gospels accurately reported what He said? I left this unanswered question behind and moved on in *Experiential Learning*. I continued my examination of *The Club*.

CHAPTER 9

SECOND CAREER

In my early 50's, my employer began downsizing and offered incentives to retire. Although I was approaching my 30th anniversary with IBM Canada, I was initially devastated. I clearly wasn't ready to retire. What would I do with my life for what might well be the next 30 or 40 years? I couldn't maintain my life style on a pension that was a little over half of my current compensation package. I enjoyed my job at IBM Canada and had recently been given the opportunity to be part of its new offering, management consulting. I didn't want to sell for a competitor. I knew nothing about entrepreneurship. I initially decided to turn down the package. However, I soon realized that if I continued to work it would be for "50% dollars", as I would be giving up my monthly pension for each month I worked. I decided it made financial sense to retire. With fear in my heart, I took the leap at 52 years of age.

Fortunately, I was able to build a management consulting practice to supplement my pension. I established a home office, which made it easier to pursue personal interests in parallel with consulting contracts. As well, it left me considerable amounts of free (if worrisome) time between contracts, which meant I could pursue those interests further.

My next *Perception* experience was reading C.S. Lewis' *Mere Christianity*[5] written in the mid-20th century. It presents a unique and convincing (at least to me) argument God exists, Christ is the Son of God and God dislikes sin (rather than the sinner). Sin includes everything we do against the will of God. Lewis concluded we need to do our utmost to discern and accomplish the will of God. He had been an atheist and

---

[5] Lewis, C.S. *Mere Christianity*. NY: Harper Collins, 1952

called himself "the most dejected and reluctant convert in all England . . . kicking, struggling, resentful and darting his eyes in every direction for a chance to escape."

The strength of Lewis' argument and the clarity of its presentation made a major impact on me. It strengthened my tentative acceptance Jesus was the Son of God and that what He said in the Gospels is *more likely than not* to be the Word of God. Although I still didn't *know* any of this, the stronger my acceptance became, the more I realized I needed to make a far more extensive study of the Gospels.

I found an attractive, leather-bound Bible[6] that highlighted the quotations of Jesus in red. The good news was this enabled me to easily focus on what the four Gospels quoted Jesus as saying without having to read all the intervening narrative.

The bad news was Jesus is quoted hundreds of times in the four Gospels. I found I was unable to connect the quotations on any specific subject in a way that permitted me to determine what His *message* on that subject was. I needed a way to see all the quotations on any one subject in one place.

Fortuitously, I found a way to do this, which I describe in PART TWO. There, you'll read how it led me to an extensive *re*-examination of *The Club* and a second correction of my knowledge of life's purpose.

---

[6] *The Holy Bible – English Standard Version*. Wheaton, Illinois: Crossway Bibles, 2001

Perception Experiences	Scientific method	My best friend
		My late wife
		Pascal's Wager
		The Catholic Information Centre
		My seminarian mentor
		Bits of the RC Catechism
		COR
		Participation House
		Marriage Encounter
		Daily Mass
		A bit of the Bible
		C.S. Lewis' *Mere Christianity*
Process Learnings	There is no proof God exists	I must accept the *possibility* God exists
	Atheism makes sense	The Church establishes a *likelihood* God exists
		The Apostle's Creed is *more likely than not* to be true
		I am *capable* of selfless love of others
		I am *capable* of selfless love of God
		The Gospels *likely* deliver God's Word
		I *knew* none of the above
Knowledge of Life's Purpose	Earthly fulfillment	Live according to Church teaching

In the meantime, looking at my evolving template, you can see how my latest (shaded) *Perception* experiences led to *Process* learnings.

COR, Participation House and Marriage Encounter had produced the *Process* learnings I am capable of selfless love of God and others.

Daily Mass, its exposure to a bit of the Bible and C.S. Lewis' *Mere Christianity* produced the *Process* learning the Gospels likely deliver God's Word.

Sadly the *Knowledge* they confirmed, that life's purpose was to live according to Church teaching, was based solely on likelihood. I still didn't *really* know it.

Earlier (as discussed in Chapters 3-5) *Experiential Learning* had *corrected* my previously established knowledge life's purpose was earthly fulfillment. Now it was *confirming* my corrected knowledge life's purpose is to live according to Church teaching.

That *Experiential Learning* can either correct or confirm knowledge it has previously established makes it a very valuable tool. We'll continue to see this valuable aspect as we continue the journey.

So far my examination of *The Club* had come up short. To strengthen my knowledge of life's purpose, I had to undertake a *re*-examination of *The Club*.

Because I had determined the Gospels likely deliver God's Word, it made sense to begin with an examination of them.

PART TWO

ACTIVE EXPERIENTIAL LEARNING

CHAPTER 10

THE GOSPELS

The first step of my examination of the Gospels was to explore how to determine what they present as Jesus' message on each of the many topics He addressed. I came up with an idea that intrigued me. If I were to assign a topic name to each of Jesus' almost-400 quotations, I could extract all the quotations on any single topic and study that topic separately. As well, if I could determine the relative importance of each topic, I could focus my attention on the most important topic first. Once I had thoroughly digested the message on that topic, I could work on the message of each of the remaining topics in the order of their importance.

But how was I to identify the relative importance of the topics Jesus addressed? It seemed to me the *number* of times Jesus referred to a topic might be a good criterion of its importance. The *length* of His discourse on a topic seemed to be a reasonable indicator as well. Now I should warn you this pursuit led to a part of my *Experiential Learning* that is admittedly a little bizarre.

I imagined an Excel spreadsheet with a *topic* column, a *quote-text* column, a *book/chapter/verse* column and a *# of words* column. I could copy the *quote-text* and the *book/chapter/verse* from each Bible passage into the spread sheet. I could assign a *topic* to each passage and sort the spreadsheet by topic. Excel could calculate the *# of words* in each passage. However, copying the text of hundreds of passages would have required an awful lot of keying.

My discovery of another valuable tool solved this problem. I searched the Internet for online bibles and found one I liked called *Logos Bible*

Software[7]. It presents the full content of many versions of the Bible including the one I had just acquired. Among its many functions is the simple capacity to enter a *book/chapter/verse* search criterion and instantly call up the passage. A simple copy and paste of each passage's *book/chapter/verse* and *quote-text* made the population of the spreadsheet fast and error-free.

Once the spreadsheet was fully populated and sorted, Excel could calculate, for each topic, its total *# of quotes* and total *# of words*.

From this, I could produce a second (much smaller) spreadsheet with a *topic* column, a *# of words* column and a *# of quotes* column. Sorting this spreadsheet twice would produce respectively a *words rank* and a *quotes rank*. Finally, sorting the spreadsheet by the sum of both ranks would produce a *topic rank*. You can see an example of the results of this process in *Figure 1* on the last two pages of this book's Appendix, which is entitled *THE SAYINGS OF JESUS*[8].

I'm sure you will now be thinking this is just the sort of approach one would expect of a computer nerd. It is admittedly a bit subjective in the assignment of a topic to a quote. The *topic-importance* ranking can also be questioned as it is a simplistic sum of the *# of words* and the *# of quotes* rankings. However, despite these limitations, adding the *topic rank* to the first spreadsheet and sorting it by *topic rank* accomplished everything I needed. It assembled everything Jesus was quoted as having said on each topic, from the most important topic down to the least important topic.

Looking at each of the most important topics one at a time was a powerful experience for me. The quotes on each topic supported each other, elaborated upon each other and reinforced each other. The overall message of each topic came through loud and clear. It was difficult to minimize the importance of what Jesus was reported to have said when so much of it was so concisely presented for one's consideration.

I was so impressed with the impact this process made on me, I next considered how I could share that impact with others. I decided to capture the eleven most important topics in a fictional account of an atheist being exposed to one of the eleven messages each day through his encounters with a mysterious stranger occupying a bench on his morning jogging route. I titled the book *The Journey*.

---

[7] https://www.logos.com/

[8] A full description of *Figure 1* is presented in the last chapter of *THE SAYINGS OF JESUS*.

The process of editing *The Journey* presented me with new *Perception* experiences, which so intrigued me that I never published the book. I took a timeout from my study of Jesus' sayings. However, much later in *Experiential Learning*, my study would resume, become more extensive and lead to my writing of another book, *THE SAYINGS OF JESUS*[9]. You'll read about this in PART FIVE. For now, let's look at how writing *The Journey* led to new *Perception* experiences.

---

[9] *THE SAYINGS OF JESUS* is a textbook for *Experiential Learning* and it is included in the Appendix of this book.

CHAPTER 11

STAGE THREE: SOUND AND SUPPORTED KNOWLEDGE

A s *The Journey* was the first book I had written and as I have had no instruction in authorship, I sought out people who would read *The Journey* and give me critique and suggestions to strengthen it. One of my friends said his daughter was a professor at McMaster (my alma mater) and he would approach her. She contacted me with an offer to read what I had written and I sent her a copy. Her critique could have been considered scathing but it set me on a whole new course.

Her main point was that the subject I wrote about was philosophy and I had better inform myself of what philosophers had written before I went any further with my own ideas, much less my writing. I told her I wasn't writing for philosophers but for lay people like myself. She insisted, despite my intended audience, I had no business writing about these things without studying philosophy. I told her I was certainly not prepared to subject myself to even a first year course in philosophy. She referred me instead to a first year philosophy text[10] and a book entitled *Philosophy for Dummies*[11]. I put aside the thought she might have been dissing me with the second referral. I decided to buy both books and study their contents.

I expected *Philosophy for Dummies* to be an easy but trivial treatment of philosophy. I found it readable and a much more thorough introduction to philosophical thinking than I had anticipated. It presented arguments

---

[10]   Baker, Ann and Bonjour, Lawrence. *Philosophical Problems – An Annotated Anthology*. NY: Pearson Education Inc., 2005

[11]   Morris, Thomas V. Philosophy for Dummies. St. Louis, Missouri: Sierra Nevada Books, 1999

on both sides of each issue it addressed. Reading both sides of an issue led me to the conclusion neither argument was conclusive. When I read one side, I thought it made sense, but when I read the opposing argument it made comparably good sense. I was left with the initial feeling no philosophical argument was conclusive.

The first year philosophy text also presented both sides of issues. The exercises it contained aimed at teaching readers to *think* philosophically and so develop their own position. This approach appealed to me. I didn't know where my pursuit of philosophy would take me but I was correct in my feeling it would be an interesting trip.

It turned out thinking philosophically enabled me to establish sound and supported *knowledge* of life's purpose. This is what I had been missing. *More likely than not* to be true continued to fail to satisfy me.

Both philosophy books presented two classic forms of reasoning and established the validity of both in defending arguments and supporting positions. Both presented the arguments of atheists as well as of theists. I decided to pursue atheism before exploring philosophy more broadly. Both pursuits would intensify my re-examination of *The Club*.

CHAPTER 12

ATHEISM

Ireasoned if atheists could establish belief in God was unfounded, everything else I had learned so far in *Experiential Learning* would have to be unlearned. Naturally I pursued atheism with more than a little trepidation. Surprisingly, it turned out the best atheistic spokespersons I could find strengthened, rather than successfully challenged, my growing conviction that God created us, loves us and offers us eternal life.

I became aware of two books that had recently been published. The better publicized of the two was Richard Dawkins' *The GOD Delusion*[12]. In a discussion I had, having read it, I was referred to a second book, Sam Harris' *Letter to a Christian Nation*[13].

My overall reaction to both books was one of surprise. Firstly, both authors were highly defensive. They repeatedly left the impression they considered atheists to be a disrespected and somewhat persecuted minority. Secondly, both were dismissive of religious thinking. They frequently dismissed it out of hand without sound argument. I expected much more, especially of Richard Dawkins, whom I knew to be a highly respected scientist.

I set my disappointments aside and undertook to identify all the arguments they both cited as proof God could not exist. As you'll see shortly, none of them are proofs God does *not* exist. They are simply poorly supported rejections of others' positions that He *does* exist.

---

[12] Dawkins, Richard. *The GOD Delusion*. NY: Houghton Mifflin Company, 2006

[13] Harris, Sam. *Letter to a Christian Nation*. Toronto, Ontario: Random House of Canada Ltd., 2008

Dawkins' primary position is that the *cosmological* argument for the existence of God, first made by Aristotle, later developed by Thomas Aquinas and still later, by other philosophers is *flawed*. The argument is essentially that all things are caused by something else and thus only two possibilities exist. Either there is an *infinite* chain of causation, which is impossible, or there must be a *first* cause that is independent of cause. That first cause, itself independent of cause, is what most people call God. Dawkins takes the position that exempting God from cause is unjustified and agrees an infinite chain of causation is impossible. He therefore concludes creation is the result of a *natural* process of life arising from non-living matter – abiogenesis – and evolution.

I found three things strange about Dawkins' argument. Firstly he fails to admit abiogenesis is founded on the *hypothesis* life created itself and has not, itself, been scientifically proven. Secondly, he doesn't seem to see a need to determine *what* caused the *Big Bang* from which the non-living matter was generated. Thirdly, he apparently does not realize the *Big Bang* and abiogenesis, even if scientifically proven, can demonstrate only *how* creation was achieved but not *what* caused it.

A secondary Dawkins' argument is a perfect being could not have created all we know because so much of what was created is *flawed*. For example, our windpipes and throats share the same passage leaving us subject to choking. He elaborates on this and other examples of what he claims are flawed aspects of creation. Dawkins is unquestionably a leading scientist but, in my view, he has wandered far from his field of expertise.

If what Dawkins is critiquing is the work of his referenced "perfect being", his intellect is puny compared with the intellect he is critiquing. To me he is like a child who learned the first line of Happy Birthday and then undertook to critique Mozart. I don't know why the windpipe and throat share the same passage, but I'm pretty sure it wasn't a mistake. It certainly doesn't impress me as an argument to reject God.

Sam Harris in *Letter to a Christian Nation* shares most of the arguments in *The GOD Delusion*. Both authors look at the world that has been created and conclude it is so lonely, cruel and evil it could not have been the work of a being that loved us. Both develop arguments shared by many other atheists.

- God holds Himself remote, untouchable and mute
- God created a world full of evil
- God exposes us to pain

- God exposes us to life-long suffering
- God chooses pain and life-long suffering over available alternatives
- God continually insists we are in sin
- God insists on us asking forgiveness of sin we can't avoid
- God insists on the sin of, and on asking forgiveness by even the ignorant
- God plays favourites, gifting us unequally
- God insists on punishment over available alternatives
- God threatens us with hell
- God is portrayed as vengeful in the Bible, the Tanach (Hebrew Bible) and the Koran
- God's religions fail to produce a consistent picture of a loving God
- God is represented by religious leaders who are evil

On the surface, these fourteen observations might seem to support atheists' arguments that what we call God does *not* exist. However, none of them hold up for me on further examination. Let's look at each one of them in turn.

God holds Himself remote, untouchable and mute. While this is indeed what most of us experience, I feel it is what God *must* do. If He loves us and wants us to love Him, He must preserve our free will to *choose* to love Him. If He were to present His magnificence to us, we would be overwhelmed, incapable of choice and reduced to puppets. If God loves us could He allow that to happen?

God created a world full of evil. While the world is full of evil, it is unlikely that is how it was created. Because we were created with the free will we experience, we must realize its byproduct is we can choose to be evil. God cannot take free will away from us without taking away our freedom to choose whether or not to love Him.

God exposes us to pain. We can understand this better if we reflect that we do the same to our children. In order for our children to grow phys-ically, mentally and emotionally, we sometimes expose them to painful experiences. For example, we put them on a bicycle from which they will repeatedly fall until they learn to control it. Later most children realize these painful experiences enabled their growth even though, at the time, all they felt was the pain. Similarly for God to enable our fulfillment, even when pain is a necessary ingredient, is an act of love even if we don't understand the need for the pain.

God exposes us to life-long suffering. As we expose our children to painful experiences for short periods in their lives, it makes sense God would do the same. While life-long suffering cannot possibly seem like a short period to us, it is most certainly a short period for an eternal God. If God has created us for an eternal life with Him, it is for us as well. If that eternal life is dependent on us developing the capacity of selfless love, which we see in sufferers and their caregivers, might life-long suffering be an act of God's love? We'll explore both of these *if*s in Chapter 13.

God chooses pain and life-long suffering over available alternatives. When we experience pain and life-long suffering, it's natural to ask God to do us no more favours. However, once again, if the most important lesson we need to learn is selfless love, pain and life-long suffering may be the only effective enablers. Although we rarely see selfless love in ourselves or others, we *do* see it in sufferers and their caregivers, in the eyes of the individual caregiver of a challenged person, in the community response to families who have lost their homes to fire and in the outpouring of global support for the victims of tsunamis, earthquakes and other natural disasters. We may need to experience (vicariously or personally) pain and lifelong suffering to develop our capacity of selfless love.

God continually insists we are in sin. Doesn't this sound like negative reinforcement? Wouldn't a loving God focus on catching us doing something right? Of course. The problem is we think we are sinless when we don't do evil. Sin is not the same as evil. Sin is not doing the will of God. If God's will is that we do our best to develop our capacity of selfless love (a possibility we'll also pursue in Chapter 13), most of us sin by falling short. We tell our children when they do something against our will in order that their awareness of these failings can enable them to correct them. Similarly, God's loving insistence we are in sin can make us aware enough of our sin that we persevere in the lifelong battle to overcome it.

God insists on us asking forgiveness of sin we can't avoid. Because, like us, our children are not perfect, we know they are subject to doing bad things. When we insist our children tell us they are sorry for going against our will, we realize we are enabling our children's internalization of their failings. This internalization enables the child to take ownership of the failing and to set about its correction. Similarly, God knows we will repeatedly sin. Might God's insistence we ask for His forgiveness of our sin be His loving enablement of our internalization and ownership of our sin and of our attempt to correct it?

God insists on the sin of, and on asking forgiveness by even the ignorant. How can God blame us for a sin of which we are ignorant? Many of us do not realize we are in sin. However, is our ignorance of our sin a product of our inability or of our unwillingness? Is it a product of our complacency? Is it because we feel we are no worse than most other people? Do we feel sinless as long as we don't do bad things? Could God's insistence we ask forgiveness of our sin be His way of helping us overcome our complacency?

God plays favourites, gifting us unequally. How can God love us equally if He showers beauty, intelligence, peace-of-mind and perfect bodies on some of us and cruelly withholds these things from others? Could it be "to whom much is given, much is expected"? If I am blessed with beauty, am I to build up the esteem of one not? If I am blessed with intelligence, am I to patiently help one less blessed? If I encounter a challenged person, am I to reach out to them? Could our inequality of gifts be a loving God's enablement of our development of selfless love?

God insists on punishment over available alternatives. If loving parents use punishment as sparingly as possible why would God continually threaten us with it? The answer may become evident when we recognize the distinction between insistence and threat. If He threatened us with punishment, it would be up to Him to inflict it. If He simply insists on it, it might be His loving warning to us we are punishing *ourselves*. When we use our free will to choose to ignore God's will, we are the authors of our own separation from God. God's insistence may be His loving way of helping us avoid deploying our gift of free will to our detriment.

God threatens us with hell. The Bible contains many terrifying descriptions of the punishments God has prepared for those whom He judges deserve them. Why would a loving God expose those He loves to this? It might help to look first at the flip side. If God has prepared heaven for those who love Him and others selflessly and unconditionally, can He permit it to be populated by those who don't? If heaven is a place of selfless and unconditional love, must we not develop that capacity to be a part of it? As long as we choose not to, is not our hell – separation from God – self-inflicted? A good scare is worth more than good advice. His insistence on the danger of (a self-inflicted) hell might be the most loving gift of a loving God.

God is portrayed as vengeful in the Bible, the Tanach (Hebrew Bible) **and the Koran.** If these Holy Books can be believed (and over half of the world's population claims belief in one or other of them) God is a vengeful, jealous and angry god who demands genocide by His beloved. However, at this point in my *Experiential Learning*, Holy Books had little credibility for me. I considered them all to have been written by fallible men and re-written by fallible men countless times over the centuries.[14] For me, they could not support an argument a loving God does not exist. Besides, it seemed to me to be a bit odd that atheists would turn to Holy Books to support their positions.

God's religions fail to produce a consistent picture of a loving God. My first-year university elective course in *Comparative Religion* validated this point. For the most part, only the three Abrahamic religions portray a loving God and even they differ in their portrayals. However, for me, religions didn't support the positions they teach. They simply demanded acceptance by their faithful of their teachings. Unsupported positions could not, for me, support an argument a loving God does not exist.

God is represented by religious leaders who are evil. While it's true we see incidents of evil being perpetrated by religious leaders, as a group they have no monopoly on evil. They are simply fallible humans like the rest of us. The fact some of *them* do evil is no more indication God is evil, or He created evil than is the fact some of *us* do evil. This observation, for me, does not support an argument a loving God does not exist.

Considered as a group, I found the arguments referencing these fourteen observations to be flawed. Rather than sound support for arguments, they are simply fourteen observations that occur to us when we turn away from, rather than towards God. This reminds me of an amusing story.

---

[14]   I have since come to realize this position is too dismissive. In Chapter 14 we'll address this issue more thoroughly.

As the dentist finished his procedure, his patient said, "Thank God that's over." The dentist replied, "I don't believe in God. How can *you* when we see so much pain and evil in the world?" The patient's response was "Well, I don't believe in dentists. How can I when I see so many people with oral diseases, cavities, pain and missing teeth?" The dentist's defensive reply was "Well I can't help them if they don't come to me." The patient replied, "It's the same with God."

Having looked at each of these fourteen challenges thrown at believers by Dawkins and Harris, a strange and unexpected thing happened. Rather than impressing me with their thinking and challenging what I had so far established through *Experiential Learning*, they unwittingly supported and confirmed what I had learned. Furthermore, they inspired me with some ideas with which I could continue my *Experiential Learning*.

It's true I haven't examined a critical mass of atheistic thinking. Still this chapter summarizes a fairly comprehensive study of the thinking of two of the most recently prominent atheists. The results of this study led me to conclude I wouldn't find a lot more of substance from pursuing atheism further.

However, I realized all I had established at this point is that the common arguments a loving God does *not* exist are flawed. I had made no progress in establishing my *knowledge* a loving God *does* exist. Until I could *know* this, I would remain unsatisfied. I could not accept a position on life's purpose based simply on it being *more likely than not* to be true. I had to *know* my position on life's purpose. My knowledge had to be sound and supported. It was time for me to pursue philosophy.

CHAPTER 13

PHILOSOPHY 101

As I mentioned earlier, my first-year university philosophy text offered guidance in forming one's own philosophical thinking. For starters it described two established modes of reasoning. Of the two, the one more familiar to most of us, is deductive reasoning. Here is a simple example.

- All people have two legs
- He is a person
- He has two legs

The conclusion (last point) necessarily follows from the premises (preceding two points). Its proof is dependent on the validity of the premises. If the premises are valid, they permit no other conclusion. If *any* of the premises can be shown to be invalid, the proof is invalid.

Inductive reasoning is less familiar to most of us. Its basis is *consistency* of observation. If I consistently observe a condition to be the case, I can *know* it is the case where I have not observed it or cannot observe it. Here's an example of inductive reasoning.

- Every person we see has two legs
- All people have two legs

The proof of this second argument is dependent on the *consistency* of the observation stated in the premise. If an exception can be observed (such as seeing a three-legged person), the proof is invalid.

Reading this second argument, did you notice the validity of the first premise of the first argument is dependent upon the validity of this second argument? You may have not previously even thought about how you know all people have two legs. You probably just took it for granted. You probably didn't realize we can only *know* it using the inductive reasoning in this second argument.

Inductive reasoning is often the *only* way we can know something. Consider another example.

- Gravity has *never* failed
- Gravity will always work

Science does not yet know what gravity is or how it works and thus cannot establish it will always work. However, *we* know it will always work. If we did not *know* this, we would have to constantly hold onto something for fear of suddenly floating off into space. How do we know it works? The only way we can know it is through inductive reasoning. Because we have never observed an exception to the premise, we can *know* the conclusion is true.

My first reaction to inductive reasoning was to question whether I could *know* what I consistently observe. At the first observation of an exception, the proof would be invalidated and what I thought I knew would be shown to be in error. What kind of knowledge is that? I quickly realized that kind of knowledge is as good as it gets. The first time an exception to the observations supporting a scientific proof is discovered, the proof is invalidated. The first time an exception to the premises in a deductive argument is discovered, the proof is invalidated. All human "knowledge" is subject to correction. We cannot know anything *absolutely*.

For me, this was a startling revelation. Everything I know is subject to error. I was reminded of the famous quote "I think, therefore I am." René Descartes, dubbed the father of modern philosophy, finding reason to doubt everything he tried to conclude he knew, finally decided, if he doubted, something must be doing the doubting and thus he could *know* the doubter (he) exists.

While I am, by nature, almost as skeptical as René, I find it impractical to maintain one knows nothing. I think back to my Dad's agnosticism. He felt articles of faith were unknowable. I would love to have had the opportunity of chatting with him while I was at this stage of *Experiential Learning*. Sadly, by this time, he had passed away.

If one rejects all knowledge, little of consequence can be achieved. For example, if the scientific community had ignored the knowledge expressed in Newton's *Three Laws of Motion*, the industrial revolution would not have occurred and we would not be the beneficiaries of much of the progress of the following three centuries. It would have been folly not to have acted on the knowledge disseminated by Newton simply because it might be proven to be in error sometime in the future. We now know it *has* been proven to be in error. It is inconsistent with the proofs of the *Theory of Relativity* and the findings of *Quantum Mechanics*. The fact that the knowledge established by Newton *has* since been proven to be not universally true does not diminish its considerable value.

I concluded it would be equally foolish to fail to act on knowledge supported by inductive reasoning simply because it might be proven to be in error sometime in the future. The best knowledge we can attain is that which we can rigorously support by scientific observation, deductive reasoning and/or inductive reasoning. I concluded all knowledge, thus supported, is sound and it is folly not to act on it. I decided to attempt to apply deductive and inductive reasoning to determining sound and supported knowledge of whether or not God created us and everything in the universe.

Knowledge God Created Us

I set about my argument in support of the knowledge God created us in two steps. The first employs inductive reasoning.

- *Everything* we observe has a cause
- Everything that *can* be observed has a cause

Although we know this (by inductive reasoning), it presents us with a problem. What caused the *first* cause? How can the *first* cause be *first* if *it* has a cause?

Let's examine this question with a mind game. We can imagine all the causes of everything we observe to be links of a chain suspended from some point beyond the clouds. As we observe what holds up any one link we see it is the link above it. However, what holds up the top link (which, by the way, we can't see)? It can't be the link above it, or it wouldn't be the top link. There must be something other than a higher link holding up the chain. What is it?

Similarly, we *consistently* observe each and everything we experience is caused by something else we can observe. However, what caused the first cause (which, by the way, we can't observe)? It can't be the cause before it, or it wouldn't be the first cause. There must be something other than the causes we *can* observe that is the cause of everything we *do* observe. What is it?

This brings us to the second step of the argument, which applies deductive reasoning in two stages.

- Everything that can be observed has a cause (prior argument)
- The first cause cannot have a cause (by definition)
- The first cause cannot be observed

The first premise is established by inductive reasoning in the prior argument. The second premise is established by definition – if it had a cause it wouldn't be the first cause. The conclusion necessarily follows from the first and second premises.

The second stage of this second argument proceeds as follows.

- The first cause cannot be observed (prior argument)
- The first cause must be independent of cause (by definition)
- The first cause caused (or created) everything that can be observed (by definition)
- The first cause must have always existed (by definition)
- The first cause cannot be observed, is independent of cause, created everything, and always existed

The first premise is established in the preceding argument. The second premise is established by definition – if it had a cause it wouldn't be the first cause. The third premise is established by definition – because it is the first cause, its effect(s) caused the following effects, which themselves caused what followed in ongoing chains that result in the creation of everything that can be observed. The fourth premise is established by definition – if it preceded everything that can be observed it must have existed from the beginning of time. The conclusion follows from the four premises.

This deductive reasoning may be easier to follow when it is expressed conversationally. Common sense tells us initially something *independent* of cause must have caused everything thereafter. Something that preceded everything must have *always* existed. We can think of "always" as meaning *independent* of time. It must be eternal. To have created everything we know, that something must be all-powerful and all-knowing. Thus, we can establish sound and supported *knowledge* that we were created by something we cannot observe – an all-powerful, all-knowing and eternal being independent of cause (which is how most people think of God).

God is what most people call a creator that is all-powerful, all-knowing and always existed. We don't yet know if this God is the God portrayed in the Abrahamic religions. However, we *do* know we were created by something we call God.

Did you find these last two pages a bit of a tough slog? Are you tempted to skip ahead? If so, please try to stay with me for a few more pages. We are about to uncover some truly life-changing knowledge.

Knowledge God Loves Us

It may be intellectually satisfying to know a being many people call God created us, but it doesn't make much difference in our lives unless we can know whether that being seeks a relationship with us and, if so, what that relationship might be. Let's apply reasoning to establish sound and supported knowledge that the being many people call God, and which created us, loves us.

By way of introduction to this argument, we note everything we observe about the creation of beings is what we experience in parenthood. We create other beings through parental procreation. What do we know about the creators (parents) of the beings they create?

- All *capable* beings that create with *intent* (parents) love what they create (children)
- God is *capable* of everything (all-powerful) and always acts with *intent* (all-knowing)
- God loves what He creates

The latter part of the second premise may need explanation. A being that is all-knowing is free from error. He knows what He is doing. He is free from unintended action. It follows He always acts with intent.

The first and second premises necessarily lead to the conclusion. If *all* capable beings that create with intent love what they create and God is a capable being that creates with intent then it follows (by deductive reasoning) the creator we simply *call* God loves us.

Your first reaction to this reasoning may be we are equating God's creation of us with our *pro*creation of our children. Upon reflection, you may realize this is not what we are doing. We are simply applying what we *consistently* observe of creation (our procreation) to what we *cannot* observe of creation (God's creation of us). Supporting knowledge of what we *cannot* observe by the consistency of our observation of what we *can* observe is the essence of inductive reasoning.

As well, your reaction to this reasoning may be that the first premise is flawed. You have likely observed too many parents who do not love the children they create. However, because God is *capable* and acts with *intent*, we need only consider the subset of parents who are *capable* and procreate with *intent*. Those outside this subset, who procreate accidently or as a result of rape (that is, without *intent*), may even abort their children. Those outside this subset may not be *capable* of love either due to not having experienced it from others or due to extreme self-centredness. Excluding these parents, we focus our observation on *capable* parents who create with *intent*. It is in this *subset* of creators that we observe the consistency stated in the first premise and upon which the conclusion is dependent.

Through this inductive and deductive reasoning, we attain sound and supported knowledge the God that created us loves us.

Knowledge God Created Us to Live with Him for Eternity

What we experience on Earth is that, at the end of our lives, we all die. What we cannot experience on Earth is eternal life. How can we know the creator we simply *call* God created us to live with Him for eternity? Once again, let's apply what we observe of creation – our experience in parenthood.

- All *capable* beings that create with *intent* (parents) intend the beings they create (children) do not predecease them
- God is *capable* of everything (all-powerful) and always acts with *intent* (all-knowing)
- God intends what He creates does not predecease Him
- God is eternal
- God intends that we live with Him for eternity

Looking at this argument, you may notice we use deductive reasoning twice. The first two premises establish a conclusion represented by the third point. The third point then becomes one of the two premises that establish the overall conclusion.

As you reflect on this reasoning, you can see it is nothing more than applying what we *consistently* observe of creation (our procreation) to what we cannot observe of creation (God's creation of us). Thus, through this inductive and deductive reasoning, we attain sound and supported knowledge God loves us and created us to live with Him for eternity.

These two items of soundly-established knowledge have life-changing implications. If our creator loves us, we need to respond. If we are created for eternal life, we need to discern the purpose of the earthly portion of our lives. Even if we took our pursuit of knowledge about God no further, it would be folly to ignore and fail to act on the sound and supported knowledge we have just established.

However, I had *not* yet established that our creator is the God described by religions. Until I could establish this, religion would remain an unsupported source of knowledge of life's purpose. As well, the failure to resolve this doubt is the cause of heated arguments between believers and non-believers. Before taking our pursuit of knowledge further, let's examine why these arguments persist.

Those who accept this knowledge – the creator we simply *call* God loves us and created us to live with Him for eternity – and those who reject it both read too much into it. Both make the completely unsupported leap of faith that the creator, to whom we have been referring, is the God portrayed by *religion*. This erroneous leap of faith is as prominent among atheists, agnostics and skeptical thinkers as it is among believers. Believers use this unsupported leap of faith to justify everything they *believe* about God. Atheists, agnostics and skeptical thinkers allow the lack of support for this leap of faith to lead them to *reject* the knowledge we have just established as sound and supported. Both arrive at their *own* convictions by going *beyond* sound and supported knowledge.

What believers, atheists, agnostics and skeptical thinkers *can* agree on is the sound and supported knowledge at which we have arrived – the creator we simply *call* God loves us and created us to live with Him for eternity.

Where can we go from here? Reflecting on the fact we do not yet *know* our creator is the God described in religion's Holy Books, let's explore if we can learn any more about our creator through Philosophy 101.

Knowledge Life's Purpose is to Love God and *All* His Children as Selflessly and Unconditionally as We Are Able

Could the creator we call God, who loves us and whose intent is we live with Him for eternity, have a purpose for our lives? To answer this crucial question, I once again applied deductive reasoning (in two steps) to what we observe of creation – our experience in parenthood.

The first step is to determine our creator's intent.

- All *capable* beings who create with *intent* (parents), intend that all their children love their siblings and them as much as they love their children

- God is *capable* of everything (all-powerful) and always acts with *intent* (all-knowing)
- God intends all His children (all of us) love Him and *all* His children *as He loves us*
- The love of a perfect (all-powerful and all-knowing) being is perfect (*selfless* and *unconditional*)
- God intends that we *selflessly* and *unconditionally* love Him and all His children

As in the prior argument, the first two premises establish a conclusion stated by the third point. The third point then becomes one of the two premises that establish the overall conclusion.

The second step is to determine if God has a purpose for our lives.

- All *capable* beings who create with *intent* (parents), intend that all their children achieve their *best*
- God is *capable* of everything (all-powerful) and always acts with *intent* (all-knowing)
- God intends all His children (all of us) achieve our *best* – as much *as we are able*
- God intends that we selflessly and unconditionally love Him and all His children (prior argument)
- Our purpose must be what our creator intends
- *Life's* purpose is to love God and all His children as selflessly and unconditionally as we are able

Once again, the first two premises establish a conclusion stated by the third point, which then becomes the third premise. The fourth premise is from the conclusion of the prior argument. The fifth premise is established by definition. The conclusion necessarily follows from the third, fourth and fifth premises.

Putting this argument conversationally, it might go like this. Since God intends that we both love as He loves and achieve our best, His purpose must embody *both* of these intents. Since God created life, life's purpose must be God's purpose – to love Him and all His children as selflessly and unconditionally as we are able.

What an amazing conclusion! I *know* life's purpose. My knowledge is sound because it is rigorously supported by inductive and deductive reasoning. Until I can find a flaw in any of this reasoning, this knowledge remains as sound as *any* knowledge I have. Because of this I cannot put off *acting* on it.

Establishing this sound and supported knowledge was a very big leap in my *Experiential Learning*. Before this, my only support for my knowledge of life's purpose was it seemed *more likely than not* to be true. As such, it was knowledge I could put aside and get on with my life. It did not compel me. However, I now realized I possessed *sound and supported* knowledge of life's purpose. I could no longer ignore it. I had to *act* on it.

Although I didn't realize it at the time, these four items of knowledge turned out to be *foundational*. Everything I came to know from this point on through *Experiential Learning* was based on this *foundational knowledge*. Because I now had established this foundation, everything else that necessarily flows from it is equally *sound and supported* knowledge. Therefore, for PART THREE through PART SEVEN of my *Experiential Learning* story, I will stop qualifying what I know as *sound and supported* knowledge. I will simply say I *know* it. If you find it follows from my *foundational knowledge* and you accept that my *foundational knowledge* is sound and supported then you will see how I *know* it as well.

Ah, but there's the rub. Can you accept that my *foundational knowledge* is sound and supported?

Sound and Supported Knowledge

It's now time to more fully justify my claim of sound and supported knowledge. As I've already noted, sound and supported knowledge is not absolute. However, it *is* knowledge. It is the best knowledge we possess as earthly human beings as long as it is rigorously supported by inductive and deductive reasoning and/or by comparative analysis of arguments (for and against a position). We can do no better than that. However, we must do *at least* that. We do ourselves great harm if we live our lives in ignorance of requisite knowledge. But are you not free to question knowledge claimed by someone else?

You are not only *free* to. To avoid *denying* yourself knowledge it is *necessary* to question it. Could you really know anything based solely on another's position? To *really* know it, would you not have to pursue that person's position as thoroughly as you are able? Of course you have the option of *rejecting* another's position because you find it sounds too much like the religious teachings you have already rejected, because it is uncomfortable or simply because you doubt it. But is that in your best interest? Let's examine these three options a bit further.

On the first point, you probably noticed that, although religion teaches what I have come to know, I did not come to know it *based* on religious teaching. In fact, it was because I could *not* know it based on unsupported religious teaching that I had to rely on Philosophy 101 to make further progress in my re-examination of *The Club*. It is sound deductive and inductive reasoning that establishes what I know. Is it reasonable to reject this knowledge simply because religion takes a similar position?

On the second point, the knowledge I have just established – life's purpose is to love God and all His children as selflessly and unconditionally as we are able – is surely discomforting. If you were to accept this as life's purpose, you would have no rational choice but to pursue it. This pursuit might very well entail more than you bargained for, as you will see it did for me. It might even compel you to significantly change your life. We find change uncomfortable. We hate to be compelled to change. However, can you reasonably reject rigorously supported knowledge simply because you find it uncomfortable?

On the third point, I have been asked if I have concluded that anyone, who doubts what I have established as sound and supported knowledge, is unreasonable. Far from it. It is not unreasonable to doubt. Doubt is inevitable. It is a part of the human condition. It is evidence of an engaged mind. It is my strong conviction it is not doubt that is unreasonable. It is the failure to fully *pursue* doubt that is unreasonable. To overcome doubt of the validity of any knowledge requires the pursuit of that doubt. That pursuit might lead to a discovery of a flaw in an argument that supports that knowledge or a counter argument that refutes it. Barring such a discovery, can it be in your best interest to reject sound and supported knowledge based solely on unsupported doubt?

Here's an example of how one reader pursued his doubt.

He took the position the scope of my argument is much too narrow in that it is limited to human beings on Earth. It ignores anything beyond earthly humanity. It excludes everything God created *except* human beings. Others have taken similar positions. My answer in a few words is that these peoples' scope of pursuit of doubt is too broad. What do I mean by this?

If we try to understand all of what the vastness of time and space entails, we are biting off much more than we can chew (or even get into our mouths). I do not pretend to know any of this. I am simply focusing on what I *can* know based on what I can personally experience on Earth.

If we try to understand the makeup of everything God created, humanity may eventually succeed but very likely not in *our* lifetimes. I don't know life's purpose for non-terrestrial beings. I don't know life's purpose for everything on Earth that is non-human. Do non-human creatures love? I don't know but almost everyone I know shares my observation that no creature consistently exhibits unconditional love more than a dog. Does God intend that plants, insects and animals exist eternally in heaven? I don't know He does, but I don't know He doesn't.

The realization I don't know any of this should not discourage me from pursuing what I *can* know. When I narrow the scope of my investigation, I enable myself to establish knowledge of what I *must* know. I must know *humanity's* life purpose. I don't *need* to know non-humans' (terrestrial or beyond) life purpose. This is why my focus is solely on God's human children. With that focus I can establish sound and supported knowledge of what I *must* know. If I permit my focus to wander beyond my limitations, I may end up feeling I can't know *anything*.

We all need to come to the realization that, if we insist that knowing *anything* is dependent on knowing *everything*, we can know *nothing*. We can't let that happen to us. It is important we establish our knowledge of what we are *capable* of knowing. It is critical we establish knowledge of life's purpose.

What compels you to establish this knowledge? To me, it is your mind. If you had no mind you would be no more compelled than are non-human earthly creatures. However, you have a mind. Is it not as important that you use *it* to the best of your ability as it is that you use anything *else* you have been given? It seems to me we are not expected to know *more* than that of which our minds are capable but we are expected to know *all* that of which our minds are capable. Because our minds are God's gift, are we not compelled to fully use them? Jesus said we are. As we'll pursue in PART FOUR, He commanded we love God with all our heart *and* all our mind.

In *my* case, at this point in *Experiential Learning*, I had largely failed at loving God with my heart. I had felt glimpses of what my heart was trying to tell me through experiencing COR, Participation House and Marriage Encounter. However, I had not used *all* my heart to the best of my ability. Others I observe fail at loving God with *all* their mind. Each of us must fully use *both* our heart and our mind. As you continue to follow my *Experiential Learning* adventure, you will see I gradually became capable of *fully* using my heart.

Now at this point, I have to warn you of a consequence of *Experiential Learning*. Once you possess sound and supported knowledge of *God's* purpose for your life, you will likely feel compelled to further re-examine *your* position on life's purpose. If you proceed, what you learn will likely lead you to change your life on Earth. It's understandable you might find such a prospect makes you wary and reluctant to take your re-examination any further. To do my best to allay such a concern, I'd like to share my experience (as an incentive).

It is true the further my re-examination of *The Club* progressed the bigger were the changes in my life. However, these changes, the thought of which had made me uneasy, turned out to enrich my life. Rather than imposing more on me they invited more of me. Rather than finding the changes I experienced an imposition, I found them to be fulfilling and joy-filled. I strongly suspect you would find the same thing.

I have *now* come to know what Jesus meant when He said, "Take my yoke upon you and learn from me, for I am gentle and lowly in heart and you will find rest for your souls. For my yoke is easy and my burden is light." (Matt 11: 25-30) Today, the more I strive towards the impossible standard Christ sets for me, the more I feel the lightness of the burden. The more I strive, the more I feel God giving me strength to strive a little more.

However, at *this* point in my *Experiential Learning*, religion had insisted Christ demanded a very great deal of me. I could not see how His yoke could be easy or His burden light. Like most things that didn't make sense to me, I put this teaching aside for quite a long time.

Perception Experiences	Scientific method	My best friend	Jesus' sayings
		My late wife	McMaster professor
		Pascal's Wager	Two philosophy texts
		The Catholic Information Centre	Dawson's book
		My seminarian mentor	Harris' book
		Bits of the RC Catechism	Sound reasoning
		COR	
		Participation House	
		Marriage Encounter	
		Daily Mass	
		A bit of the Bible	
		C.S. Lewis' *Mere Christianity*	
Process Learnings	There is no proof God exists	I must accept the *possibility* God exists	Atheism is unfounded
	Atheism makes sense	The Church establishes a *likelihood* God exists	God created us, loves us and offers us eternal life with Him
		The Apostle's Creed is *more likely than not* to be true	God wants us to love Him and all His children as selflessly as we are able
		I am *capable* of selfless love of others	
		I am *capable* of selfless love of God	
		The Gospels *likely* deliver God's Word	
		I *knew* none of the above	
Knowledge of Life's Purpose	Earthly fulfillment	Live according to Church teaching	Love God and *all* His children as selflessly and unconditionally as we are able

In the meantime, *Experiential Learning* had already enabled a very thorough re-examination of *The Club*.

My template shows the next major (shaded) *Perception* experiences, to which the strength of C.S. Lewis' arguments had led me. My study of Jesus' sayings in the Gospels led to a unique organization of them that produced my book, *The Journey*. Pursuit of its critique led me to the McMaster professor who introduced me to philosophy. This led to my re-examination of atheism (using Dawkin's and Harris' books) and my application of inductive and deductive reasoning. All of this provided several (shaded) *Process* learnings.

My re-examination of atheism led to the *Process* learning it has no foundation. My pursuit of sound reasoning led me to the *Process* learnings that 1) God created us, loves us and offers us eternal life with Him and 2) God intends that we love Him and *all* His children as selflessly and unconditionally as we are able.

Because our creator's intent must be life's purpose, these *Process* learnings had led me to sound and supported *Knowledge* that life's purpose is to love God and *all* His children as selflessly and unconditionally as we are able.

Experiential Learning had corrected rather than confirmed the knowledge of life's purpose that I had previously established. My continuing re-examination of *The Club* had lead (and may continue to lead) to correction of my knowledge. However, I had to act on this sound and supported knowledge *now* and *continue* acting on it until whenever in the future it might be corrected.

In the meantime, I had fully pursued all I could establish *without* reliance on religious teaching. My re-examination of *The Club* had to shift focus to its charter, its founder and its fallible human leadership.

Was its charter really the revealed Word of God? Was its founder really the Son of God? Was the Roman Catholic Catechism, produced by its fallible human leaders, really the revealed Word of God? These questions are fundamental. Their answers establish or undermine the foundations of *The Club*.

PART THREE

FOUNDATIONS

CHAPTER 14

THE BIBLE – THE OLD TESTAMENT

As you know, *The Club* charter is composed of the Old and New Testaments of the Bible.

Like many people I know, my knowledge of the Bible was cursory at this point in my *Experiential Learning*. I had used my *Logos Bible Software* from time to time to do a keyword search to answer particular questions I had. I had read the four Gospels. Like most people, I was familiar with the Bible's creation story, told in the first two chapters of Genesis, because of the controversy over evolution and creation. I knew the creation story and the four Gospels to be a very small part of the Bible. I was just not prepared to subject myself to a reading of the whole of the Old Testament. I wondered if any précis of the Bible existed.

I learned there are several and they provide good synopses of the Bible's content. They permit the reader to get a summary of each book of the Bible in five to ten minutes of reading. Anyone can Google them anytime. I focused my attention on the first seventeen books of the Bible, as well as the book of Daniel and excepting 1 and 2 Chronicles. Doing the math, you'll see this took only about three hours. In all, these books comprise almost half of the Old Testament.

I decided this would be enough of the Old Testament for me to determine if it is the revealed Word of God as Christian teaching claims. Two things caused me to seriously question this claim. Firstly, its many inconsistencies made it suspect. I had concluded Jesus' words were *more likely than not* the Word of God. However, much of what I read in the Old Testament was *inconsistent* with Jesus' teachings. As well I felt a creation story, inconsistent with science, could not be the Word of God. Secondly, how could fallible men have *received* the Word of God? I had decided God does not talk to us. If God did not talk to the Bible's authors, how else could they have received the Word of God?

Addressing the second question first, I realized, because God *is* all-powerful and all-knowing, He assuredly *could* reveal His Word to Man. However, because I was sure He didn't *talk* to us, I didn't see *how else* He could. One day, thinking further about this, it occurred to me God *could* simply put what He chose to reveal directly into our minds. If He did, we would not *hear* it, we would just *discover* it. That would be a very effective means of communication, but how *likely* is it?

Have you ever wondered why things pop into your mind? When they had done for me, I had rarely ever thought about where they had come from. I started paying attention to that. I realized most of these ideas were likely triggered by my human experience – something I had read, heard or seen. However, I was unable to relate *some* of these ideas to *anything* I had experienced. Where did *those* ideas come from?

Could it be an all-powerful, all-knowing God had decided to put them into my mind? If so, nothing could prevent Him. It was at least possible He does this often to each of us. Because we wouldn't be able to *hear* Him, most of us would remain unaware He was doing it. Recognizing this possibility, I realized there was nothing to say He didn't reveal things to the authors of the Old Testament in this way. If so, what He revealed *was* the Word of God. My realization God *could* do this, raised the question why God *would* do this.

This technique has two obvious weaknesses. Most intended recipients would be likely to miss the communication altogether. Even those who did discover it could very easily misinterpret what was not put into words. Why would God choose non-verbal revelation?

As I pondered this question, I thought about the teachers I had during my formal schooling. Most told me (repeatedly) what they wanted me to learn. They *dictated* to me. A few created a way to lead me to *discover* what they wanted me to learn. I realized I had learned much more from the latter. Why was this?

I have concluded it was because I was *engaged* in the learning process. I remember the saying we learn more from *doing* (including thinking) than from being shown or being told. My best teachers inspired me to think through what they revealed to me rather than dictating what I should think. If the *best* teachers choose that method, would it not be likely the *perfect* being, God, would also? Might He choose to reveal His Word by putting messages directly into our minds and leaving their interpretation to us?

This led me to an "Aha" moment that addressed the first question. If God chose to reveal His Word rather than to dictate it, then how that revelation would be *recorded* in the Old Testament would be how it was *interpreted* by its authors. Inconsistencies might be only misinterpretations. What they recorded of the Word of God might be simply the best interpretation of which they were capable. God may very well *have* revealed His Word to the Old Testament authors and then patiently awaited its correct interpretation. If the inconsistencies are simply misinterpretations, they don't preclude the claim the Old Testament is the revealed Word of God. Its authors were simply human and thus fallible.

I decided to catalogue all the inconsistencies I had discovered that call the Old Testament into question. Could it be God *intended* the creation story in Genesis to be different than the scientific explanation? Could it also be, despite the Old Testament's inconsistencies, what God *revealed* to its authors *was* consistent with what Jesus later revealed to us?

I first tackled the apparent inconsistency of the Genesis story of creation with the *Big Bang* and the *Theory of Evolution*. In the end, I found the Genesis account to be consistent with science. I concluded it was not an account born of the ignorance of the author(s) of Genesis. Instead, its inaccuracy could have been God's intention rather than the result of its authors' misinterpretation.

If God were revealing the *Big Bang* and evolution to people with no exposure to science or education, the account of His revelation in Genesis would seem to be a pretty good explanation. The Genesis account starts out describing what could have been the *Big Bang* 13 billion years ago. It then describes a progression of life forms, similar to those described in *On the Origin of Species* published by Darwin in 1859, which began about 3500 million years ago.

The opening words – "In the beginning, God created the heavens and the earth. The earth was without form and void" – seem to refer to creation from nothing. "And God said, 'Let there be light' and there was light" certainly sounds like the *Big Bang*. What it describes God doing on each of the next five days sounds much like evolution. After separating heaven from earth, God created the continents as water receded. From cells and organisms, life forms in the water became, progressively, amphibians, land-based creatures and eventually humans were created.

The Genesis story isn't specific about whether humans were created from scratch or as a product of evolution. As far as six days is concerned, a few billion years here or there for God is comparable to a short afternoon for us. God could have said six days or six years, but several billion years would not have resonated with those to whom He revealed His Word.

It appeared I could no longer maintain the conviction the Genesis account of creation and the scientific discoveries of the *Big Bang* and the *Theory of Evolution* contradict each other. It seemed more likely God revealed His Word to the author(s) of Genesis, in a way to which they could relate, of how He created everything.

When we talk to children, the best of us manage to talk to them at their level. We strive to discern what, of what we know, can be understood at their level of development and then to express ourselves accordingly. I found it fascinating to think God might have been doing this same thing in the Word He revealed from the earliest days the Bible records through to the time of Christ.

To me, the Genesis story of creation has God's fingerprints all over it. I concluded no part of this content of the Old Testament supports the claim the Bible is not the revealed Word of God.

I next identified six repeated Old Testament themes that appeared to be inconsistent with Jesus' teaching of God's unconditional love of *all* His children.

- God's punishment of Adam and Eve (and each of us thereafter)
- God's restriction of His love to Abram[15] and his descendants
- God's instruction to Moses to expel the Canaanites
- God's repeated outbursts of wrath at humanity
- Moses' and Joshua's insistence God's love is conditional
- God's repeated instruction that the Jewish people commit genocide

Let's pursue each of these apparent inconsistencies one at a time.

Following its account of creation, the Old Testament describes the fall of Adam and Eve. I have concluded Adam and Eve represent *all* humanity rather than a specific man and a specific woman. When I interpret this event as God's punishment of us *all*, it does not seem to be consistent with an unconditionally loving God. However, if I focus on what happened, a different picture emerges. Adam and Eve were (and we are) given a paradise and a free will to accept or reject God's will and His love. They chose to put their will above God's will much as we do to this day.

---

[15] When God made the covenant with Abram (which means *exalted father*) and his descendants, God changed his name to Abraham (which means father of a multitude). (Genesis 17: 5)

It occurred to me, rather than paying for Adam's and Eve's sinfulness, we are repeating it.

God appears to have lovingly accepted Adam's and Eve's (and our) choices and to be now patiently awaiting our choice to return to Him. To me, God's gift of our free will, His acceptance of our choice to reject His will and His unlimited patience in awaiting our choice to accept His will are all consistent with an unconditionally loving God. I conclude God is not punishing us. He is warning us against misusing our free will to separate *ourselves* from Him. I concluded no part of this content of the Old Testament supports the claim the Bible is not the revealed Word of God.

Things began to look up when God made His covenant with Abram and his descendants. God's covenant reveals a God who loves His people. However, this covenant raises the next two issues I found to be *inconsistent* with Jesus' teaching of God's unconditional love of *all* His children.

Firstly, why did God restrict His love to Abram and his descendants? Why did He select only a *subset* of His children to be His chosen people? It occurred to me God could have made a covenant with Abram and his descendants non-exclusively. Does God's choice of Abram and his descendants necessarily exclude the rest of us from His love? It's clear the Jewish people *interpreted* His love as exclusive to them. However, Jesus later made it clear God's covenant with them excluded no one. God revealed His love *firstly* to the Jewish people. It was only their interpretation of what God revealed that is inconsistent with a God that loves *all* His children unconditionally. I concluded no part of this content of the Old Testament supports the claim the Bible is not the revealed Word of God.

Secondly, why did God instruct Moses and Joshua to expel the people living in and around the land of Canaan?[16] God promised His chosen people they would inherit the "Promised Land". Much later, Jesus revealed God's promise is our inheritance of eternal life. In hindsight, it is understandable Moses and Joshua would interpret the "Promised Land" as land rather than as eternal life. They had to pick the land they thought God meant and they picked Canaan. It must have seemed clear to them they had to expel the present inhabitants if they were to inherit it for themselves. With this mind-set, they would naturally so interpret God's promise. After all, tribes had been taking each other's lands repeatedly as long as anyone could remember. The Word of God promised His chosen people a "Promised Land". I concluded it was only their *interpretation* the "Promised Land" was land inhabited by others. I concluded no part of

---

[16]   Joshua 24: 1-13

this content of the Old Testament supports the claim the Bible is not the revealed Word of God.

The Old Testament goes on to describe the continual ups and downs of the Jewish people's (and our) relationship with God. It describes what they interpreted as God's wrath at His people. It describes Moses' and Joshua's insistence God's love is conditional. It describes what was interpreted as God's instruction that the Jews wipe out everyone in their path. Do these descriptions reflect God's revelation or were they simply the Jewish leaders' misinterpretations of what God had revealed to them?

It doesn't take too much reading of the Old Testament to encounter many descriptions of *terrible* manifestations of God's wrath. In one passage alone, in Deuteronomy[17], God threatens everything from pestilence, famine and incurable illnesses to sieges so devastating that starving men will eat their children and starving women will eat their afterbirth. Fierce wrath is clearly inconsistent with an unconditionally loving God. Either the Bible's authors misinterpreted the Word of God or this Old Testament content is not the revealed Word of God.

I set about looking at the mindset of those who did the interpreting. I knew the Jewish people were the first to conceive there was only one God, He was good and He loved them. This idea was conceived at a time when other religions promoted multiple gods who were capricious – as likely as not to be angry and punishing – and who thus needed to be placated. Primitive societies interpreted every unexplained bad occurrence as a sign one of their gods was angry with them.

The Jewish society in Biblical times was likely rampant with every type of horrific evil – torture, murder, incest, sodomy, you name it – as was every other society of the day. The Jewish people knew they were evil and felt their God must be angry with them when they were evil. Like everyone else, they interpreted bad things as signs of God's anger and punishment. The Word of God revealed God's love to the Jewish people. It was only their interpretation of God's revelation that led them to conclude He was horribly threatening and punishing them. It was only their interpretation that is inconsistent with a God that loves all His children unconditionally. I concluded no part of this content of the Old Testament supports the claim the Bible is not the revealed Word of God.

This also explained to me why Moses and Joshua interpreted God's love as *conditional*. They witnessed the repeated sinfulness of their people and did their best to convince them they needed to repent. Their

---

[17]   Deuteronomy 28: 15-68

message to their people was any unexplained good occurrence (such as the manna given them in the desert) or battle won was a sign of God's mercy and any unexplained bad occurrence (such as a plague or famine) or battle lost was a sign of God's jealousy, anger and vengeance in response to their sinfulness. Only centuries later did Jesus reveal God's love for us is *unconditional*. God's revelations of His love are not inconsistent. Once again the Old Testament's authors misinterpreted them. I concluded no part of this content of the Old Testament supports the claim the Bible is not the revealed Word of God.

All this still left me with the many descriptions of God's instruction to the Jewish people to commit genocide. One passage in Numbers[18] gives a shocking example. Moses' interpretation of God's Word was ". . . kill every male among the little ones, and kill every woman who has known man by lying with him. But all the young girls who have not known man by lying with him keep alive for yourselves." Genocide is clearly inconsistent with unconditional love. Either God's revelation was again misinterpreted by the Jewish people or it could not be the revealed Word of God.

What was the mindset of those doing the interpreting? The Bible and other historical writings report an endless cycle of wars and short-lived truces between tribes. The only love that existed at that time was within one's own tribe. It is understandable the message God *revealed* – He loved the Jewish people – would be *interpreted* as He loved them exclusively. This belief was only reinforced by their knowledge other tribes did not worship God and thus He must be angry, jealous and vengeful towards them. It was a logical conclusion God meant the Jewish people to wipe out the sinfulness they found in the tribes surrounding them and His revealed Word was thus misinterpreted. Sadly Muslim extremists hold a similar misinterpretation of their Koran to this day. I concluded no part of this content of the Old Testament supports the claim the Bible is not the revealed Word of God.

So, in summary what did my analysis of the content of the Old Testament tell me about whether or not it is the revealed Word of God?

Most convincingly, I had determined it makes sense God would *want* to reveal Himself to us. I based this on my recently established *foundational knowledge* God wants us to love Him and *all* His children as He loves us. Because God wants us to *choose* to love Him, He must make Himself known to us in a way that is unprovable. In the period when the Old Testament was written, no other repository of God's revelation

---

[18]   Numbers 31: 1-18

existed. God *needed* a vehicle whose content was unprovable as is the Old Testament content. Because God *needed* such a vehicle, and the Old Testament *is* such a vehicle, I concluded the Old Testament *was* that vehicle. God revealed His Word *spiritually* to the authors of the Old Testament and left its interpretation up to them. I suspect He has been continuing to reveal Himself spiritually to each one of us ever since, but because He places His revelations in our minds, rather than putting them into words, we remain largely unaware of it.

Secondly, I had resolved the issue surrounding the Genesis account of creation by seeing it in light of our growing understanding of how our universe was created. I saw its description as what we would expect a loving God to reveal of His creation to people with no scientific knowledge. Seen this way, the Genesis account seemed to me to be almost assuredly the revealed Word of God.

Thirdly, I had countered all the reasons I could identify for determining the Old Testament *cannot* be the revealed Word of God. My difficulty with God's punishment of Adam and Eve had been resolved by my realization the punishment we share is self-inflicted. My difficulty with God's act of choosing to make a covenant with only Abram and his descendants had been resolved by my realization the covenant excluded no one. My difficulty with the expulsion that resulted from God's offer of the Promised Land had been resolved by Jesus' revelation God's promise is humanity's inheritance of eternal life. My difficulty with the descriptions of God's repeated wrath and vengeance had been resolved by my realization they were erroneous interpretations of God's revelation. My difficulties with Moses' and Joshua's interpretation of God's love as conditional and God's exhortations to genocide had been similarly resolved. In summary, I had concluded the errors of interpretation made by the Old Testament authors simply reflect their human limitations and God's patience in letting us approach a true knowledge of His Word at our own pace. I concluded none of the human misinterpretations in the Old Testament support the claim it is not the revealed Word of God.

All this led me to the conclusion the arguments for the position the Old Testament is the revealed Word of God are supported and, against it, are refuted. Until I am presented with new arguments (or shown flaws in these arguments), I retain my *knowledge* the Old Testament *is* the revealed Word of God.

However, my inherent skepticism presented me with what I found to be inconsistencies in the New Testament as well.

- Christ died for our sins. Would a loving God horribly punish His Son?
- Non-believers are doomed to unquenchable fire. Would a loving God abandon us?
- It is harder for a rich man to enter into heaven than for a camel to pass through the eye of a needle. Would a loving God make heaven unattainable to anyone?

I needed to resolve my doubts this content of the New Testament could be the revealed Word of God.

CHAPTER 15

THE BIBLE – THE NEW TESTAMENT

The first issue, for me, was my understanding of my Church's interpretation of a Bible teaching. It taught Christ died to atone for the sins of each one of the descendants of Adam and Eve. I understood this teaching to mean Jesus accepted God's *punishment* for our sins on our behalf. God punished His Son rather than us. As before, my problem with this interpretation was punishment by an unconditionally loving God didn't make sense to me.

After further study I learned *atone*ment means becoming "*at one*" with God by making reparation or amends for wrongs one has done. I should have better interpreted Jesus' death as making reparation for our sinfulness. It is clear human sinfulness has been present in billions of people over many millennia. No one of us can atone for a sin this great. Only God Himself could accomplish our atonement. Because His love is unconditional, I concluded the Incarnate God atoned on our behalf because we are incapable.

I next searched for the meaning behind the horror of Christ's death. Here's how I see it. God saw the *silent* revelation of His Word in the Old Testament was not enough to reach us. He sent us Jesus so we could hear the Word of God *spoken* to us. However, God knew we could accept Jesus was God Incarnate only if He were resurrected. God knew a shocking experience was needed to get us to pay attention.

All this led me to three conclusions. God did not punish His Son. People did. Secondly, God *allowed* us to crucify His Son so, having looked in horror at what we had done, we would sit up and take notice. Thirdly, God could only show us His promise of eternal life by resurrecting Christ, which could not have happened unless He had died. I concluded no part of this content of the New Testament supports the claim the Bible is not the revealed Word of God.

The second issue, for me, was my understanding of the Bible's teaching non-believers would be punished in an unquenchable fire. After more study, I arrived at an understanding unquenchable fire is a metaphor. *Fire* is a metaphor for a horrible separation from God. *Unquenchable* means God cannot quench it without taking away our free will. Because God won't allow Himself to prevent me from separating myself from Him, then only *I* can take away my separation from God by discerning and accomplishing His will. Jesus made it explicitly clear to us the danger we face of self-inflicting a separation from God. I concluded no part of this content of the New Testament supports the claim the Bible is not the revealed Word of God.

Thinking through this second issue gave me a better understanding of what leads one to heaven, purgatory or hell.

- **Heaven**   God judges that you do His will to the best of your ability ("... as it is in heaven"[19])
- **Purgatory** God judges that you are not yet doing His will to the best of your ability
- **Hell**   You *persist* in rejecting God's will

I conclude hell is not an option for God.

The third issue, for me, was my understanding of Jesus' assertion it is easier for a camel to pass through the eye of a needle than for a rich man to enter into heaven. To me (as well as to His disciples) this meant it was impossible. I had already concluded we are incapable of avoiding sin. Our human nature is one of self-indulgence, self-possession and self-absorption. As such we are all incapable of perfect selfless love.

I finally understood the real message. I am as incapable of doing God's will on my *own*, as is a camel of passing through the eye of a needle on its *own*. However, nothing is impossible for God. I can adequately prepare myself for heaven only if I ask God to help me. I have to *ask* because God can't *impose* His help without taking away my free will. Sending Jesus to tell me I need to ask God for help and God will "top up" my best efforts is a loving act. I realized God is not saying it is impossible. It was only *my* interpretation of Jesus' teaching that led me to conclude He meant it was impossible. I concluded no part of this content of the New Testament supports the claim the Bible is not the revealed Word of God.

Having resolved what I had found to be inconsistencies in the New Testament, I discovered another indication the New Testament is the revealed Word of God. Jesus' messages are unprovable. I realized they

---

[19]   I find this to be a very *telling* clause in the Lord's Prayer

must be to preserve our *choice* to accept the will of God. We can choose to reject Jesus' messages but we would lose that choice if they were provable. To preserve our choice, God needs a vehicle for revealing His Word that is unprovable. The content of the New Testament is unprovable. The facts that God *needs* such a vehicle and the New Testament *is* such a vehicle both support the argument it is the revealed Word of God.

All this led me to the conclusion the arguments for the position the New Testament is the revealed Word of God are supported and, against it, are refuted. Until I am presented with new arguments (or shown flaws in these arguments), I retain my *knowledge* the New Testament *is* the revealed Word of God.

As a result, I *know* the *whole* Bible is indeed the revealed Word of God.

Perception **Experiences**	Scientific method	My best friend	Jesus' sayings
		My late wife	McMaster professor
		Pascal's Wager	Two philosophy texts
		The Catholic Information Centre	Dawson's book
		My seminarian mentor	Harris' book
		Bits of the RC Catechism	Sound reasoning
		COR	Much of the Bible
		Participation House	
		Marriage Encounter	
		Daily Mass	
		A bit of the Bible	
		C.S. Lewis' *Mere Christianity*	
Process **Learnings**	There is no proof God exists	I must accept the *possibility* God exists	Atheism is unfounded
	Atheism makes sense	The Church establishes a *likelihood* God exists	God created us, loves us and offers us eternal life with Him
		The Apostle's Creed is *more likely than not* to be true	God wants us to love Him and all His children as selflessly as we are able
		I am *capable* of selfless love of others	The Bible *is* the revealed Word of God
		I am *capable* of selfless love of God	
		The Gospels *likely* deliver God's Word	
		I *knew* none of the above	
Knowledge of **Life's Purpose**	**Earthly fulfillment**	**Live according to Church teaching**	**Love God and *all* His children as selflessly and unconditionally as we are able**

Experiential Learning had presented me with the next (shaded) *Perception* experience in my template. I had discovered a précis that simplified the study I needed to undertake of *The Club's* charter.

My study led me to the (shaded) *Process* learning that the Bible is indeed the revealed Word of God. I could no longer let its obvious misinterpretations lead me to discount it and ignore what it revealed of God's Word. I concluded the Bible (***B**asic **I**nstructions **B**efore **L**eaving **E**arth*) was very likely my Owner's Manual.

My *Process* learning had further *confirmed* rather than corrected my *Knowledge* of life's purpose. Of course, this knowledge, like all knowledge, will always be subject to correction.

My *Perception* experience is "a gift that keeps on giving". I had digested only about half of the Old Testament and only the Gospels in the New Testament. I need to continue my re-examination of *The Club* charter by more fully digesting more and more of it. Whenever I encounter a reading that appears to refute my *Process* learning that the Bible is the revealed Word of God, I need to fully pursue that reading until I can establish whether it confirms or corrects this latest *Process* learning.

I realize, in order for *you* to accept that the Bible is the revealed Word of God, you may need to explore other sources to pursue issues that cause you to question it. Your pursuit may uncover new arguments, or flaws in *my* arguments that refute my knowledge. As you make your study of the Bible, I hope you will share the results of your study with me at delsmith@rogers.com just as I have shared the results of my study with you. I very much need your piece of glass.

Meanwhile, the next part of my re-examination of *The Club* focused on its founder. I realized I still had *not* arrived at the *knowledge* Jesus is the Son of God. The only way I could *know* Jesus' reported teachings are the Word of God was to know *Jesus* is the Son of God. How could I know this? As well, the Bible claims it reports what Jesus taught. How could I know the Bible reliably reported His words?

CHAPTER 16

JESUS CHRIST – SON OF GOD

Having established to my satisfaction the Bible is the revealed Word of God, it made sense to me to use *it* to explore whether or not Jesus is the Son of God.

I was aware the Old Testament contained prophecies of the coming of a Saviour. I discovered six of these prophecies among the many more the Old Testament reports. When I placed the six in chronological order, I realized each subsequent prophecy came a little closer to what the New Testament claims actually happened.

Prophecies of the Son of God

The earliest prophet I discovered was Nathan who prophesied at the time of David.[20] God revealed to Nathan a message for David that He would make an offspring of David a warrior king who ". . . will give you rest from all your enemies." God would establish the throne of His kingdom forever and ". . . will be to Him a father and He shall be to me a son." This *interpretation* of the revealed Word of God was consistent with the Jewish people's view that God would continuously save them from defeat by their enemies. This prophecy also establishes, even from this early point, the saviour would be God's Son.

The next prophet was Isaiah who prophesied a prince of peace.[21] "For to us a child is born, to us a son is given; and the government shall be upon His shoulder and His name shall be called Wonderful, Counselor,

---

[20]   2 Samuel 7: 8-14

[21]   Isaiah 9: 1-6

Mighty God, Everlasting Father, Prince of Peace." He would come to us as a new-born infant. He would become a governor rather than a warrior. He was still seen as God's Son but also as one who would be God, a Father to us.

The third prophet was Micah who prophesied the Son of God would be born in Bethlehem.[22] His interpretation of the revealed Word of God was the king would "... shepherd His flock in the strength of the Lord, in the majesty of the name of the Lord His God. And they would dwell secure, for now He shall be great to the end of the earth. And He shall be their peace." His protection of His people would be like that of a shepherd of his sheep.

The next prophet was Zephaniah who prophesied He would be a forgiving, loving God.[23] "The Lord your God is in your midst, a mighty one who will save; He will rejoice over you with gladness; He will quiet you by His love; He will exult over you with loud singing." He would be a God of love.

The fifth prophet was Jeremiah who prophesied during the time of the Babylonian captivity.[24] Jeremiah prophesied God would "... raise up for David a righteous Branch and He shall reign as king and deal wisely and shall execute justice and righteousness in the land. In His days Judah will be saved and Israel will dwell securely." Jeremiah prophesied the Son of God would be righteous, just and wise as well as equally protecting and loving.

The last prophet was Malachi who prophesied John the Baptist as well as Jesus.[25] "Behold, I send my messenger and he will prepare the way before me. And the Lord whom you seek will suddenly come to His temple; and the messenger of the covenant in whom you delight, behold, he is coming, says the Lord of hosts. But who can endure the day of His coming and who can stand when He appears? For He is like a refiner's fire and like fullers' soap." Malachi's interpretation of the revealed Word of God was of an awe-inspiring, all-powerful king who would purify and perfect us.

Each subsequent prophecy yielded an interpretation closer and closer to the saviour the New Testament portrays – from a warrior king who would be a son of God, to a prince of peace who would be

---

[22]   Micah 5: 2-5a
[23]   Zephaniah 3: 14-17
[24]   Jeremiah 23: 5-8
[25]   Malachi 3: 1-4

a Father to us, to a shepherd king who would be born in Bethlehem, to a God of love, to a king who would be righteous, to a purifying king preceded by a messenger, John the Baptist. I conclude God allowed the prophets their interpretations of the Word He revealed, patiently waiting for those interpretations to come closer and closer to the true Word of God.

I am aware some scholars do not accept that these passages prophesy Jesus' divinity. To support their rejection, they present evidence that some of the Bible's prophecies were back-dated by its authors. If so, they are manipulations of the truth rather than revelations of it. However, these six prophecies do not fit that evidence.

If they were made up by Jesus' disciples after His resurrection, it's unlikely they would have contained descriptions the authors had already seen to be false. For example, they would not have contained descriptions of a warrior king, of a governor and of a reign where Judah will be saved and Israel will dwell securely.

The evidence *some* prophecies may have been back-dated, is not evidence *all* prophecies were.

After preparing us through the prophets, God sent His Son to *tell* us and *show* us He was God Incarnate.

Jesus' Claim to Be the Son of God

God next gave us Jesus' direct *spoken* Word to supplement the unspoken revelation that had been afforded the Jewish prophets. Listening to Jesus, people were amazed He taught as one with authority, but the idea of a man being God didn't make sense. So Christ repeatedly (and uniquely) claimed He was God. In fact, *THE SAYINGS OF JESUS*[26] shows Jesus referred to God as His Father many dozens of times. When people rejected His claim, Christ repeatedly performed miracles to attest to His power. People liked the miracles but they made it clear they still didn't believe He was God.

Finally, God chose a communication medium no one could possibly miss. He staged a horrible human death and then presented the resurrected body of Jesus Christ. His disciples witnessed His presence and His words even after He had died. They could no longer be in

---

[26] *THE SAYINGS OF JESUS* is a textbook for *Experiential Learning* and it is included in the Appendix of this book.

doubt. They thought no one else would remain in doubt either. They were wrong.

I found I was not much different than the Jewish priests of the day. I could not get over my doubts a man could be God in disguise. As I struggled with processing my doubt, I recalled what C.S. Lewis had written in *Mere Christianity*.

> Jesus' claim He was God, He forgave sins, He always existed, He will judge the world at the end of time was quite simply the most shocking thing that has ever been uttered by human lips. The claim He could forgive sins is preposterous unless the speaker is God. A man can forgive offences against himself but not sins done against someone else. To forgive sins against others can only make sense if the forgiver is God whose laws are broken and whose love is wounded in every sin.
>
> Christ says that He is "humble and meek" and we believe Him, not noticing, if He were merely a man, humility and meekness are the very last characteristics we would attribute to some of His sayings.
>
> I am trying here to prevent anyone saying the really foolish thing that people often say about Him: I'm ready to accept Jesus as a great moral teacher, but I don't accept His claim to be God. That is the one thing we must not say. A man who was merely a man and said the sort of things Jesus said would not be a great moral teacher. He would either be a lunatic, on the level with the man who says he is a poached egg, or else he would be the Devil of Hell. You must make your choice. Either this man was, and is, the Son of God, or else a madman or something worse. You can shut Him up for a fool, you can spit at Him and kill Him as a demon or you can fall at His feet and call Him Lord and God, but let us not come with any patronizing nonsense about His being a great human teacher. He has not left that open to us. He did not intend to.

Although I found this argument powerful, I still found it to be but one argument. I decided to seek out what other scholars have concluded about whether or not Jesus Christ is the Son of God.

I Don't Have Enough Faith to Be an Atheist

In an intriguing book entitled *I Don't Have Enough Faith to Be an Atheist*[27], the authors present, as part of a thoughtful analysis of the Christian Bible, several arguments on this question. Two chapters provide additional rationale for the position Jesus Christ *is* the Son of God[28] and for the reliability of the New Testament's reports of what Jesus said and did.[29] For example, they suggest the Gospel writers would not have included embarrassing details about themselves or about Jesus if they were simply making up their accounts. If they simply wanted to attract adherents, they wouldn't have included difficult and demanding sayings of Jesus. If they feared being discovered as liars, they wouldn't have included verifiable facts and miracles that could easily be disproved. Only if they were absolutely certain of what they had witnessed, could they have abandoned long-held Jewish beliefs and practices, adopted new ones and refused to deny their testimony under persecution, threat of death and death itself.

The Case for Christ

In an easily readable book entitled, *The Case for Christ*[30], Lee Strobel, former legal editor of the Chicago Tribune, cross-examines a dozen experts with doctorates from schools like Cambridge and Princeton who are recognized religious authorities, each in his own field of expertise. An atheist, the intent of Strobel's cross-examination was to establish facts to prove the resurrection did *not* happen. The facts uncovered in his interviews established just the opposite.

One expert makes the point that Paul's conversion occurred within two years of the resurrection and, as little as three years thereafter, he had learned the key facts about Jesus' death and the names of eye witnesses to whom He had appeared in resurrected form. These eyewitness accounts were captured within five years of the crucifixion.

---

[27]   Geisler, Norman L. and Turek, Frank. *I Don't Have Enough Faith to Be an Atheist*. Wheaton, Illinois: Crossway Books, 2004

[28]   Ibid Chapter 13: *Who is Jesus: God? Or Just a Great Moral Teacher?*

[29]   Ibid Chapter 11: *The Top Ten Reasons We Know the New Testament Writers Told the Truth*

[30]   Strobel, Lee. *The Case for Christ*. Grand Rapids, Michigan: Zondervan Publishing House, 1997

Four other experts establish, with scientific evidence, the reliability of the New Testament documents, their accurate transmittal through history, extensive corroboration by ancient historians and others and how archaeology underscores their trustworthiness.

A sixth expert rebuts the challenges by *The Jesus Seminar* and a minority of other academic writers. These academics insist some of the Gospel quotations attributed to Jesus were, in reality, made up by His followers after His death. This sixth expert makes the point, because of the sensationalism of their assertions, these challengers get more air time than their share of academic opinion warrants.

A psychologist establishes Jesus believed He was on a divine mission to redeem the people of God; this was humanity's last chance; no one less than God could save humanity and He was the Son of God and the final Messiah. As C.S. Lewis had noted, if He did not intentionally deceive His followers or was not a mad man, He must have been asserting the truth. The psychologist establishes He was not mad and notes no one supports a suggestion He was an intentional deceiver.

Another expert establishes the likelihood Jesus could falsely fulfill all the Old Testament prophecies (which total over one hundred) is negligible.

A medical doctor references the American Medical Association's acceptance of his paper describing historical and medical evidence Jesus *did* die on the cross. His evidence includes the debilitating blood loss from His scourging with metal-tipped whips, the collapse of His lungs resulting from pressure exerted from being hung by His arms and the fact that water, as well as blood, flowed from the piercing of His side which is a result of death by asphyxiation.

A historian maintains that Jesus' body was absent from the tomb. He notes that the location of the tomb was well known by the surrounding community and thus that its emptiness would have been witnessed by believers and skeptics alike. Those who had a strong motivation to refute the resurrection never located a dead body.

The Gospel writers recorded it was women who first discovered the empty tomb. Because testimony of women was accepted as being suspect, they would not have included this detail unless it had actually happened.

Another expert notes that the Apostles would have had no incentive to make up claims of seeing, touching and eating with Jesus after the resurrection. Because they knew their conviction would result in their deaths, their testimony had to have been the result of their absolute certainty their claims were real.

A medical doctor establishes that Jesus' sighting by over 500 people could not be a mass hallucination as is commonly claimed. Hallucinations are personal experiences like dreams. No one would have had the capability or incentive to hypnotize 500 people.

A final expert offers what he calls circumstantial evidence – things that could only have occurred if Christ were indeed the Son of God. He cites five things: the willingness of the disciples to die for what they experienced, the revolutionized lives of skeptics like James and Saul, the radical changes in social structures cherished by Jews for centuries, the sudden appearance of Communion and baptism and the amazing emergence and growth of the Church.

I found the evidence in these two books alone to be powerful and convincing. Before this, my skepticism had been fired by the popularization of the many academic challenges to belief in Jesus. I now realized, despite the fact these challengers represent a minority of religious scholars, their prominence is due to their newsworthiness. Although I found it impractical to research a critical mass of religious scholars, the arguments advanced by the many scholars reported in these two books convinced me the majority of scholastic evidence supports belief Jesus is the Son of God.

My Case for Christ

The last step in my re-examination of *The Club*'s founder was to construct my own argument Jesus was God in human form. Earlier, I had established my knowledge God needs to tell us enough about Himself to enable us to *choose* to accept and do His will. He has to tell us about Himself without disclosing His awesome majesty and obliterating our free will.

As you have read in Chapter 14, I have concluded He "talks" to us by placing non-verbal messages directly into our minds. However, many of us don't believe this and don't pay attention. He sent His prophets to interpret His revealed Word, but some of us question their prophecies. Although He could not verbally talk to us as God without overpowering our free will, He could talk to us directly as a man so we could hear and read His words. However, this would require Him to *become* Man.

It made sense to me God would choose this last vehicle to talk to us when we had demonstrated our inability to hear Him by any other means. Nothing could prevent an all-powerful God from becoming Man if He so chose. Because God *needed* to do this and was *able* to do this, it follows, for me, He *did* this. After all, what God wants, God gets.

Because I find all these arguments for the position Jesus is the Son of God are supported, and the arguments against it are refuted, I conclude I *know* Jesus Christ is the Son of God.

Perception **Experiences**	Scientific method	My best friend	Jesus' sayings
		My late wife	McMaster professor
		Pascal's Wager	Two philosophy texts
		The Catholic Information Centre	Dawson's book
		My seminarian mentor	Harris' book
		Bits of the RC Catechism	Sound reasoning
		COR	Much of the Bible
		Participation House	Religious scholars
		Marriage Encounter	
		Daily Mass	
		A bit of the Bible	
		C.S. Lewis' *Mere Christianity*	
***Process* Learnings**	There is no proof God exists	I must accept the *possibility* God exists	Atheism is unfounded
	Atheism makes sense	The Church establishes a *likelihood* God exists	God created us, loves us and offers us eternal life with Him
		The Apostle's Creed is *more likely than not* to be true	God wants us to love Him and all His children as selflessly as we are able
		I am *capable* of selfless love of others	The Bible *is* the revealed Word of God
		I am *capable* of selfless love of God	Jesus was human and God Incarnate
		The Gospels *likely* deliver God's Word	Jesus' words *are* the Word of God
		I *knew* none of the above	
***Knowledge* of Life's Purpose**	**Earthly fulfillment**	**Live according to Church teaching**	**Love God and *all* His children as selflessly and unconditionally as we are able**

By this stage of my *Experiential Learning*, I had accumulated additional *Perception* experiences. In my template they all fall into the (shaded) category of religious scholars. C.S. Lewis established the most compelling argument Jesus Christ was the Son of God. Norman Geisler and Frank Turek provided the most extensive analysis of the divinity of Jesus and of the reliability of the New Testament's quotations of Jesus. Lee Strobel's many religious scholars added sound rationale Jesus was the Son of God. *My* case for Christ was supported by a majority of religious scholars.

Thinking through this multi-faceted *Perception* experience firmly established two (shaded) *Process* learnings. Firstly, Jesus was both human and God Incarnate. As we've seen, the evidence for the *Process* learning Jesus is God Incarnate is extensive. It follows Jesus' words are the Word of God. Because Turek and Geisler establish the Bible accurately presents Jesus' message (albeit repeatedly translated) the Gospels give me access to the Word of God.

Both *Process* learnings confirm my *Knowledge* of life's purpose. Because *The Club*'s founder's teachings are the Word of God, my ongoing study of them, which we'll explore in PART FIVE, will further confirm or correct my *Knowledge*.

However, having confirmed *The Club*'s founder is the Son of God, I found myself experiencing the nagging feeling it was almost too good to be true. Could I internalize this knowledge and direct the rest of my life according to its dictates? Yes, nothing could *prevent* God from becoming Man, but could I count on the knowledge He *did*? I couldn't overcome my inherent skepticism. I wasn't sure.

In the depths of my doubt, I was reminded of *Pascal's Wager*. I thought it could be restated as follows. Either Jesus is the Son of God or He is not. If He is not and I direct the rest of my life as if He is, I have lost little. Worst case is I benefit from the wisdom of this man's teachings. However, if He *is* the Son of God and I fail to direct the rest of my life according to His teaching of the Word of God, I risk everything. I grab Pascal's crutch whenever I question the overwhelming evidence Jesus Christ is indeed the Son of God.

As with the Bible, you may need to make your own study of the validity of the claim Jesus was God Incarnate. When you do, I hope you'll share your piece of glass with me at delsmith@rogers.com.

Looking back at my *Experiential Learning* journey to this point in my life, I realized I had now established knowledge of the main tenants of Christianity. I *knew* God created me. I *knew* God loves me unconditionally. I *knew* it is God's will I live with Him for eternity in a state of selfless love. I *knew* He has made the realization of His will dependent on my discernment, acceptance and accomplishment of it.

The next step in my re-examination of *The Club* was to focus on the Roman Catholic Catechism, which its fallible human leadership claims to be the revealed Word of God. To accept this, I had to resolve the instances where I found it in conflict with Jesus' teachings.

However, before launching into this next step, I'd like to present to you my first *Experiential Learning* case study.

CHAPTER 17

MY FIRST CASE STUDY

This case study describes a very painful tragedy in my life and the life of my family. The episode produced two learnings that became a significant part of my *Experiential Learning* journey.

Shortly after her retirement and a few years after mine, Peggy began to experience hip pain. It would be most severe while we skied – a sport our children and we had enjoyed until their early adulthood and we continued to enjoy as empty-nesters. Her stoicism permitted us to continue skiing, but she began to need longer and more frequent rest stops. One day at the Whistler Blackcolm resort in British Columbia, she could ski no further. She took off her skis and worked her way slowly down the half-mile slope sliding in a sitting position as I carried her skis and poles.

After we returned home from Whistler, the pain got worse and worse, month by month. Several visits with specialists over this period resulted in succeeding diagnoses of arthritis, bursitis and rheumatism. Finally, she requested a hip replacement. She was told there would be a several month wait time. She told me, on hearing the news, she did something she had never done before. She cried in her doctor's office. A woman's tears are hard to resist and he managed to schedule the operation within a few weeks.

After the procedure, the surgeon came to see me. He told me the operation was successful and he was pleased with the result. Parenthetically, he briefly mentioned he'd found a small "spot" and made a circle about the size of a nickel with his thumb and forefinger. I had had no experience with the way doctors sugar-coat bad news.

When I was able to talk with Peggy, she told me they had found cancer in her hip. Thinking she was looking at the worst possible scenario,

I encouraged her to think maybe the "spot" was something else. She was far too capable a nurse to be in doubt. She assured me it was bone cancer (which represents less than one percent of all cancers), it had likely metastasized (as it often starts elsewhere) and she would die before long. An incurable optimist, I hoped she was wrong. It later occurred to me, because she had been a palliative care nurse, I should have known she was right. I soon realized her detailed foreknowledge of what was in store for her made all she had to endure even worse.

She began chemo treatments along with radiation. The oncologists were unsuccessful in discovering trace elements that would indicate the source of the cancer. This left Peggy blaming herself for years of smoking (which she had successfully ended a decade or two earlier). It also left the oncologists with no choice but to administer a "cocktail" of chemo to cover all the bases. As a result the chemo was even more debilitating than usual.

When they finally discontinued the treatments, her hair began to slowly grow back and I resigned myself to the inevitability of her death. We set up palliative support in our home. Peggy began to spend her days resting on a living room sofa. We shopped for a kitten for her, which she named Heidi. Heidi was a beautiful white Siamese blue point (we had always had Siamese cats) and she would lie with Peggy for hours.

As the months dragged on, Peggy had to discontinue her short walks up and down our block. Her pain became intolerable. I learned bone cancer is one of the most painful diseases. Her oncologist prescribed morphine with a handheld pump with which she could control how much she administered. As she needed more and more morphine, she began to hallucinate. At one point she was certain there were bats in our bedroom (which I believe were the rotating blades of the ceiling fan).

She became more and more dependent on my presence. Whenever one of her nieces or a cousin came to enable me to do errands, she would repeatedly ask, "Where is Del?" She needed to feel my presence 24/7.

Peggy's sister from New York came to be with her as her death approached. One evening, she showed me the blue under my wife's fingernails and toenails. She told me, based on her experience as a nurse, this was a sign Peggy's body was beginning to shut down. Within hours she passed away. She had received the Sacrament of the Anointing of the Sick a few days earlier.

My immediate reaction was one of thanksgiving her suffering was over. Her siblings often said, "If Peggy isn't going to heaven, none of *us* are going there." Like them, I was confident she would not long await eternal life with God. I prepared her eulogy and delivered it during each of the three visitations. I organized a reception for her many friends and family members to celebrate her life with us. As was her wish, she was cremated.

As I look back over the whole experience, I realize it was an important part of my *Experiential Learning*. It immersed me in selfless love as well as providing me symptoms with which to diagnose my self-centredness.

Regarding the first of these two lessons, as Peggy's dependence on me gradually increased and as my care of her intensified, we both realized we were experiencing a greater intimacy than we had enjoyed before her diagnosis. I knew selfless love was not dependent on attraction, but I had not realized it could provide the profound intimacy we treasured. It was evidence of the reason God allows bad things to happen to good people. Terminal illness had triggered selfless love.

As for the second lesson, I saw my self-centredness in my complete absorption in *my* loss. For almost the whole period of processing my grief, I didn't give nearly enough thought to the loss my children had experienced. The way I saw it was I had lost my life partner and was left alone. On the other hand, my sons still had their partners and they and my daughter still had fulfilling lives ahead of them. It didn't register with me all three had lost the mother who had been their main source of love for most of their lives. I realized my self-centredness is so deeply engrained that I need to be able to recognize each symptom with which I am presented if I am ever to succeed even to a small degree in overcoming it.

Sometimes *Experiential Learning* is a school of hard knocks.

Grief takes a long time to work itself out. When it finally did I reapplied myself to *Experiential Learning*. I recalled it was now time to determine if the Catechism, produced by *The Club*'s fallible human leaders, is the revealed Word of God.

CHAPTER 18

THE ROMAN CATHOLIC CATECHISM

I f the Roman Catholic Catechism is the revealed Word of God, its study is as important as is study of *The Club*'s charter, the Holy Bible. In fact, its study may be even *more* important, as it is more specific on the issues of our time than is the Bible.

There are two reasons to conclude the Roman Catholic Catechism is very likely the revealed Word of God. Firstly, Jesus chose Peter upon whom to build His Church and promised to send it the Holy Spirit to guide it. Secondly, on almost all issues, the Catechism's positions are consistent with the teachings of Jesus.

However, if it were to take a position contrary to the teachings of Jesus, it could *not* be the revealed Word of God. Where this appears to be the case, the only way to confirm one's conclusion that it *is* the revealed Word of God is to resolve the apparent conflict. To resolve it, one must determine if the position is, in reality, consistent with Jesus' teachings, simply a misinterpretation of them or truly contrary to them. Occasionally there may be no good case to be made for any of these three possibilities.

The Church places the responsibility of discerning the Word of God entirely on our shoulders. It informs conscience rather than policing it. It believes its Catechism to be absolute truth and thus its best vehicle for informing conscience. However, as I learned as a catechumen, and outlined in Chapter 4, individual Catholics can conscientiously question specific positions.

The Church prohibits its members from *rejecting* any of its teachings and strongly advises them not to ignore them. I find both positions are sound. On the first one, I and all its members are at least as subject to misinterpretation as are its authorities (the Pope and Bishops). On the second position, it is much more dangerous to ignore the Roman Catholic Catechism than it is to conscientiously question its positions. For anyone who accepts even the *possibility* it is the revealed Word of God, it is folly to ignore it.

However, it may very well be some of its *interpretations* and resulting articulations of what the Holy Spirit revealed to it *are* flawed. Just as the Bible is the product of fallible human beings, so is the Catechism. Just as fallible Jewish prophets, on occasion, misinterpreted God's revelation, as we explored in Chapter 14, it is possible that at times the fallible Popes and Bishops have misinterpreted what the Holy Spirit has revealed to their Church. In order for me to *know* the Catechism is the revealed Word of God, I needed to resolve the inconsistency I found between several of its positions and the teaching of Jesus Christ.

Before I could begin to question these positions, I had to understand the thinking supporting them. The treatise that most thoroughly supports the positions of the Catechism that I question is John Paul II's *Theology of the Body*[31]. When I decided its study was too challenging, I was referred to a more readable interpretation of it, entitled *Fill These Hearts: God, Sex and the Universal Longing*[32]. It is produced by the COR Project[33], whose worldwide mission is to enable understanding and internalization of John Paul II's thinking.

I learned *Theology of the Body* refers to what we can learn of God, whom we can't physically experience, from our bodies, which we do experience. In order to discern and accomplish His will, we must take every opportunity to get to better *know* God. What does *Theology of the Body* tell us we can learn about God from what we experience in our bodies?

It teaches us God's will in giving us three gifts. God gave our bodies the physical ecstasy of sexual arousal to give us a glimpse of the spiritual ecstasy of loving Him in heaven. He gave us the sexual act to enable us to be as much inside each other as physically possible so as to give us a glimpse of the heavenly ecstasy of being spiritually in Him and having Him in us. He gave us the capacity of procreation and its experience of parental love in order to give us a glimpse of His fatherly love of each of us. His will is that we use each of these gifts as expressions of the selfless and unconditional love Christ modelled rather than as a source of selfish pleasure.

[31] John Paul II. *Man and Woman He Created Them: Theology of the Body.* Boston: Pauline Books and Media, 2006

[32] West, Christopher. *Fill These Hearts: God, Sex, and the Universal Longing.* New York: Image, an imprint of the Crown Publishing Group, 2012

[33] https://www.corproject.com

"A new commandment I give to you, that you love one another: just as I have loved you, you also are to love one another." (John 13: 34-35)

Theology of the Body teaches us the attributes of the love Christ modelled.
- **Freely given**   I lay down my life. No one takes it from me. (John 10: 12-18)
- **Without limit**   I speak . . . that they may have my joy fulfilled in themselves. (John 17: 11-19)
- **Faithful**   I am with you always, to the end of the age. (Matt 28: 18-20)
- **Fruitful**   Whoever abides in me and I in him, he it is that bears much fruit. (John 15: 1-6)

I find John Paul II's interpretation of the Holy Spirit's revelation extends Christ's teachings in a way that is largely consistent with them.

However, what I question is how the Catechism *extends* the teachings of *Theology of the Body* and Jesus. For examples, it teaches us the act of love cannot be *fully* fruitful unless it enables procreation and love cannot be limitless and faithful unless it enjoys the graces attendant to the Sacrament of Marriage.

Having understood the basis for the Catechism's positions, I was now ready to pursue those I question. In my pursuit, I found the first three positions to be the revealed Word of God, the next four to be misinterpretations of the revealed Word of God and the last to be indeterminate. I found *none* of these positions that I questioned to be *contrary* to Christ's teachings.

- Masturbation
- Abortion and Euthanasia
- Christian Exclusivity
- Pre-Marital Sex
- Contraception
- Homosexuality
- Celibacy and Female Ordination
- Adultery

Masturbation

For over half of my life, I questioned the teaching masturbation is against the will of God. Because God gave us the gift of sexual arousal, it didn't make sense to me that it was His will that we not satisfy it. However, once I accepted John Paul II's teaching of God's *purpose* in giving us this gift, I saw that masturbation does not accomplish God's will. It is not a non-verbal expression of the love for one another that Christ modelled.

I conclude the Catechism's position that masturbation is a sin is a correct interpretation of the revealed Word of God because it goes against God's will. It is a lesser sin, because it hurts no one other than God and the practitioner, but it is a sin nevertheless.

Abortion and Euthanasia

Right to life is a controversial and unpopular position taken by the Catechism. It took considerable study for me to adequately question this position. I had determined that God loves all His children, that science can show us a fetus' humanity within weeks of conception and that the Bible is the revealed Word of God. What could these three pieces of knowledge contribute to my study?

The Bible's *Ten Commandments* tell us we are not to murder. (Exodus 20: 13) No reasonable doubt remains that a fetus is a human being.

Specifics from the creation story indicate we don't have dominion over human life. The Bible tells us that on the sixth day God said,

> Let us make man in our image, after our likeness. And let them have dominion over the fish of the sea and over the birds of the heavens and over the livestock and over all the earth and over every creeping thing that creeps on the earth. (Genesis 1: 26)

The Word of God is very specific about what we have dominion over. It does not include human life.

Even when society legalizes euthanasia and abortion we are not free to obey what goes against God's will. When the Jewish leaders ". . . strictly charged (Peter and the apostles) not to teach in this name", they answered, "We must obey God rather than men." (Acts 5: 29)

Job realized, because God gives life, only God can decide when to end it. "The Spirit of God has made me, and the breath of the Almighty gives me life." (Job 33: 4) Much of Job's life was one of continual suffering but he realized only God had the right to end his life. He concluded Man's ". . . days are determined, and the number of his months is with you (God) and you have appointed his limits that he cannot pass." (Job 14: 5)

My common sense tells me we don't have the right to end a life. Our lives are God's gift and it cannot be God's will that we reject that gift.

On the other hand the issue is replete with difficulty, pain and challenge. A woman who conceives unintentionally or under force bears a terrible burden if she has no alternative but to sacrifice her life for an unwanted child. The caregivers of a pain-ridden, chronically ill relative bear a terrible burden if they have no alternative but to helplessly witness for decades the unavoidable pain of their loved one. It seems to me we all are called to do everything we can to ease that suffering short of ending the life of *any* child of God including the unborn and the chronically ill.

For me, the litmus test on this issue, as on every issue we face, is the will of God. Which action follows the will of God? Would God want us to terminate the life of one of His children or would He want us to further develop our capacity of selfless love by doing everything of which we become capable to ease the suffering of His child. I have concluded it is inconceivable God would want us to terminate a human life.

I conclude the Catechism's position that abortion and euthanasia are sins is a correct interpretation of the revealed Word of God because both are opposed to what we can discern to be the will of God.

Christian Exclusivity

Before my questioning, my early understanding of the Catechism's position was that only Roman Catholics could reach heaven. Later, I was led to believe it was that only Christians could. Neither seemed consistent with Jesus' teaching that God loves all His children. I was reminded of an amusing story.

> As St. Peter was touring the saved through heaven, one of them noticed a high wall in the distance. When asked what it was, St. Peter replied, "Oh, that's the section reserved for Roman Catholics. They still believe they are the only ones up here."

Still, at first, one of Jesus' assertions seems to exclude non-Christians from heaven.

> I am the way and the truth and the life. No one comes to the Father except through me. (John 14: 1-7)

105

My questioning led to my understanding Jesus was excluding no one from heaven and that this had never been a position taken by the Catechism.

Jesus frequently talked of Himself as being one with God. As such, His statement could be better interpreted as God can only be reached through God. Only God can provide us the fullness of truth. Individual religions can provide only incidents of truth. This interpretation is completely consistent with Jesus' teaching that it is easier for a camel to pass through the eye of a needle on its own than for a rich man to enter into heaven on his own. The Catechism's position is we cannot adequately prepare, on our own, for eternal life with God. We must ask for and accept God's help. Christians have the teachings of Jesus and access to the Roman Catholic Catechism to help them know this. For non-Christians, *any* way they can know they need God's help can lead them to ask God to grant them it.

The Roman Catholic Church's prayer on Good Friday – *The Solemn Intercessions* – illustrates the Catechism's true position on who can reach God. After several prayers for the Roman Catholic Church and its catechumens (those preparing to join the Church), it prays that Protestant Christians, the Jewish people, those who do not believe in Jesus Christ and those who don't believe in God will become one with God. This inclusivity is evidence the Catechism's position is that God will show His mercy to *all* humanity. The *sequence* of the prayers illustrates the Church's position that *its* establishment by Jesus Christ means it is most able to lead its faithful to open their hearts and their minds to the love of God and to the discernment and accomplishment of His will. The *inclusivity* of its prayers illustrates its position that God may have many ways of reaching Protestant Christians, Jewish people, non-Christians, atheists and agnostics.

I conclude the Catechism's position that God welcomes *all* His children is a correct interpretation of the revealed Word of God because of its consistency with Jesus' teaching.

Pre-Marital Sex

Theology of the Body teaches that pre-marital sex (as well as sex in general) is sinful when it is used as a source of selfish pleasure rather than as an expression of the faithful, fully committed and selfless love that Christ modelled. However, the Catechism's position is that such faithful commitment to each other can *only* be assured by the Sacrament of Marriage because of the graces that it claims are attendant to that sacrament alone. Marriage is an effective means of formalizing the commitment we must make to each other before we engage in sex. However, it is unclear to me that commitment is *dependent* on sacramental graces.

Only God, and the two people engaging in sex, can know whether their love for each other follows the model of Christ's love of us. It seems to me God doesn't need our marriage vows in order to recognize our commitment. It seems to me God wills the *commitment* rather than *how* it is formalized.

I conclude the Catechism's position on pre-marital sex is a misinterpretation of the revealed Word of God. It misinterprets the role of marriage. Marriage is an enabler rather than a prerequisite of a commitment to love one another as Christ modelled. Rather than pre-marital sex being a sin, it is selfish, pleasure-seeking, uncommitted sex that is a sin. Non-married couples are capable of the commitment that is God's will.

Contraception

Theology of the Body teaches that using God's gift of sexual arousal and the sexual act solely to provide ourselves selfish, non-loving, fleeting pleasure through the use of others' bodies is a sin. To me this is a correct interpretation of the revealed Word of God. If it went no further, the teaching would be that the sin is in the *use* we make of contraception rather than in contraception itself.

However, *Theology of the Body* does go one step further. It teaches that contraception is *always* against God's will because it unnaturally separates the gifts of sexual expression and procreation. I can find nothing in the teachings of Jesus to support the claim that God's gifts are a package deal.

In the absence of contraception, the only way to use God's gift of procreation responsibly is abstinence. However, abstinence separates God's gift of the sexual act from the expression of the faithful, fully committed and selfless love for which He *gave* us the sexual act. To me, abstinence is just as much a separation of God's gifts as is contraception.

It seems clear God wants us to use His gift of procreation responsibly. He cannot want us to procreate every time we express our faithful, fully committed and selfless love for each other. Is the Holy Spirit's revelation that we should exercise our responsibility with abstinence or with contraception? Abstinence requires that we sacrifice by foregoing God's gift of the sexual act. To me this contravenes Jesus' teachings that God does not want our sacrifice.

> Go and learn what this means "I desire mercy and not sacrifice." (Matt 9:13)

> And if you had known what this means "I desire mercy and not sacrifice." you would not have condemned the guiltless. (Matt 12: 7)

> {Scribe: . . . to love Him with all the heart and with all the understanding and with all the strength and to love one's neighbour as oneself, is much more than all whole burnt offerings and sacrifices.} {Jesus:} You are not far from the kingdom of God. (Mark 12: 33-34)

It seems clear to me God's will is that we love as Jesus modelled rather than that we sacrifice through abstinence.

I conclude the Catechism's position that contraception is a sin is a misinterpretation of the revealed Word of God. The misinterpretation is that the possibility of procreation must be part of *every* use of the sexual act in order to love as Christ modelled. It remains true that the use of contraception, to enable selfish, non-loving, fleeting pleasure through the use of others' bodies, *is* sinful because it is not the will of God.

Homosexuality

The Catechism's position that homosexual relationships are sinful is questionable because we now realize that homosexuality is a condition rather than a choice. A person has no more control over the sexuality God gave them than they do over their sex.

When I was still a child, my mother taught me that each person is part male and part female. Most are predominantly one or the other so we rarely see their less dominant side. Some are physically male and emotionally female and vice versa. God created each person's sexuality. God loves all His children. Because this thinking made great sense to me, I revisited Christ's teaching.

> But from the beginning of creation "God made them male and female. Therefore a man shall leave his father and mother and hold fast to his wife and they shall become one flesh." So they are no longer two but one flesh. What therefore God has joined together, let not man separate. (Mark 10: 6-9)

We now know it is only in the *majority* of cases God makes each of ". . . them (predominately) male or female". God makes *some* of His children *both* male and female. I conclude that Jesus' teaching that a person ". . . shall leave his (or her) father and mother and hold fast to his (or her) partner and they shall become one. . . " applies to homosexuals as much as it does to heterosexuals. For them, as well as for heterosexuals, "What therefore God has joined together, let not man separate."

For me, it follows homosexuals have all the rights *and* responsibilities of marriage and of sustaining a committed, loving relationship. Homosexual sexual relations, outside a loving, committed relationship, are just as sinful as those of heterosexuals. Homosexuals must love as God loves.

The Catechism's position is that a homosexual, loving relationship is sinful because it cannot result in procreation, and thus cannot produce the fruitfulness that is an essential attribute of the love Christ modelled. We now have seen countless examples of a loving, homosexual relationship being fruitful in the couple's adoption and parenting of children (much as Joseph adopted Jesus). The fruitfulness of those in a homosexual relationship can be their love and care of their family and others of God's children.

I conclude the Catechism's position on homosexuality is a misinterpretation of God's Word. The misinterpretation is that homosexuality is a choice and that a homosexual relationship is abnormal and unfruitful. Rather than homosexuality being a sin, just as with heterosexuals, sin exists only when homosexuals use their sexuality for selfish, pleasure-seeking, uncommitted sex.

Celibacy and Female Ordination

The Catechism's position is that priests must not marry and females are not permitted to become priests.

For many years, I assumed the rationale behind this was that Christ did not marry, was male and appointed only male apostles. The Church was simply following Christ's example. This didn't make sense to me for two reasons. Firstly, I couldn't find any scripture to suggest that Christ demanded His apostles remain celibate or that He prohibited female disciples. Secondly, as far as I could determine He had many disciples who were married and/or female. It seemed to me, in appointing only male apostles, Jesus was simply following the culture of His time.

Theology of the Body takes a more complex position. God gave us marriage on Earth to prepare us for marriage to Him in heaven. However, marriage of two people is not the only vocation that can accomplish God's will. The Catechism teaches Jesus married the Church. It concludes that vocations where priests marry the Church and females marry Christ prepare their practitioners even better for marriage to God in heaven. I question this position for two reasons.

First of all, the only three references in the Bible to a bridegroom leave a lot of room for doubt. John the Baptist once referred to Jesus as a bridegroom when he met Him at the River Jordan.

> The one who has the bride is the bridegroom. The friend of the bridegroom, who stands and hears him, rejoices greatly at the bridegroom's voice. (John 3: 29)

Christ's use of the term bridegroom occurs in only two of His parables.

> Can you make wedding guests fast while the bridegroom is with them? The days will come when the bridegroom is taken away from them and they will fast in those days. (Luke 5: 34-35)

> Then the kingdom of heaven will be like ten virgins who took their lamps and went to meet the bridegroom. Five of them were foolish and five were wise. For when the foolish took their lamps, they took no oil with them, but the wise took flasks of oil with their lamps. As the bridegroom was delayed, they all became drowsy and slept. But at midnight there was a cry "Here is the bridegroom! Come out to meet him." Then all those virgins rose and trimmed their lamps. And the foolish said to the wise "Give us some of your oil, for our lamps are going out." But the wise answered, saying "Since there will not be enough for us and for you, go rather to the dealers and buy for yourselves." And while they were going to buy, the bridegroom came and those who were ready went in with him to the marriage feast and the door was shut. (Matt 25: 1-10)

It seems to me that these parables are metaphors as are many parables. If Christ meant that He was married to His Church and that anyone who leads His Church must be also, would He not have stated that explicitly?

Second of all, even if vocations other than marriage of two people *are* God's will, God must be giving us a choice whether or not to marry a person, the Church or Christ. I can find no place where God Incarnate *insisted* that those who devote their lives to Him and/or the Church must not marry another person. If God Incarnate didn't insist on it, I can find no justification for the Catechism to insist on it. I wonder if Jesus would tell the Roman Catholic Church what He told the Pharisees.

> You leave the commandment of God and hold to the tradition of men. And many such things you do." (Matt 15: 1-9, Mark 7: 5-13)

In questioning this position, I realize it has no impact on me or on anyone except priests, religious and candidates for these two vocations. However, it is troubling to me for three reasons.

Firstly, the exclusion of women from any field, including priesthood, is an unjustified legacy of male domination. While male domination still persists in much of today's world, it is equally true women have demonstrated they are as capable as men in most things and superior to men in many things. I'm reminded of a quote. "Any woman who strives for equality with a man has little ambition."

Secondly, the non-participation of women in the Roman Catholic Church, as in any organization, limits what can be accomplished. The exclusion of female candidates for the priesthood cuts the supply line in half. The requirement of celibacy likely deters many male candidates for the priesthood. The result is harmful to the Church and to its members. The Church fails its members where it can't provide them a priest. Recognizing this shortfall, the Church ordains deacons. Sadly, it excludes women from this role as well.

Thirdly, the Church takes the position that non-celibate priests would be unable to focus all their energies on their parishioners and/or the Church. It seems to me priests would likely be far less troubled and far more effective if they were married. Leaders in government and industry consistently maintain that their spouses were of immense support in achieving their success. Why would this not be true of priests (as it has been shown to be in most Protestant and Eastern Orthodox churches)?

I conclude the Catechism's position on celibacy and female ordination is a misinterpretation of the revealed Word of God. The misinterpretation is that the Bible's references to bridegroom mean that Christ is married to the Church and thus the leaders of His Church must be as well.

Adultery

I find the Catechism's teaching, that a loving adulterous relationship cannot be permanently forgiven, very difficult to understand and thus very difficult to satisfyingly question.

> But from the beginning of creation "God made them male and female. Therefore a man shall leave his father and mother and hold fast to his wife and they shall become one flesh." So they are no longer two but one flesh. What therefore God has joined together, let not man separate. Whoever divorces his wife and marries another commits adultery against her and if she divorces her husband and marries another, she commits adultery. (Mark 10: 6-12)

> I say to you: whoever divorces his wife, except for sexual immorality and marries another, commits adultery. {Disciples: If such is the case of a man with his wife, it is better not to marry.} Not everyone can receive this saying, but only those to whom it is given. For there are eunuchs who have been so from birth and there are eunuchs who have been made eunuchs by men and there are eunuchs who have made themselves eunuchs for the sake of the kingdom of heaven. Let the one who is able to receive this receive it. (Matt 19: 4-12)

> Let him who is without sin among you be the first to throw a stone at her. Woman, where are they? Has no one condemned you? {Woman, accused of adultery: No one, Lord.} Neither do I condemn you; go and from now on sin no more. (John 8: 7-11)

I do not understand what is meant by "one flesh", "What ... God has joined together", "Whoever divorces ..." and "sin no more".

Since "one flesh" is visibly not a physical oneness, could it refer to the oneness of the love of each other, which a couple shares? If so, "What . . . God has joined together, let not man separate" would refer to that love rather than to the couple's cohabitation. Divorced and separated couples "separate" that love only when they fail to retain its every attribute except sexual love. Where both parties maintain their commitment to selflessly supporting each other and their children, it seems to me they are honouring their commitment to love each other freely, faithfully and fruitfully. Of course, where divorce and separation are used to enable selfish, sexual pleasure at the expense of one's partner, it is clear to me they are sins.

Does "What . . . God has joined together" happen only in the Sacrament of Marriage? If so, are those who marry outside the Roman Catholic Church or who live common law exempt? Does "Whoever divorces . . ." mean that the victim of the divorce is not subject to adultery? If so, it would seem it applies to both only where both choose to divorce.

Does "sin no more" mean do not, *again*, separate what God has, once again, joined together or do not *resume* the adultery that I have just forgiven. If the former, I read it as when you commit yourself to a new partner, do not commit adultery again in *that* relationship. If the latter, I read it as you must not resume the adultery I have just forgiven.

In my puzzlement, I next turned to *Theology of the Body*. John Paul II teaches God's will in giving us our sexuality is to allow a couple's love for one another on Earth to be as close as possible to what our love of Him will be like in heaven. If God gave us this gift, I conclude He can't want us to reject it when we make a new commitment to love another. God knows that, when a young couple makes a sincere marriage commitment to each other, neither has control over whether they will grow together or apart. When a couple grows apart, they can't will a return of the sexual love that was lost. If they maintain their commitment to love each other in every way over which they *have* control, it seems to me God would still want them to use His gift whenever they make a new commitment to love another.

Jesus taught we are to love one another as we love ourselves. When a couple can no longer love each other as man and wife, they can still love one other as they love themselves. They can want the best for each other and their family. They can free their children from an environment absent of love and continue to cooperate in their love and support of their children. They can free each other from a commitment they can no longer keep and from confinement to a non-loving spousal relationship. They can do all this even after they have made a loving commitment to another.

On the other hand, the Catechism takes the position that Jesus' forgiveness was dependent upon not repeating the adultery He forgave. Because adultery applies to *every* sexual *act* outside marriage, the Church's interpretation of the Holy Spirit's revelation seems consistent with Jesus' teaching.

I can find no satisfactory argument to show the position of the Roman Catholic Church to be consistent with Jesus' teaching, simply a misinterpretation of it or truly contrary to it. As well, because I can understand neither Jesus' teaching nor the Church's position, I am left uncertain whether or not the Catechism's position that a loving adulterous relationship cannot be permanently forgiven is the revealed Word of God.

Conclusions

My thorough questioning of each of these positions has had immense benefit for me. Without questioning the Catechism's positions, I would not have discerned God's will on the first three of these positions. Without questioning its position on all but the last of the remaining issues, I could not have concluded the Catechism is not contrary to the revealed Word of God, but simply a misinterpretation of it. It has also helped me better understand sin.

The Church teaches that we sin only when we know we sin. Those who have had no opportunity to know (such as infants) or too little access to knowledge (such as primitive societies) are not guilty of sin. However, we *are* guilty of sin when we are culpably ignorant because we have failed to inform ourselves, to the very best of our abilities, of what is sinful.

I have concluded several things. Our conscience is our interpretation of what the Holy Spirit is revealing to us. The Holy Spirit does not dictate what it reveals to our conscience by putting its revelation into words. It leaves it up to us to translate its revelation into words. When we fail to do our very best to interpret what the Holy Spirit reveals, we abandon ourselves to sin. When we fail to fully inform our conscience, we are guilty when we sin.

The Catechism is Christ's Church's interpretation of what the Holy Spirit is revealing to it. It contains the combined wisdom of the Popes and Bishops over more than 2000 years. The Catechism is the very best interpretation of what the Holy Spirit reveals of which the Church has been capable to date. However, just as God left it up to fallible Jewish prophets to interpret His revelation in the Bible, the Holy Spirit leaves it up to the fallible Church leadership to interpret its revelation in the Catechism to the best of its ability.

Because the content of the Catechism is revealed by the Holy Spirit and because its interpretation of that revelation is largely consistent with the teachings of Christ, I conclude I can *know* the Catechism is indeed the revealed Word of God. That a handful of its positions *appear* to me to be misinterpretations, in no way refutes this conclusion. They are the inevitable result of human (mine or the Church's) fallibility. They are no indication that the Catechism is not the revealed Word of God. I can't let my conclusion, that some of its positions are, or may be, simply misinterpretations of the revealed Word of God, keep me from knowing the Catechism *is* the revealed Word of God. As my mother often cautioned "Don't throw the baby out with the bath water."

I cannot fully inform my conscience without *fully* internalizing what the Catechism teaches. To fully internalize its teachings, I must thoroughly study and question, to the best of my ability, all of them that affect me personally. I must continue to question what I learn in order to fully inform my conscience. As long as I fail to do this to the very best of my ability, I am leaving myself subject to sin. I will have no excuse for such failure.

The Catechism is uncompromising as I feel it must be. If it were to yield to popular opinion, it could not be the revealed Word of God. I conclude, where individual interpretations are inconsistent with the teachings of Christ, the Church's continuing discernment of the Holy Spirit's revelation will eventually produce a modification of its positions to bring them in line.

The renowned Canadian Jesuit, Bernard Lonergan, observed, "The Church inevitably arrives on the scene, late and a little out of breath."

Pope Francis appears to be pursuing further discernment of the Holy Spirit's revelation. He has apparently concluded that married men should be able to join the priesthood even though his position is still not supported by a consensus of the Bishops. This consensus will be hard to achieve because of its implications. If married men can become priests, what can justify preventing priests from becoming married men? Hopefully Pope Francis' practice of continuing discernment will be institutionalized.

Once again, you may need to make your own study of the Roman Catholic Catechism to establish *your* knowledge whether or not it is the revealed Word of God. I strongly recommend you undertake this study. Even if you feel the Catechism is only *possibly* the revealed Word of God, can you ignore such a possibility? When you do undertake your own study, I'd welcome your piece of glass at delsmith@rogers.com.

Perception Experiences	Scientific method	My best friend	Jesus' sayings
		My late wife	McMaster professor
		Pascal's Wager	Two philosophy texts
		The Catholic Information Centre	Dawson's book
		My seminarian mentor	Harris' book
		Bits of the RC Catechism	Sound reasoning
		COR	Much of the Bible
		Participation House	Religious scholars
		Marriage Encounter	RC Catechism
		Daily Mass	
		A bit of the Bible	
		C.S. Lewis' *Mere Christianity*	
Process Learnings	There is no proof God exists	I must accept the *possibility* God exists	Atheism is unfounded
	Atheism makes sense	The Church establishes a *likelihood* God exists	God created us, loves us and offers us eternal life with Him
		The Apostle's Creed is *more likely than not* to be true	God wants us to love Him and all His children as selflessly as we are able
		I am *capable* of selfless love of others	The Bible *is* the revealed Word of God
		I am *capable* of selfless love of God	Jesus was human and God Incarnate
		The Gospels *likely* deliver God's Word	Jesus' words *are* the Word of God
		I *knew* none of the above	The RC Catechism *is* the revealed Word of God
Knowledge of Life's Purpose	**Earthly fulfillment**	**Live according to Church teaching**	**Love God and *all* His children as selflessly and unconditionally as we are able**

At this point, I took stock of where I was in my re-examination of *The Club*. Looking at the last row of my evolving template from left to right, we recall it had begun with my re-examination of my first position on life's purpose. It had continued with my re-examination of my second position on life's purpose – it is *more likely than not* to be to live according to Church teaching. That re-examination produced my current knowledge that life's purpose is to love God and all His children as selflessly and unconditionally as we are able. Prior to what I have just shared with you in this chapter, my re-examination of my current knowledge of life's purpose had focused on *The Club*'s charter and founder.

My latest (shaded) *Perception* experience was my re-examination of *The Club*'s fallible human leadership and of its Roman Catholic Catechism. My re-examination resulted in the (shaded) *Process* learning that, where it is consistent with Jesus' greatest commandment, the Roman Catholic Catechism is the revealed Word of God.

All four of the most recent *Process* learnings, resulting from my re-examination of *The Club*, confirmed my *Knowledge* of life's purpose.

Of all my *Process* learnings, the most compelling is Jesus *is* the Son of God. As long as I had simply accepted the *likelihood* of Jesus' divinity, I had remained a lukewarm member of *The Club*. Once my re-examination of its founder established my *knowledge* Jesus is the Son of God, I began to suspect I was irrevocably moving towards fervent membership.

Where would my re-examination of *The Club* take me next? Jesus gave us the Word of God in the twin commandments "Love your God with *all* your heart, *all* your mind, *all* your strength and *all* your soul and your neighbour (*all* God's children) as yourself." I decided my next step was to more fully understand what Jesus meant by all those *all*'s in *The Club*'s greatest commandments.

PART FOUR

COMMANDMENTS

CHAPTER 19

THE GREATEST COMMANDMENT – LOVE YOUR GOD

At this stage of my *Experiential Learning*, I had three important issues to think through about this first portion of the greatest commandment. Why does God command us to love Him? What does this commandment demand of me? How am I to be able to obey it?

Why

Earlier in *Experiential Learning*, I had begun to resolve the puzzle of why we are commanded to love God. You'll recall, it had seemed to me, since God is self-sufficient, He has no *need* of our love. Why would God even *value* our love when it pales in comparison with His selfless and unconditional love? I finally realized He is asking this for *our* sake rather than for His. God is simply asking us to *return* His love *in kind*.

What do I mean by *in kind*? As you read in Chapter 13, sound reasoning established my knowledge, because God is perfect, His love must be perfect – selfless and unconditional. To love Him *in kind* our love must be selfless and unconditional. God wills this because He wants us to be with Him in heaven. Why must we love selflessly and unconditionally to be in heaven?

Jesus gives us the answer. He teaches us in the Lord's Prayer "Thy will be done on earth as *it is* in heaven." (Italics mine) It is noteworthy Jesus did not add "by some of the people some of the time." It follows *everyone* in heaven does God's will. They love Him and all His children with selfless and unconditional love to the very best of their ability. It seems to follow those, who don't, can't yet fit into heaven.

I conclude God commands us to love Him not for *His* good but for *our* prerequisite self-development.

This thinking satisfied the "Why?" question for me.

The question of *what* this commandment demands of me is answered by its qualification. The *way* we are to love the Lord, our God, is with *all* our heart, with *all* our strength, with *all* our mind and with *all* our soul. I determined this commandment demands a great deal more of me than I had blithely assumed. It seemed clear I am commanded to love God to the *best* of my ability. I must love God with *all* my faculties. This realization caused me to look at each faculty, one at a time.

With All My Heart

What does it mean to love God with *all* one's heart?

I decided to reflect on which type of *earthly* love most engages my heart. As a child, I loved my parents based on my dependence on them. As an adult, I loved my late wife based initially on my attraction to her. As a parent, I loved my children based on my procreation of them. Of these, the love of my late wife most absorbed me and most engaged my heart. After all, we lived together more than I lived with anyone, including my children. To love God with *all* my heart, I must love Him with *at least* as much of my heart as I loved Peggy. What characterized loving her with all my heart?

Firstly, I chose Peggy. I chose her initially because I was deeply attracted to her. As I got to know her, my choice was continually reaffirmed because I respected her values and trusted her. Secondly, I wanted to be with her as much of each day as I could. I wanted to luxuriate in the feeling of intimacy we had. I sought out her input on every important decision I faced. Thirdly, I put what she wanted before what I wanted. This was less selfless than it may first appear. I quickly realized what she wanted was usually better for us both than what I wanted. Fourthly, I wanted to give her everything I could. I was more fulfilled in giving to her than in getting from her. Fifthly, I put my love for her above all the other loves of my life. It was not that I did not love others. It was simply, because I devoted more of my life to her than to anyone else, I loved her more than anyone else. As well, I got better at more frequently telling her how much I loved her and how much she meant to me. Finally, I spent my life working at my love for her, as she undeniably worked at her love for me. My love was an act of will, driven by the intensity of my heartfelt love of her.

I have concluded that to love God with all my heart means my love of God has to be at least as deep as was my love of Peggy. My love of God must embody, at the very least, all the elements of my love of her. Let's look at these elements in the same order as I have just recalled them.

Firstly, I need to *choose* to love God and deepen my attraction to God by increasing my awareness of all He has given to me, all He has done for me and all He has created around me. I need to internalize God's values and trust completely in God. Secondly, I need to make time every day for God and exclude from my attention all that can distract me from Him. I have to do my best to develop an intimacy with God. I need to "talk" to (that is, direct my mind towards) God about everything that is important in my life. I need to "listen" to God (that is focus my attention on what He has put directly into my mind). Thirdly, I have to put God's will before my will. Fourthly, I need to offer my *all* to God including everything I accomplish, everything I acquire and everything with which I am blessed. Fifthly, I need to make God more important than *anyone* else in my life. I have to profess my love for God as often as I can and at least daily. I need to thank Him for His unconditional love of me. Finally, I need to spend my life renewing daily the act of will to do all these things to the best of my ability. I need to fully engage my heart in my love of God.

My sister recently shared a quotation with me. "What would happen if you awoke this morning and saw all you had left was what you had thanked God for yesterday?"

With All My Strength

What does it mean to love God with *all* one's strength?

I concluded one of the most important aspects is to *discern* the full extent of one's gifts. God has given each of us different gifts and different degrees of these gifts. To love God with *all* my strength I need to develop and apply *all* these gifts. Some of us are good listeners; some excel in observation; some think more logically or more imaginatively than others; some are more empathetic than others; some excel in will power and so on and so on. I need to think about the gifts I have been given rather than take them for granted and ignore them. I need to discern my stronger gifts and fully apply them. I need to continually develop my weaker gifts. To not fully develop and apply *all* the gifts God gave me is not loving God with *all* my strength.

A second aspect is to *use* these gifts to accomplish the will of God to the best of my ability. If I am a good listener, I need to actively pursue opportunities to listen to others. I have to afford them as much of my time as it takes to fully explore what matters to them. If I excel in observation, I have to acknowledge what I see in others and pick up on others' body language. If I think more logically or more imaginatively than others, I need to respectfully share the benefit of my thinking. If I am more empathetic than others, I have to offer my empathy where others can't. If I excel in will power, I need to take every occasion to apply that will power for the benefit of others. When I put my *all* into doing these things for *all* God's children at *every* opportunity, I love God with *all* my strength.

Finally, I need to discern the *extent* of my capabilities. Most of us are unaware of how extensive our capabilities are. God knows. I have come to the realization that the only way for *me* to know I am using all the capability God gave me, is to do a little more with each capability today than I did yesterday. A sports analogy is "One more rep." As in golf, I'm playing against myself. It is only when I repeatedly find I can do no better that I can know I've achieved my personal best. To do anything less than my best is not loving God with *all* my strength.

I find I forget these three aspects of loving God with all my strength whenever I complacently conclude I am good. Why are we satisfied with being good? Why do we not strive to become better? Why do we not continue that striving until we become as good as we can be?

With All My Mind

What does it mean to love God with *all* one's mind?

To me, the most important aspect is to doggedly pursue *each* question one has of one's faith. As an example, the Roman Catholic Catechism teaches that during the Eucharist the bread and wine become the body and blood of Jesus Christ. Although I questioned this teaching, I failed to fully pursue it for most of my life. I must pursue each question, like this one, that I experience. I must pursue it until I come to *know* it is or is not the case. Whenever I choose not to pursue a question, I am failing to love God with all my mind.

A priest once told me "When you question your faith, you are loving God with your mind."

A second aspect of loving God with all my mind is to pursue *all* opportunities to better *know* Him. For example, early in *Experiential Learning*, I doubted the Bible and the Roman Catholic Catechism were the revealed Word of God. As a result, I ignored both and what they could teach me about God. I didn't give either any serious thought for a considerable period of time. In so doing, I definitely was *not* loving God with all my mind.

As you read in Chapters 14, 15 and 18, I have come to the conclusion I can no longer ignore either. To reach this conclusion I had to re-examine my skepticism. As you'll recall this involved identifying the things I found inconsistent with what I had come to know at that stage and resolving those inconsistencies. The result was I came to the knowledge both are the revealed Word of God and I need to continue to study them to better *know* God. The mental effort and discipline involved in my studies is an act of loving God with all my mind.

Many other avenues of pursuit have been presented to me over the decades. It has been up to *me* to fully pursue each opportunity. You have come across many of my avenues of pursuit in what you have read so far. They include the rare occasions when I meet people who will pursue my thinking about God and share theirs. They include philosophy, the writings of atheists and religious academics, other readings *they* reference and reflection on experiences such as COR, Participation House and Marriage Encounter. These avenues of pursuit are the *Perception* experiences of my *Experiential Learning*. Loving God with *all* my mind means fully pursuing *all* these avenues of better *knowing* God.

A third aspect of loving God with all my mind is to set aside time each day to reflect on what I have *experienced* that day. I now firmly believe every interaction in my day can teach me something. Every interaction needs at least some of my attention. Interactions may include the readings and homily at Mass, the people I see and talk to, aspects of the world news, an article I have read and many similar daily occurrences. I need to discern whether any of these interactions raise new questions for me or whether they reinforce and strengthen what I know. I believe each interaction is a gift of God. To ignore even one of them is not loving God with all my mind.

With All My Soul

What does it mean to love God with *all* one's soul?

Sadly, I *still* do not know what this means. I hardly know what comprises my soul. However, I don't lose a lot of sleep over this. I consider I have my hands full loving God with all my heart, strength and mind.

How

The final question I had to resolve was how. How am I to love a God I can't physically experience? As I pursued this question, I was reminded of the stages of human love most of us experience. It occurred to me my earthly love experiences are part of my *Experiential Learning*. Perhaps they could teach me how to love God.

As I observed in Chapter 7, our first experience of love is based on dependence and our second is of falling in love. As we age, we learn a more selfless love. We love our children; we love our teenage children even when their actions are unlovable. As Harold S. Hulbert observed, "Children need our love, especially when they don't deserve it." We love selflessly those who become dependent on our care. We *will* a selfless love of people who need our love. I concluded this progression in human love might provide a model for me with which I could work towards a selfless love of God.

I might first focus on my total dependence on God. Every capacity I have is a gift of God. Every achievement, for which I take credit, is only possible because of a gift God gave me. Every breath I take is mine because God has allowed me one more instant of life on Earth. Every acquisition I make and think is mine, is something God has entrusted to my use (as to a steward). God has given me the free will to use the gifts, of which I am a steward, either according to His will or according to my will.

Jesus said, "You can do nothing apart from God." (John 15: 1-17) The more I reflected on this, the more I internalized my total dependence on God. Of course, I had realized I had been dependent on God from the instant of my conception. I simply didn't think about it, admit it or focus on it. Now that my dependence on God was in my consciousness, it was natural and maybe even inevitable I would *feel* a love for God just as a child loves its parents.

Having experienced a love based on dependency, I might next focus on falling in love with God. I could sharpen my perception of all His works and wonders. I could marvel at all the sights, sounds, smells, tastes and touch that are given to me to enjoy. I could grow my awareness of the plants that beautify my world, feed me and heal me. I could become more aware of the animals that feed me, help me and entertain me. I could see how God's creation reflects the boundless beauty and goodness that is God. Thomas Aquinas wrote this in the 13th century.

God brought things into being in order that His goodness might be communicated to creatures and be represented by them; and because His goodness could not be adequately represented by one creature alone, He produced many and diverse creatures, so that what was wanting to one in the representation of the divine goodness might be supplied by another. For goodness, which in God is simple and uniform, in creatures is manifold and divided.

Amazing Grace[34] and *How Great Thou Art*[35], are two well-known hymns that bring God's beauty to mind.

I could see God as beautiful beyond my imagination and wildest dreams. I could *allow* myself to fall in love with Him. The more I reflected on all God's beauty, the more I *felt* like I was falling in love. Of course, I already knew the world was a beautiful creation but I had taken its beauty for granted. I didn't even notice it. However, now I disciplined myself to focus throughout the day. At a breakfast of fruit, I marvel at how delicious each of those fruits is. I marvel at their design. Citrus fruits are sectioned into bite-size pieces. Clumps of grapes and berries offer us individual mouthfuls. We are given the ability to combine a huge variety of delightful meats, seafood, vegetables, grains, fruits and spices into scrumptious meals and satisfying beverages. On my morning walk, I began to notice the beauty and scent of flowers, the scent of freshly mown grass, the marvel of birds' flight and the sounds of animals I couldn't see. Being retired, I had many occasions throughout the day to look around me. In bed at night, I found myself looking forward to seeing the beauty around me when I awoke. It was like being in love.

Having fallen in love with God, I began to *actively* love Him. What enabled active love was my newfound faith in prayer.

Earlier, in my examination of the Old Testament (in Chapter 14), I had concluded God reveals His Word to each of us by placing it directly into our minds. Could those ideas that pop into our minds, that we are unable to source, have any other source but God? I have since concluded even *this* idea could have had no other source but God.

As I began paying attention to those ideas, I developed a growing conviction they were the result of God "talking" to me. As I began processing

---

[34]   http://library.timelesstruths.org/music/Amazing_Grace/

[35]   http://www.sharefaith.com/guide/Christian-Music/Hymns/How_Great_Thou_Art.html

those ideas, I shared what I was thinking with God. Sometimes, I put those thoughts into words as one does in traditional prayer. Sometimes I simply left them in my mind for God to pick up on His next delivery to me. More and more, I considered this "prayer" to be a two-way conversation. I was "talking" to God and He was "answering" my prayers.

I began thinking about God throughout my day. On my morning walks, I began saying prayers of thanksgiving and offering my day and myself to God. When I approached someone, I thought about what God's will might be for that encounter. Whenever I read or watched the news, I looked for inspirations and ideas about how I might better discern and accomplish God's will.

I realized I was beginning to put God's will ahead of my own just as, in our marriage, I had begun to put Peggy's will ahead of mine. As I had done with her, I was beginning to focus more of my day on communication with the One I loved. What had enabled a more selfless love of Peggy was now enabling me to *actively* love God more selflessly.

Having progressed in loving God with all my heart, strength and mind, it was time to turn my attention to the second half of the greatest commandment – to love my neighbour (*all* God's children) as myself. As an introduction to my study of this commandment, I'd like to share with you my second case study.

CHAPTER 20

MY SECOND CASE STUDY

Throughout Peggy's career as a palliative care nurse, and more and more in its latter stages, I would talk to her peers whom I had come to know. Without reservation or exception, they would repeatedly tell me what an excellent nurse she was. Of course, they would be unlikely to tell me she was a bad nurse. Even so, the consistency of their unsolicited feedback confirmed to me the sincerity of their comments.

My belief in their feedback was supported when I learned why she preferred the night shift. She had always had difficulty sleeping after night shift. She would get a few hours' sleep in the early morning and then be unable to fall back to sleep. When she had a few night shifts in a row, the lack of sleep would impact her severely. I asked myself how she could prefer night shift. Finally I asked *her*.

She told me night shift gave her more time with her patients. There were fewer procedures to perform, fewer distractions and fewer demands on her time. She would regularly spend up to an hour with individual patients. She would do their nails or their hair. She would talk to them and more importantly, listen to them. I had long ago recognized she was an excellent listener and what a blessing it is to have a good listener with whom to converse.

In talking about her night as we shared our "day" together, I was regularly reminded of what a unique and special person she was. I realized few, if any, of her peers did what she did for her patients. I realized her patients would feel loved when she attended to them.

Most importantly, when I saw what a toll the night shift took on her, I realized I was witnessing selfless love. For me, this was an example of the selfless love we all need to acquire. I concluded God gives us many personal and vicarious experiences like this to learn how to prepare ourselves to live in selfless love with Him and *all* His children for eternity. I also realized the experience had been personal for Peggy. For me it had been only vicarious. However, that was about to change.

After Peggy died, I decided I would volunteer to visit patients on her palliative care ward. I thought of how much her patients treasured the time she spent with them and felt the institutionalized might benefit from a regular visit from me. I realized my many conversations with Peggy had uniquely prepared me for what would be a difficult place to volunteer for most people. I signed up for weekly Wednesday afternoon visits.

On my first visit I was introduced to the nursing staff. One of them recognized me as Peggy's husband. She told me I had to come in to see the staff room bulletin board. Prominently displayed was a beautiful picture of Peggy in her nurse's uniform. The nurses told me no one was allowed to take that picture down. I was reminded once again of how respected she was. As well, I was reminded of my sadness that the nurses' uniform is a thing of the past and that patients have lost the reassurance it provided.

I still visit the palliative care unit regularly and intend to do so as long as I am able. I have come to see why it is so difficult for most people to make such visits. For those who doubt eternal life, it is uncomfortable to be with people who are about to die. For those who fear rejection, it is uncomfortable to approach people whose reaction is unpredictable. Some patients make it explicitly clear they don't want to talk to a stranger. Some are too weak or depressed to talk. Nevertheless, I have learned most patients still appreciate the presence of a person who demonstrates love of them. As well, *some* patients want to talk and say how much they enjoy my visits. Most family caregivers want to talk. Each of them feels my unconditional, selfless love.

This experience provided the best opportunity I had found to this point in *Experiential Learning* to develop my capacity for selfless love. It continues to be challenging and rewarding. It gives me the opportunity to personally experience loving selflessly. I was no longer limited to vicarious experience.

All this, of course, brought me to the second half of the greatest commandment. I could not do God's will without following that second half to the best of my ability. It turned out it was even more difficult than the first half of the greatest commandment.

CHAPTER 21

THE GREATEST COMMANDMENT – LOVE YOUR NEIGHBOUR

As you'll recall from Chapter 13, I had come to know God loves me and everyone because He created each of us. I had established sound and supported knowledge all creators want all their created to love as they love and that God loves all His created (us) selflessly and unconditionally. It necessarily follows His will is *I* love everyone selflessly and unconditionally. The more I thought about God's will, the more I concluded it is even tough to selflessly and unconditionally love *any*one.

My Limitations

I love my wife. I am blessed to have found her after Peggy's passing and to have her by my side every day of my life. Her happiness is more important to me than my own. However, at times, I'm not conscious of how much I love her. At times, I don't act as if I love her. Even when I am conscious of what would make her happy, at times, I put my own happiness above hers. I may feel it's my turn. I may feel my choice is more important to me than her choice is to her. It may simply be my self-centredness kicking in. At these times, I am far from a selfless love of the most important person in my life. I am far from a selfless love of the person for whom a selfless love is easiest.

I love my children and my siblings. I have loved them all the days of their lives. However, there are incidents when I fail to love them selflessly. On these occasions, I forget my love, withdraw, lose my patience, become judgemental or even lose my temper. At these times, I am almost always focused on how the incident affects me rather than on how it impacts them. I think of myself first and only when I get over my self-centredness do I begin to think of them. *After* such occasions, I realize self-centredness is sadly a part of my makeup. I realize I am far from a selfless love of my immediate family.

I grew up with a small immediate family. It is limited to one sister, one brother and one cousin. However, I am blessed with two large "families-in-law" and one "stepfamily". All three have accepted me as part of their families and they greatly expand my own. They have provided me with many occasions to develop a selfless love of them.

However, at times when we are together, my engagement with them is proportional to how much our topic interests me at that moment. If the topic of conversation is mine, I am joyfully engaged. If the topic of conversation is of interest to me, I am fully engaged. However, I am engaged in the topic rather than with the person. I am thinking less about how I can make that person's day a little brighter and more about my enjoyment. I am missing the opportunity to actively pursue whatever is on their minds or in their hearts unless it resonates with me. I realize I am far from a selfless love of my extended families.

In all my years of *Experiential Learning*, I have accumulated a rather large group of acquaintances, peers and friends. I want the best for them. I keep in touch and get together with many of them. However, I see the same limitations in my love for them as I do for my extended families. Ideas distract me from focusing on people. To selflessly love, I need to listen more than I expound. I need to pick up non-verbal signals rather than ignore them. When I don't, I'm thinking of myself rather than of them. I am far from a selfless love of those who are a part of my life.

Are you beginning to see why I find this second half of the greatest commandment the more difficult of the two halves? I am far from selfless love of the people it should be easiest for me to love. What about the people who are not as easy to love? What about those who don't appeal to me? What about those I actually dislike? What about those I feel I am *right* to dislike?

When I am part of a gathering of people largely unknown to me, I tend to seek out people whose appearance makes me think I might find them interesting. Whenever I see people who appear standoffish, I avoid them. Whenever I see people who are monopolizing conversation, bragging, apparently avoiding me or exhibiting any other behaviour I interpret as negative, I avoid them.

I have now come to realize these people need attention, caring, support and selfless love. The apparently standoffish may need an invitation to become engaged. Those who monopolize need someone to engage them in more selfless conversation. The braggarts need recognition. Those who seem to be avoiding me may need me to make the first move. Not only do these things occur to me upon reflection, they have been *shown* to me to be the case on the occasions when I have selflessly reached out. Now, of course, people like these outnumber those close to me. They are the many more people I *should* selflessly love.

And then there are the people I dislike. These are the people whose behaviour I find unappealing or offensive, who I feel are taking advantage of others, who are hurting (or who I feel are hurting) the people I love, who put other people down and who focus on critique rather than corrective initiative. I am even further from a selfless love of them than I am of anyone. Except for the *bad* people.

These are the people who abuse others emotionally, mentally and/ or physically, who prey on the elderly, the alone and the vulnerable and who destroy the reputations of others by rumour, lies and manipulation. The worst of these are sadists, rapists, pedophiles, murderers, terrorists and despotic dictators. These are the people from whom I am furthest in selfless love. Surely Jesus is not commanding me to love them. Or is He?

Heredity and Environment

One of my most rewarding lessons in *Experiential Learning* came from the discovery of a book by Robert Blatchford entitled: *Not Guilty: A Defense of the Bottom Dog*[36]. It was published about one hundred years ago. An extract from it was one of the readings included in the first year philosophy text I had had recommended to me.

Blatchford persuasively develops the argument we are all products of our heredity and our environment over which we have no control. Because of this, none of us can claim credit for what is good in us nor be blamed by others for what is bad in us. I realized, if this is indeed the case, society must help perpetrators rather than judge them. If Blatchford is right, all our efforts should be directed to helping rehabilitate offenders, wounded by their heredity and environment, rather than to punishing them. We should selflessly and unconditionally love perpetrators. Of course we may have to protect society by, when necessary, capturing, prosecuting and incarcerating dangerous offenders until they are rehabilitated.

---

[36] Blatchford, Robert. *Not Guilty – A Defense of the Bottom Dog*. New York: Boni and Liveright, 1918

Because this argument was foreign to me, I was fascinated by it. In his book, Blatchford raises every objection I could think of to his argument and then systematically refutes each of them. Objection 1: Two siblings share a common heredity but one rises above it while the other does not. Objection 2: Two siblings share a common environment, in that they are raised by the same parents in the same home and go to the same schools, but one rises above it while the other does not. Objection 3: Even if our childhood environment is out of our control, we have the ability to pick our adult environment and we are responsible for the environment we choose. We experience free will so surely we are responsible for how we exercise it.

The argument for the lack of control over one's heredity is the easiest to make. We know our genes are inherited from our ancestors and they are all in place before we are even born. But what if one sibling is good and the other bad? If both share the same heredity, *it* can't be the cause of the bad sibling's behaviour. However, this raises the question of whether the heredities of siblings are the same.

We know each of us inherits some genes from our mother and some from our father. We also know they inherit genes from each of their parents and successive inheritances go back further than we can trace. To me, it follows that the mix of genes one sibling inherits is almost always different from the mix another sibling inherits.

I suspect your own experience confirms this. In many families you observe, you probably marvel at how different the children are from each other. Does this not show us the heredities of children of the same parents are different?

The bad sibling has no more control over his or her heredity than does the good sibling.

The argument for the lack of control over one's environment is harder to make. It is easier in the case of one's childhood (formative) environment than of one's adult environment so Blatchford starts there. His approach is the same as for heredity. He allows, if both siblings share the *same* formative environment, it can't be the cause of the bad sibling's behaviour. However, he questions the assumption the formative environments of siblings are the same.

He makes the point one's environment is a product of *every* interaction one experiences. It is not limited to interactions in the home and in school. It is a product of *every* person that comes into one's life. Even within a family, one child's home environment may be more influenced by the mother and the other's more by the father. One child may be influenced by an aunt, uncle or grandparent differently than the other. In the school, one sibling may have different teachers than the other sibling. Where they have the same teacher, that teacher may find it easier to reach one child than the other. In the childhood neighbourhood, one sibling may be exposed to different friends (and enemies) than the other sibling. Blatchford claims, and it follows for me, the chances two children from the same family experience the same formative environment are infinitesimal. The fact they turn out differently is what we would expect.

The bad sibling has no more control over his or her formative environment than does the good sibling.

The third objection is, although this may be the case during one's formative years, in our teen and adult years we have more control over our environment. We can pick our friends. We can choose the places where we congregate. We can take advantage of good influences in our lives or ignore them. We can avoid bad influences in our lives or cultivate them. Rather than refute the obvious truth of these observations, Blatchford qualifies them. He observes that the choices we make to influence our later environments are, in most cases, limited to those *enabled* by our heredity and formative environments over which we have no control. The traits that are developed in our formative environments are well-engrained by the time we assume some choice over our later environments.

This third argument made sense to me, but I looked for confirmation. I decided to test this part of Blatchford's argument against, firstly, the experience of a friend of mine and, secondly, my own experience.

My friend's father abandoned him before he was born. His mother was incapable of raising him and gave him up to a series of foster homes. He was a ward of the Children's Aid Society for the first twenty-one years of his life with the result he lacked the parental loving, nurturing and support that most of us enjoy. It would seem, if Blatchford's third argument were sound, my friend's heredity and formative environment would have resulted in his being unable to choose a good adult environment. However, this was not the case.

He earned acceptance at the University of Pennsylvania, an Ivy League school. While there, he set an outdoor meet record in the triple jump with a leap of 16.02 metres. He was named to Canada's 1980 Summer Olympic Team. He is the recipient of a National Aboriginal Achievement Award. The choices he made in his later environment do not seem to have been limited to those enabled by his heredity and formative environment. If he could overcome his heredity and formative environment, what was to say others could not? This seemed to refute Blatchford's argument.

However, on further reflection, I realized my friend's achievements were exceptional. He was able to achieve *more* than his heredity and formative environment enabled. You may know of others who have done as well. However, you may share my observation they represent the exception that proves the rule. The observation that *exceptional* people can rise above what their heredities and formative environments enable does not refute the argument that *most* people cannot. I concluded Blatchford's third argument holds true for the vast majority of people. Did it hold true for me?

In my case, heredity and formative environment led to good choices in my adult environment. My heredity produced bad eyes and bad teeth. I was the butt of abuse as the only five-year-old any of my classmates had ever seen wearing glasses in the 1940's. In my teens, my front four upper teeth abscessed and were replaced by a partial plate, which made me feel like a freak and shattered my confidence. My *formative* environment lacked a male influence while my father was away throughout the Second World War. As a result, I never learned to throw, catch or bat a ball and failed in all sports. Because of my heredity and formative environment, my only chance for recognition was to excel in school. I worked harder in school than my friends did. This led me to realize any limitation of my gifts could be overcome by dogged perseverance in whatever I pursued. In my teens, I joined a rowing team to make up for my lack of athleticism. I survived army basic training and, as a result, acquired new competencies in it and in officer training a year later.

As you can see, the choices I made to influence my adult environment were the consequence of my heredity and formative environment. It follows I can claim no credit for these good choices. For others, the choices they make to influence their adult environment are *limited* to those enabled by their heredity and formative environments. Similarly, they cannot be blamed for their bad choices.

The bad person has no more control over his or her heredity and environment than does the good person.

My friend's and my experiences supported Blatchford's argument. This led me to wonder if his argument could be taken one step further. Do we really have free will? Unless we do, we are even less accountable for what is bad in us.

Free Will

I was bothered by free will's apparent conflict with predestination. I know God knows everything because He created everything. If so, He must know what I am going to do before I do it. If He knows ahead of time what I am going to do, how can I be free to choose what I do or to change my mind? I concluded if God knows everything then my will is not free.

Earlier in *Experiential Learning*, you'll recall, I studied *Mere Christianity* by C.S. Lewis. An excerpt from the book addresses this question I had about the reality of free will. He addressed the argument of predestination versus free will in this way.

> If God foresaw our acts, it would be very hard to understand how we could be free not to do them. But suppose God is outside and above the timeline. In that case, what we call "tomorrow" is visible to Him in just the same way as what we call "today". He does not remember you doing things yesterday; He simply sees you doing them because, though you have lost yesterday, He has not. He does not "foresee" you doing things tomorrow; He simply sees you doing them because, though tomorrow is not yet there for you, it is for Him. In a sense, He does not know your action till you have done it; but then the moment at which you have done it is already "Now" for Him.

About the same time, I came across another book that also addressed the idea of dimensions beyond those we experience. This entertaining book is entitled *Flatland: A Romance of Many Dimensions*[37] and was first published in the late-1880s by Edwin A. Abbott (1838 to 1926). Flatland is a place inhabited solely by two-dimensional beings of which *Mr. A. Square* is one. One day he visits *Sphere*, a three-dimensional being who shows *Square* his world, Spaceland. *Square*, whose experience has been limited to Flatland, has difficulty following and believing what *Sphere* is describing. He can't see the third dimension to which *Sphere* is referring and, in fact, sees *Sphere* as a mere flat circle. Towards the end of the book, *Square* becomes convinced the three-dimensional world that *Sphere* is describing may actually exist. He realizes he is going to have to tell his

---

[37] Abbott, Edwin A. *Flatland – A Romance of Many Dimensions*. Mineola NY: Dover Publications Inc., 1884

fellow close-minded Flatlanders the world may have more dimensions than they have experienced. He realizes this may be an impossible quest. How can they accept what they cannot see and experience? Those of us, who have difficulty accepting the possibility of a time dimension because we cannot see and experience it, can empathize with poor *Mr. A Square*.

I had been exposed to the hypotheses of a time dimension and even of a fifth and additional dimensions. It seemed to me the fact I could not experience more than three dimensions was more a limitation of earthly beings than an indication a time dimension could not exist. I accepted the likelihood of a time dimension.

Although many more academic arguments for free will exist, I found this argument simple and convincing. For me, it eliminated the apparent conflict between free will and predestination. I concluded we all have complete freedom of choice even though God has already seen the choice we will make before we make it.

All this led me to four conclusions. Firstly, we all *do* have free will. Secondly, our range of choices *is* limited by our heredity and formative environment. Thirdly, because none of us have control over either, we can take no credit for the good choices we make or blame others for the bad choices they make. To paraphrase Jean Vanier, there are no bad people – just people to whom bad things have happened. Fourthly, none of this gives perpetrators a free pass.

We must hold perpetrators accountable for the *results* of the bad choices they make. We must incarcerate perpetrators who threaten us. However, because they have no control over what shaped them, we need to help them rather than judge or punish them. The objective of incarceration must be to protect society and help the offender rehabilitate.

I could see I have to selflessly *love* offenders even when I hate what they do. I will have no excuse for not selflessly and unconditionally loving the worst offenders.

My third case study will show how my next two *Perception* experiences – the incarcerated and parolees – helped me develop a selfless love of those who are among the least loved of society. My re-examination of *The Club* had, to this point, been predominantly the product of my mind. To fully understand the perpetrator I had to involve my heart in my re-examination.

CHAPTER 22

MY THIRD CASE STUDY

Sometime in the latter stages of my *Experiential Learning*, I received a shocking phone call. One of my close friends, whom I had known for several decades, had been charged with a serious crime. The charge was soon in the newspapers and known all over town. Most of his family and friends ostracized him during the trial and subsequently. Fortunately a few souls continued to offer him support.

As for me, I was initially in a state of disbelief. Our two families had been friends together for years. In our latter years, my wives and I had had conversations with him and his wife that were the most satisfying I have experienced. There was no subject off limits. Especially unique was his comfort with discussing any aspect of faith. I liked him and treasured our times together.

As his trial agonizingly progressed, I came to realize it was unlikely the things he had been accused of having done were a fabrication. He slowly began to admit some of the charges were indeed true. After some months, he was convicted and sentenced to several years in prison. Because of my long standing and close relationship, my wife and I made several trips to where he was incarcerated and talked with him about his experience in custody.

His first experience was in a wretched jail full of hardened criminals. His jail mates continually threatened him. Fortunately he had established an ability to stand up to the worst of bullies in his childhood. I shudder to think what I would have experienced had I been in his place.

After some months, he was moved from the jail to a prison to serve the remainder of his sentence. Here the living conditions were vastly superior. Of course he sadly missed his wife, who had remained faithful to him. He missed his freedom. However, he valued the psychological services that were made available to him and the process of rehabilitation they enabled. He took full advantage of these services and told me how much he was benefiting from them.

Throughout our earlier times together I had heard snippets of conversation about the strangeness of his parents, especially his father. Some of this strangeness was evident on the few occasions when I was with his parents. During the time he was in prison, I learned how horrible his upbringing was. He rarely, if ever, experienced nourishing love. His father abused all the members of his family and my friend often had to fight his father to protect his siblings or mother. Aha, that's where he learned so much about defending himself! Is this not a pretty clear case for the effects of formative environment? As he unburdened himself of these memories, he expressed a closeness to his father. He shared with me that his father had survived an abusive environment, largely absent of nourishing love as well. His grandfather often got his axe out of the basement during family altercations. Is not the presence of such traits in three consecutive generations a pretty clear case for the effects of heredity?

Finally, my friend was granted parole, which enabled more frequent conversations. He described at length the process of his rehabilitation and the empathy and effectiveness of his counsellors. It was obvious to me he had made excellent progress. He understood himself much better and recognized the demons that lay beneath the surface. I find his experience speaks loudly for a greater focus on rehabilitation than on punishment.

I began to wonder if I could do jail visitation. In Florida, where we wintered, it was easier to arrange than in Toronto. Our diocese had an established visitation process and after somewhat pedantic preparation, I earned the opportunity to visit groups of prisoners in the Broward County Main Jail twice a month. The visits were billed as religious services. Most of my fellow visitors would prepare scripture readings and expound on them. I was surprised at how well the inmates knew their Bibles and how much they got out of the services.

However, for me, what was lacking was open communication between equals. I began to structure my part of the services as a series of questions with which I could invite discussion. This was even more popular with the inmates. It enabled us to get to know each other so much better than did largely one-way presentations with occasional response. The frankness with which they described their lives and the crime they had committed surprised me. It enabled me to better understand their heredity and formative environment. I found most of them to be sincere and deeply appreciative.

Inmates could request one-on-one meetings with any member of our team. Unfortunately the process an inmate had to go through to get permission for a meeting was onerous and unreliable. Once finally approved, the approval could be rescinded at any time before the meeting was to take place. Despite these problems, I was successful on one occasion in having several private meetings with an inmate. I learned almost as much about him as I had learned about my friend. I could easily see how his heredity and formative environment had shaped him. They had limited his choices in his adult environment. His heredity and formative environment had clearly led him to his crime.

I began to feel a stronger and stronger love for all the prisoners I met. Of course the feeling was stronger for some than for others, but it was there for them all. I discovered the love I had for these men was selfless and unconditional. It was genuine. I realized the whole process had been a huge lesson in selflessly loving *all* God's children.

My experience with the Canadian penal system was different but equally rewarding. I was initially disappointed in my inability to get a first meeting with the chaplain of the Don Jail. After many phone calls over several weeks I finally reached him. He explained the demands on his time were overwhelming and he was unable to add my request to the pile.

When I shared my disappointment with a deacon in our church, he offered to introduce me to the manager of the Keele Correctional Centre, a Toronto halfway house for parolees. I met with him and he introduced me to a number of the parolees. My wife and I attended a dinner with the parolees at the Keele Centre, prepared and served by a group from our church led by the deacon and the Keele Centre manager.

When the latter asked me if I would be willing to meet regularly with a parolee to offer support, I readily accepted the invitation. I was unsure what I had committed to, but felt I could probably handle it. My experience with my first parolee was fascinating and rewarding. He has a quick mind and has a lot of accomplishments under his belt.

Most impressive of these was his and his partner's earlier ownership of a restaurant. He told me one night they were followed back to their home where they took the cash from the day's business. He was beaten and robbed and suffered damage to his internal organs and his brain. He subsequently turned to drugs to support his prolonged recuperation. This led to dealing and his conviction.

When I first met him he was still in a halfway house from which he could get daytime passes. He was searching for an apartment in which he could live when he was released. His search took place in a sellers' market but through perseverance he found an affordable basement apartment, which needed a lot of renovation. He made a deal with the landlord that, if he would furnish the materials, my new friend would do the labour. He still owned a garage where he set up a workshop to resurface furniture for resale. He took training to become a SMART facilitator. SMART offers addicted people self-help to overcome alcoholism as well as drug and other addictions. He has volunteered with Meals on Wheels and wanted to explore palliative ward visitation by shadowing me on mine.

That such a capable person could get into so much trouble is hard to understand. However, an environment, which he didn't choose, definitely shaped him. He undergoes biweekly drug testing and has been caught using twice. At the time of this writing, he had completed his parole obligation. He sought counselling to help him deal with the abrupt withdrawal of support. I expect to remain friends with him as long as he welcomes my friendship. In the meantime, I had begun regular meetings with two more parolees.

What all this experience has taught me is how important it is for prisoners and parolees to experience selfless and unconditional love. Everyone needs to be loved. It has also taught me I can make a difference by reaching out. I am capable of selfless love. There will be no excuse for me to not have selflessly loved.

Well, if I have to love the worst offenders, it looks as if I have to love *every* one of God's children. Having found "bad" people loveable, I now had to think about the people I dislike, those who don't appeal to me and even the people I like but don't love selflessly.

My Challenges

I realize I have good reason to dislike the things some people do but I have no good reason to hate the people who do them. My late wife explained this concept to our grade school children quite simply and effectively. When they would complain they hated little Billie, she told them they should not hate little Billie but it was right to dislike the bad things little Billie did. As I reflected on her counsel, I found myself applying it to the people I dislike.

I should not dislike the people who I feel are taking advantage of others, who are hurting (or who I feel are hurting) the people I love, who put other people down or who focus on critique rather than corrective initiative, but it is right to dislike what these people do. Once I focus on what they do rather than on them, I can apply Robert Blatchford's argument. Is it not likely the people, who take advantage of others, hurt others, put others down and focus on critique rather than on corrective initiative have experienced the same things in *their* formative environments? Is it not possible they have inherited these tendencies from parents (and ancestors) who have experienced the same things during their lifetimes?

Why do they choose to do the things they do? Are not the choices they make as constrained by their heredity and formative environment, as are the choices of perpetrators? I was reminded of the quotation "There, but for the grace of God, go I." I realized I need to build *up* these people. I need to selflessly love them.

What about the people to whom I am not attracted? They include those who monopolize conversation, who brag and who act as if they are better than anyone else.

Why do they choose these behaviours? Are they even conscious choices? Might those who monopolize conversation have been ignored in their formative environments? Might those who brag have been discounted in their formative environments? Might those who act as if they are better than others have been dismissed as less than others in their formative environments? Are any of these possible causes a reason for me to fail to love them? Are any of these people undeserving of my selfless love?

Lastly what about the people I like but fail to selflessly love? Why do I find it so difficult to selflessly love them? It took me almost all my time in *Experiential Learning* to find the answer to this question. As I think about my epiphany, I am reminded of a once-famous quotation from Walt Kelly's cartoon character, Pogo. In thinking about the world's problems, Pogo concluded, "We have met the enemy and he is us." I was my own worst enemy. I had fallen (largely unconsciously) into the trap of looking at many interactions in my life as either a source of my entertainment and gratification or not and avoiding those that were not.

I realize I have to force myself out of this trap. I need to focus on making each interaction as good an experience for the other person as I am able. It should have been obvious to me long ago. To love selflessly, I need to forget myself and focus on others. Of course coming to this conclusion is a far cry from applying it. I'm sure it will take me to my last day on Earth to master selfless love. It may even take some posthumous remedial training.

At this stage of *Experiential Learning*, I *knew* God's will is I love Him and *all* His children as selflessly and unconditionally as I am able. I'm pretty sure it does not matter to God whether I *like* each person with whom I interact. What matters is I selflessly love them and put their needs before mine. I'm pretty sure it does not matter to God whether I accomplish His will better or worse than *anyone else*. What matters is I do it to the best of *my* ability. What's more, to the best of my ability means I cannot simply selflessly love those with whom I *happen* to interact. I need to *actively* pursue opportunities to interact with others who need my selfless love. I need to discern *my* gifts to determine if they are suited to the selfless love of the homeless, the homebound, the despairing, the grieving, the prisoners, the parolees, the institutionalized, the lonely, the hospitalized or other such segments of society.

Praying for God's Grace for Others

I next pondered what I realize is a very controversial question. How could I have discerned, not simply *my* purpose, but life's purpose? The question has two parts. Is what I have discerned *really* life's purpose? If so, how could *I* have succeeded in discerning it?

As you'll recall from Chapter 13, I had already established the answer to the first part of the question. My *foundational knowledge* of life's purpose is sound because it is rigorously supported by deductive and inductive reasoning. Let's review colloquially the reasoning that establishes this knowledge. *All* capable beings that create with intent want *all* their children to love their siblings and them as they love their children and want their children to achieve their best. Our God, who is all capable and who is not susceptible to unintentional action, must want *all* His children (each of us) to love Him and *all* His children as He loves them and must want each of us to achieve our best. Since God's love must be perfect (selfless and unconditional), to love as He does we must love selflessly and unconditionally. Since God wants us to achieve our best, His intent must be that we *all* love as He does *as well as we are able*. Since God created all life, His intent must be life's purpose.

If you find this sound reasoning as flawless as I do, *you* know life's purpose as well. If you find it flawed, you can likely at least see why I will continue to claim I know life's purpose until you can help me discover the flaws in the reasoning. This leads to the second part of the question.

How could *I* have succeeded in discerning life's purpose? I surely hadn't accomplished this on my own. Jesus taught, "I am the vine; you are the branches. Whoever abides in me and I in him, he it is that bears much fruit, for *apart from me you can do nothing.*" (Italics mine) (John 15: 5) Like any of us, I could have discerned this knowledge only through the grace of God. God's grace is a gift offered to *each* of us, but forced on none of us. It is a gift we must ask for, pursue and act upon. Incapable of prayer until long after I had discovered life's purpose, how could I have asked for God's help?

Do you see a Catch-22 here? I was unable to pray for God's grace because I was not close enough to God to effectively pray. I couldn't get close enough to God to effectively pray without God's grace. How can anyone escape such a paradoxical situation? How could I have obtained the grace to discern life's purpose while I remained unable to pray for it?

I finally concluded, because *I* couldn't ask for God's grace, someone else must have asked on my behalf. I will probably never know *who* did, but I know someone, and maybe several people in my life must have.

From my personal experience I know it is difficult for most people to ask God for this grace. How can someone ask for something from a being whose existence they doubt or with whom they feel no communication? If people I love cannot ask for God's grace, the only way it can be asked for on their behalf is for *someone else* to ask. How can I love someone to the best of my ability and not ask God for what I know is of utmost importance to them? I must ask God for the grace of soundly supported faith for all those I love. I must pray they receive what is most important to them – that their eyes and ears are opened. I need to ask God to open their hearts and minds to His love and to the discernment and accomplishment of His will.

Having realized I must pray for God's grace for others, I began to wonder if I could do more. Might there be another way to help people *discover* life's purpose? Maybe if I could help others see the big picture it would help them better discern life's purpose.

CHAPTER 23

THE PUZZLE

O ne day as I thought about this, I watched my wife work on a 1000-piece jigsaw puzzle. I saw how difficult it was to construct the picture while focusing on each of the 1000 pieces. As she succeeded in getting small sections of the puzzle assembled, the picture of which they were a part began to take shape. However, one could see the whole picture only after all the pieces were interconnected and in place.

A project began to take shape in my mind. Could I construct a jigsaw puzzle where each piece represented a part of the big picture of life's purpose? What emerged from this thinking was a 40-piece jigsaw puzzle and a book entitled *The Puzzle*. Each piece of the puzzle and each chapter of *The Puzzle* represent a part of the knowledge of life's purpose. The completed puzzle shows a big picture of life's purpose.

The premise of *The Puzzle* is that a group of friends, attending a weekend reunion, get increasingly involved in a debate about whether or not God exists, and about what the answer to that question implies about life's purpose. The debate serves to philosophically develop each of the 40 items of knowledge contained in the jigsaw puzzle. A first time participant is excused from the debate but is welcomed to observe it.

Before the next annual reunion, he conceives of the puzzle and builds it. He uses each of the items of knowledge that had been debated, as a piece of the puzzle. At the following reunion, he gives a set of the 40 jigsaw puzzle pieces to each participant and invites each to complete the puzzle. The participants then share with each other what they found to be the big picture of life's purpose.

Feedback I've received on *The Puzzle* indicates it is a bit of a heavy read. The debates get a little protracted and in some cases are more than a bit difficult to follow. The book's conversational style demands considerably more writing skill than its author had developed at that point. As a result, I never published the book. However, writing it generated a lot of my thinking, a critical component of *Experiential Learning.*

Looking back on this project, I believe it did a pretty good job of illustrating the thought processes necessary to establishing knowledge of life's purpose without relying on the content of Holy Books and Church teaching. That was my purpose at the time. I wanted to engage the minds of those who had rejected religion and its teachings.

As in most things, its strength was also its greatest weakness. Its philosophical approach relied solely on the mind. It did not engage the heart. The full engagement of the heart is as critical a component of *Experiential Learning* as is the full engagement of the mind.

I now realize each of us has a predominant strength and one less developed. Because my predominant strength is my mind, I tended to discount or ignore my heart. I wasn't mad at my heart. I just didn't get what it was trying to tell me. I simply lacked confidence I could get anything meaningful out of pursuing whatever my heart felt it had to offer.

Looking more closely at others, I see their predominant strength is the heart. The mind is a strength they have not fully developed. I see this in conversations we have. They refer to how they feel, to what they believe, to their faith, which are all products of the heart. Their eyes glaze over as I share my thinking – the product of my mind. Meanwhile I lose interest in what to me are their unsubstantiated feelings. This is a most unsatisfactory situation for me and for them.

The process of *Experiential Learning* can eliminate this sad situation. The key is we fully identify all our *Perception* experiences. Each person's personal *Perception* set is unique, rich and varied. It takes deep reflection to identify the experiences of one's *Perception* set that do not initially resonate with one's predominant strength. For example, I was slow to pursue people and events that could lead me to more fully engage my heart. As a result, my understanding was very limited for a very long time. Those whose predominant strength is the heart may be in similar danger of missing readings and their study that could lead them to more fully engage their mind.

My hope is you will pursue *Experiential Learning.* I hope you will discover parts of your *Perception* set that lead you to more fully engage your mind and your heart. I now understand even more why Christ insisted we have to love God with all our heart and all our mind. Loving God and all His children is a challenging task. It's clear to me Christ knew we would need to fully use both faculties in order to do our best to love God and all His children.

Perception **Experiences**	Scientific method	My best friend	Jesus' sayings	The dying
		My late wife	McMaster professor	Blatchford's book
		Pascal's Wager	Two philosophy texts	Abbott's book
		The Catholic Information Centre	Dawson's book	The incarcerated
		My seminarian mentor	Harris' book	Several prisoners
		Bits of the RC Catechism	Sound reasoning	Several parolees
		COR	Much of the Bible	
		Participation House	Religious scholars	
		Marriage Encounter	RC Catechism	
		Daily Mass		
		A bit of the Bible		
		C.S. Lewis' *Mere Christianity*		
Process **Learnings**	There is no proof God exists	I must accept the *possibility* God exists	Atheism is unfounded	I must fully understand and carry out Jesus' message to the best of my ability
	Atheism makes sense	The Church establishes a *likelihood* God exists	God created us, loves us and offers us eternal life with Him	
		The Apostle's Creed is *more likely than not* to be true	God wants us to love Him and all His children as selflessly as we are able	
		I am *capable* of selfless love of others	The Bible *is* the revealed Word of God	
		I am *capable* of selfless love of God	Jesus was human and God Incarnate	
		The Gospels *likely* deliver God's Word	Jesus' words *are* the Word of God	
		I *knew* none of the above	The RC Catechism *is* the revealed Word of God	
Knowledge of **Life's Purpose**	**Earthly fulfillment**	**Live according to Church teaching**	**Love God and *all* His children as selflessly and unconditionally as we are able**	

My evolving *Experiential Learning* template shows my many new (shaded) *Perception* experiences. My second case study had introduced me to the dying and showed me I could selflessly love them. Blatchford's book had shown me no one has control over their heredity and formative environment. Abbott's book had helped me see that predestination does not preclude existence of our free will. My third case study had led me to a realization that the incarcerated and parolees have no more control over their heredity and formative environment than do any of us. In all this, my re-examination of *The Club*'s greatest commandment had involved my heart as well as my mind.

All these *Perception* experiences had led to a most fundamental *Process* learning. They had enriched my understanding of Jesus' greatest commandment. I came to the realization that, to achieve life's purpose, I must fully understand and carry out Jesus' message to the best of my ability.

The Club founder's greatest commandment had confirmed my *Knowledge* of life's purpose. My study had increased my *understanding* of life's purpose. I realized my love for God must be limitless. It must exceed regular church attendance and asking for what I decide I need. It must be the greatest love of which I am capable. As well, my love for *all* God's children must exceed requited love of those I like. I must show agape love to those closest and farthest from me. Finally, I must pray for God's help in this for myself and others.

It also led me to further study. If what Jesus expressed in a single sentence demands so much of me, how much more would His 400-plus teachings demand of me? It became clear the next step of my re-examination of *The Club* must be to much more fully re-examine *The Club*'s teachings.

I recalled my earlier project, *The Journey* (described in Chapter 10), which *captured* everything Jesus said. As you'll recall, it identified the Bible book, chapter and verse of each and every saying of Jesus, organized them by topic and ranked the topics in order of their importance. I eagerly returned to *The Journey*'s spreadsheet. Could it become my textbook for life?

PART FIVE

TEACHINGS

CHAPTER 24

THE SAYINGS OF JESUS – 1

My eagerness quickly turned to disappointment. As I read through what I had thought might become my textbook for life, I realized I had a faulty edition. Quotations were incorrectly assigned to topics and topics were overlapping or missing altogether. Even after I had corrected every error I could find, the spreadsheet remained, and still is subjective and imprecise in its assignment of quotation to topic. As well, some quotations deal with more than one topic.

However, the section of the spreadsheet addressed to each topic adequately covers most of what Jesus said on that topic. It is the best presentation of everything Jesus said that I have found. The size of the spreadsheet prevents me from showing it to you. However, its *content* is fully presented in the body of the Appendix of this book, *THE SAYINGS OF JESUS*. A summary of the spreadsheet is portrayed in *Figure 1* on the final two pages of the Appendix.

A quick scan of the Appendix shows a great deal of effort went into producing *THE SAYINGS OF JESUS*. You may question whether it was worth the effort it took to produce it. As well, you may question whether it is worth the effort it would demand of *you* to study it. Why is *THE SAYINGS OF JESUS* such an important resource in determining Jesus' overall message?

Undoubtedly, one could eventually discern Jesus' *overall* message by simply re-reading the Bible as many times as one needed. However, for me, it didn't work. I had read and listened to all four Gospels so many times, I thought I knew all I had to know about what Jesus said. I had essentially boiled down His message to "Play nice." I had taken away no overall message on any individual topic.

One problem, with relying solely on the Bible as a source, is I read it as I do any book. I start at the beginning of a Gospel and read each page in sequence until I get to the end. Each Gospel tells Jesus' story as a narrative. As a result when I come across something He said on a topic of interest, I don't have access to what else He said on that topic. As I continue in the Bible narrative, my attention is diverted to something He said on another topic. When later He again addresses the earlier topic, I have forgotten (and can no longer even locate) His first commentary. I find each Gospel to be a compelling story of Jesus' ministry, but a scattered portrayal of his message on any given topic.

I have a second problem. When I'm reading Mark, I can't relate what I'm reading to Matthew, Luke or John. I have to read all four Gospels to see *everything* Jesus is quoted as saying on any given topic. I can't keep track of a topic while reading *one* Gospel, let alone *four*. I am unable to see all His teachings on any one topic together. As a result, I cannot see how they support, expand on and reinforce each other to produce an *overall* message on that topic.

A third problem is trying to cope with the volume of Jesus' sayings. In the four Gospels, Jesus is quoted almost 400 times. He addresses almost five dozen topics. I can't internalize five dozen topics at the same time. I need to be able to pick a topic and focus on it before tackling a second topic. Like many of us, I can only do one thing at a time.

Finally, I need to be able to focus my attention on the most *important* topics Jesus addressed. Ideally, I would like to start with *the* most important topic. I could focus on it until I had discerned its overall message. Only then would I be ready to tackle the second most important topic. However, using the Bible alone, how could I know the order of importance of 55 topics?

THE SAYINGS OF JESUS solves these problems. It assembles everything Jesus is quoted as having said on each topic in a separate chapter, determines the relative importance of topics and sequences its chapters in order of importance. This sequencing is revealing. The five most important topics account for *over one third* of what Jesus was recorded as saying. The fifteen most important topics account for *over two thirds* of what Jesus was recorded as saying.[38]

To me, this says Jesus considered these fifteen topics to be the most important parts of His message. If so, I can understand most of His

---

[38] How all of what this paragraph states was determined is described in the final chapter of *THE SAYINGS OF JESUS* that is entitled *The Research that Produced THE SAYINGS OF JESUS (for nerds only)*.

message by focusing, one at a time, on just those fifteen out of the 55 topics. So what does my textbook establish as the fifteen most important topics Jesus addressed throughout His three-year ministry?

The top five topics, in descending sequence of importance, are *Passion and Death, Discipleship, Authority, Close of the Age* and *Guidance. Passion and Death* contains what Jesus said during the tragic end of His ministry. *Discipleship* contains what Jesus said about the commitment demanded of those of us who aspire to be His disciples. *Authority* addresses the many quotations where Jesus asserted and supported His claim to be the Son of God. *Close of the Age* addresses what He told us will happen when we meet God face to face. *Guidance* contains what Jesus said about how we are to live our lives.

The next ten topics, also in descending sequence of importance, are *Faith, Kingdom of God, Laws, Preparedness, Pharisees et al, Rejecting Jesus, Salvation, Miracles, Riches* and *Commandments. Faith* describes the incidents where Jesus insisted faith is a prerequisite of His healing and of receiving the gifts we ask of God. *Kingdom of God* contains Jesus' descriptions of heaven and what it takes to get there. *Laws* contains Jesus' claim to be Lord of the Sabbath, His insistence not one iota of the law is void and the distinction He made between earthly laws and God's laws. *Preparedness* tells us what we must discern of God's will and what we must do to accomplish it. *Pharisees et al* expresses Jesus' hatred of the hypocrisy we share with the Jewish leaders. *Rejecting Jesus* makes clear there is no excuse for rejecting what He has so clearly, compellingly and repeatedly told us. *Salvation* establishes that *doing* God's will is a prerequisite of salvation and describes God's joy when sinners repent. *Miracles* contains what Jesus said as He performed His miracles. *Riches* describes what we are to do with the blessings God gives us. *Commandments* summarizes what Jesus demands of us.

The remaining 40 topics contain many gems of enlightenment dotted throughout their approximately 120 quotations.

In this chapter and in Chapter 26 you will find what for *me* are Jesus' teachings on fourteen of the fifteen topics, as well as what *I* take to be His overall message on each topic.

In *THE SAYINGS OF JESUS*, I go one step further. Having identified what *I* have concluded to be the overall message of each of the fifteen most important topics, I have synthesized all fifteen *topic* messages into what *I* discern to be Jesus' *overall* message. The process of synthesis I used is described in *THE SAYINGS OF JESUS*.

In each of its chapters, you'll find a suggestion to write down in a personal journal what for you is Jesus' message on its topic. At the end of *THE SAYINGS OF JESUS*, you'll find a suggestion to try out my process of discerning what for you is Jesus' overall message.

Of course, the value of all this study is dependent upon how *accurately* the Bible quotes Jesus' teachings. It is true there is much scholarly debate about the Bible's accuracy. I am not qualified to even participate in such debate. However, it is clear to me that, even if *some* passages are misquoted, it is extremely unlikely they *all* are. Any error in a single passage would stand out by its inconsistency with the rest of the quotations on that topic when they are all viewed together. *THE SAYINGS OF JESUS* provides such a view.

As you continue reading here, you'll occasionally see where one quotation clarifies, supports, reinforces and expands on another. This mutual support significantly reduces the likelihood of misconstruing Jesus' message. The organization of PART FIVE shows how Jesus' teachings on each of fourteen topics support each other. *THE SAYINGS OF JESUS* does the same for all topics.

If you make your *own* study of *THE SAYINGS OF JESUS*, you'll see this mutual support more often, as you will have access to *all* Jesus said on all 55 topics. Your *own* study, of the first fifteen chapters in *THE SAYINGS OF JESUS*, may produce different interpretations of Jesus' teachings, different *topic* messages and a different overall message than my study did. This is a good thing. It enables us to learn even more whenever we have occasion to share our pieces of glass.

Before continuing to read Chapter 24 and 26, you may want to have ready access to a Bible. As you will see, my commentary on any teaching is supported, in these two chapters, by only a few phrases from the full discourse on that teaching. Where you are unfamiliar with the full discourse, you can find it in *THE SAYINGS OF JESUS* as well as by using the Bible citations in these two chapters.

Passion and Death

Many of us are familiar with most of this topic. It describes the transfiguration where Jesus foretold His death, (Mark 9: 12-13, Matt 17: 7-12) the preparations for the triumphant entry into Jerusalem, (Mark 11: 2-3, Luke 19: 30-40, Matt 21: 2-3) the triumphant entry into Jerusalem, (John 12: 12-36) the preparations for the Last Supper, (Luke 22: 8-12, Matt 26: 18, Mark 14: 13-15) the institution of the Eucharist, (Luke 22: 15-22, Matt 26:

26-29, Mark 14: 22-25) the forecast of Judas' betrayal, (Matt 26: 21-25, John 13: 21-27, Mark 14: 18-21) the forecast of Peter's denials, (Mark 14: 27-31, Matt 26: 31-35, Luke 22: 31-34) Judas' betrayal, (Matt 26: 49-56, Mark 14: 44-49, Luke 22: 47-53, John 18: 1-11) Peter's denials, (John 18: 17, 25-27) Jesus' trials, (Luke 22: 67-71, Mark 14: 60-64, Matt 26: 62-68, Mark 15: 2-15, Matt 27: 11-23, John 18: 28 - 19: 16) Jesus carrying the cross (Luke 23: 27-31) and Jesus' crucifixion and death. (John 19: 17-30)

The fact Jesus spent more time talking about His passion than about any other topic indicates He felt its message was the most important of all the things He needed to tell us. However, its content does not teach us specific lessons as does His discourse on all the other topics. I conclude its importance is due to the need for us to fully internalize the *extent* of Jesus' love for us and our *need* to respond to that love and to learn to love as He does.

I am most impacted by the humanity of Jesus' appeal to God to take this cup from Him and at the same time His acceptance of God's will over His own. (Mark 14: 32-42, Matt 26: 36-46, Luke 22: 40-46) It reinforces for me I must pray God helps me unite my free will with His divine will. How much easier this must be for me than it was for Jesus, foreknowing what He faced.

Jesus' expressions of His love for us in the midst of His passion show the intensity of that love. He said, "How often would I have gathered your children together as a hen gathers her brood." (Luke 13: 32-35, Matt 23: 37-39, Luke 19: 41-44) He said in His Father's house there are many rooms and He goes to prepare a place for us. (John 14: 1-7) In the midst of His agony on the cross He said, "Father, forgive them, for they know not what they do." (Luke 23: 34-43) The intensity of Jesus' love models for me how intensely I must grow my love of God and my neighbour.

Jesus' *humanity* was dramatically demonstrated in His final lament "My God, my God, why have you forsaken me?" (Mark 15: 34, Matt 27: 46) The desperation in that lament shouts out how much the human being, Jesus, suffered to save our souls. How can human beings not respond with all their heart, their mind, their soul and their strength?

I *know* Jesus was a man and how much He suffered for us.

Discipleship

Jesus is demanding of me and of others who aspire to be His disciples. Everyone who would follow Jesus must ". . . deny himself and take up his cross daily and follow me." (Luke 9: 23-27, Matt 16: 24-28) Of the two evangelists, only Luke adds the word *daily* but it is surely implied in the quotation from Matthew. I conclude this means I must put Jesus' teachings and God's will first. I must put them ahead of anything else in my life *every single day* of the rest of my earthly life.

Jesus went further and said, "Whoever loves father or mother more than me is not worthy of me." (Matt 10: 34-39) and, more forcefully, "If anyone comes to me and does not hate his own father and mother and wife and children and brothers and sisters, yes, and even his own life, he cannot be my disciple." (Luke 14: 26-33) Luke's quotation uses the word *hate* while Matthew's does not. Reading both we can see Jesus is using *hate* as *love less*. We can love our family, but we must love them *less* than Jesus. We must put Jesus before everything. In answer to a question, Jesus told Peter "Everyone who has left houses or brothers or sisters or father or mother or children or lands, for my name's sake, will receive a hundredfold and will inherit eternal life." (Matt 19: 28-30) In answer to the people who told Jesus His mother and brothers had asked to speak to Him, Jesus replied, "Whoever does the will of my Father in heaven is my brother and sister and mother." (Matt 12: 48-50)

We are taught we must proclaim the gospel to the whole of creation. (Matt 28: 18-20, Mark 16: 15-18) I conclude, in our individual cases, we are to proclaim the Word of God to *our* part of the whole of creation. We have to be the salt of the earth and the light of the world. (Matt 5: 13-16, Luke 14: 34-35) In proclaiming the Word of God we need to have fire in our tummies. We need to pray others join us. (Luke 10: 2-9, Matt 9: 37-38) I conclude Jesus is telling us to proactively *share*, what we understand of His teachings, with each other and with all those we encounter.

When we have done all this, we must be content we have merely done our duty. (Luke 17: 7-10) Christ is making it clear, when we do our best to be what He demands of His disciples, we are earning no bonus points. Instead we need to be thankful we have been given the grace to recognize our duty. As He told the sons of Zebedee ". . . whoever would be great among you must be your servant and whoever would be first among you must be your slave" and ". . . to sit at my right hand or at my left is not mine to grant, but it is for those for whom it has been prepared by my Father." (Matt 20: 21-28, Mark 10: 36-45) When the apostles rejoiced over the power that had been given to them, Jesus told them ". . . do not rejoice in this, that the spirits are subject to you, but rejoice that your names are written in heaven." (Luke 10: 18-20) When we see the fruits of the gifts we have been given, we need to rejoice that we are the instruments of God's will rather than rejoice in our accomplishments.

We must not be discouraged when we are rejected in one place, but must persevere elsewhere. (Luke 10: 10-16, Luke 9: 3-5, Mark 6: 10-11, Matt 10: 5-15) When we are rejected and even accused of intruding, we need not search for a response. Our best response will be whatever the Holy Spirit puts in our minds at that instant. Although we will very likely escape the apostles' fate, we *will* face rejection, by even our families, of our attempts to share our understanding of God's will. However, those who love selflessly and endure rejection to the end will be saved. (Luke 21: 10-19, Matt 10: 16-23, Mark 13: 9-13) Jesus advised us to let those, who are dead to the Word of God, tend to those who are dead. (Matt 8: 20-22) I conclude Jesus is telling us to share our knowledge of God's will and to accept its rejection by others.

Most scary of all these teachings is "No one who puts his hand to the plow and looks back is fit for the kingdom of God." (Luke 9: 58-62) This says to me anyone who knows the teachings of Jesus but who ignores them is at much more peril than one who is ignorant of Jesus' teachings.

I *know* I must love Jesus more than anyone, emulate Him daily and proclaim God's Word zealously despite rejection. I am fully accountable for dutifully following all His teachings.

Authority

Jesus seized a great number of opportunities to make it clear He was God.

The first of these opportunities was after John the Baptist had been arrested. In his doubt, John sent his disciples to ask Jesus "Are you the one who is to come, or shall we look for another?" Jesus' reply essentially said actions speak louder than words. (Luke 7: 22-23, Matt 11: 4-6) His miracles attest He is God.

Later, after ridiculing the notion Satan casts out Satan, Jesus again pointed to His deeds ". . . if it is by the finger of God I cast out demons, then the kingdom of God has come upon you." (Luke 11: 17-23, Matt 12: 25-32, Mark 3: 23-29)

In the synagogue, He said in the same breath ". . . your sins are forgiven" and ". . . pick up your bed and go home". He used the healing of the paralytic to prove ". . . the Son of Man has authority on earth to forgive sins." (Mark 2: 5-11, Matt 9: 2-6, Luke 5: 20-24)

When Philip said, "Lord, show us the Father and it is enough for us." Jesus replied, "Whoever has seen me has seen the Father. Believe me that I am in the Father and the Father is in me, or else believe on account of the works themselves." (John 14: 8-14)

To those who challenged His authority, Jesus refused to "... tell you by what authority I do these things." (Mark 11: 29-33, Luke 20: 3-8, Matt 21: 24-27) He explained His refusal on another occasion by saying "If anyone's will is to do God's will he will know whether the teaching is from God or whether I am speaking on my own authority." (John 7: 16-24) He will tell anyone who truly wants to know, in no uncertain terms, but He will not respond to the challenges of those who do not want to know.

Jesus used John's testimony to substantiate He is from God but says "... the testimony that I have is greater than that of John. For the works that the Father has given me to accomplish, the very works that I am doing, bear witness about me that the Father has sent me." (John 5: 30-36) Countering the belief, shared by His disciples, that being born blind was the result of sin by the person or his parents, Jesus explained, in curing him, he was born blind so "... that the works of God might be displayed in him." (John 9: 3-11)

On two occasions, He used conversation to assert He is God. He responded to the woman at the well who said, "I know that Messiah is coming (He who is called Christ). When He comes, He will tell us all things." He told her "I who speak to you am He." (John 4: 7-26) When He asked the blind man "Do you believe in the Son of Man?" the blind man replied, "And who is he, sir, that I may believe in him?" Jesus replied, "You have seen Him and it is He who is speaking to you." (John 9: 35-38)

On many other occasions, Jesus claimed He is God in differing wordings. "For as the Father has life in Himself, so He has granted the Son also to have life in Himself." (John 5: 25-29) "He who sent me is true and Him you do not know. I know Him, for I come from Him and He sent me." (John 7: 28-29) "If you know me, you would know my Father also." "You are from below, I am from above." "I speak of what I have seen with my Father and you do what you have heard from your father." (John 8: 12-38)

Jesus boldest claim was in using God's words themselves. "Before Abraham was, I AM." (John 8: 48-58)

Finally, to Pilate's challenges, Jesus said, "You say that I am a king. For this purpose I was born." (John 18: 34-37) To Pilate's direct question "Are you the King of the Jews?" Jesus replied, "You have said so." (Luke 23: 3)

I *know*, based on His words and actions alone, Jesus was God Incarnate.

Close of the Age

The message stated most strongly on this topic is the separation of the sheep from the goats. (Matt 25: 31-46) The criteria for separation are *acts* of selfless love including feeding the hungry, giving drink to the thirsty, welcoming strangers, clothing the naked, visiting the sick and those in prison. Christ is explicit. The sheep who do, inherit the kingdom. The goats who don't, don't. It's clear to me I must take this literally but I must also go beyond the literal. Beyond visiting and giving food, drink and clothes, I must feed the hearts and minds that hunger, clothe hearts that have grown cold, heal those who have experienced heartbreak and loss and love those who feel no love. I must proactively love.

A related message is we need to do much more than simply *like* and *listen to* Jesus. (Luke 13: 24-30) How much more we need to do is indicated by how few will succeed. We need to apply every gift we have been given to "Strive to enter through the narrow door. For many, I tell you, will seek to enter and will not be able." To me this says complacency is the biggest danger I face.

Jesus repeatedly warned us to not be led astray. (Matt 24: 4-14, Matt 24: 23-28, Mark 13: 5-8, Luke 21: 8-9) "For many will come in my name, saying, 'I am the Christ' and they will lead many astray." To me, this means many self-proclaimed authorities and experts will refute the Word of God that Jesus taught and these voices will confuse and distract most people.

I find this to be the greatest stumbling block faced by those born in the second half of the 20th century and beyond. The awareness of most of those born earlier was largely limited to what they were taught by their parents and their church. Few would want such limitations to be perpetuated, but they did have a protective aspect. Few ideas competed with the truth proclaimed by Jesus.

Those born since have greater access to university where both wise and foolish ideas abound. Television is relatively unrestricted in what it presents. The Internet drowns people in information. News networks, hungry for audience, champion those who refute and ridicule what Jesus taught rather than those who articulate it. I conclude all these are the "false prophets" of which Jesus is warning us. Without a sound grasp of Jesus' teachings, there is little to help people separate the kernels of wheat from the sand storms of chaff.

Having studied *THE SAYINGS OF JESUS*, I know I need to examine every new idea with which I am presented and test its congruence with the knowledge I have accumulated to date of Jesus' teachings.

A second repeated warning is to stay awake. (Matt 24: 36-44, Mark 13: 32-37, Luke 12: 35-40) "The Son of Man is coming at an hour that you do not expect." This strongly suggests to me it is *urgent* we *now* apply all our heart, mind, soul and strength to discerning and accomplishing God's will. It's clear to me I am playing with fire if I put off until tomorrow what I could be doing today. We do not know when we will be judged.

Jesus taught there will be a Second Coming at the end of the world. (Luke 17: 20-37, Luke 21: 25-28, Mark 13: 14-27, Matt 24: 15-31) His descriptions definitely sound like the end of the world. ". . . fire and sulphur raining down from heaven"; ". . . the sun will be darkened and the moon will not give its light and the stars will fall from heaven"; ". . . the roaring of the sea and the waves, people fainting with fear and with foreboding of what is coming on the world" and ". . . the powers of the heavens will be shaken".

However, in the very next verses of *each* of these passages, He adds ". . . this generation will not pass away until all these things take place." (Luke 21: 29-36, Mark 13: 28-31, Matt 24: 32-35) I found the latter verses contradicted the former. If the Second Coming did not come during Jesus' generation, His statement, that it would, is false. As a result, I comfortably dismissed both teachings. Taken together they seemed to be nothing more than another false prediction of the end of the world.

However, by this time I had come to know Jesus was God Incarnate. This knowledge made it very difficult to dismiss anything He said. After some time, another explanation came to light. Could the Second Coming have happened to *each* of His generation at the moment of death (which would be the end of the world for each of them)? Could it happen to each of *us* at the moment of our own death?

Jesus' descriptions do not seem consistent with what we experience of others' human deaths. Still, none of us knows *what* we will experience at the moment of our *own* death. Interestingly, reported near-death experiences do not seem too far removed from His descriptions. Could Jesus' descriptions of the end of the world refer to the end of the world for *us* when we die? If so, He is saying He will come back to judge us at the moment of our deaths.

What Jesus is teaching us is consistent with the Roman Catholic *ex cathedra* teaching, which we examined in Chapter 4. "A person worthy of heaven at the time of death would immediately go there rather than waiting until the final judgement." All things considered, I conclude our judgement will come when we die (". . . at an hour that you do not expect").

Jesus' final teaching on this subject provides a unique incentive to discern and accomplish God's will. (Matt 24: 45-51, Luke 12: 42-46) The faithful and wise manager whom his master has set over his household to give them their food at the proper time and whom the master finds so doing, will be set over all the master's possessions. From this I gather the message is those who do God's will on Earth will be given even more fulfillment in heaven.

I *know* I will be judged at the moment of my death as one of the few sheep or one of the many goats. Because my death may occur at any moment, I must prepare now. To avoid being led astray I must test every idea against a *full* understanding of Jesus' teaching.

Guidance

Jesus set an impossible standard. "You therefore must be perfect, as your heavenly Father is perfect." (Matt 5: 43-48) What good is a standard that cannot be met? Might the purpose of this standard be to motivate us to continuously *strive* for perfection, knowing all along we cannot fully achieve it?

I conclude we are given this standard to protect us from the complacency of the Pharisee who prayed "God, I thank you that I am not like other men", while a tax collector prayed "God be merciful to me, a sinner." (Luke 18: 10-14) While I am striving for perfection, I need to continuously pray, like the tax collector, for God's forgiveness each and every time I fall short. It is only in this way I can demonstrate I *want* with all my heart to do God's will. God knows I cannot be perfect but wants me to do my best to approach perfection.

Christ taught us to approach God's perfection by saying ". . . be sons of the Most High, for He is kind to the ungrateful and the evil. Be merciful, even as your Father is merciful." (Luke 6: 32-36) and ". . . be sons of your Father who is in heaven. For He makes His sun rise on the evil and on the good and sends rain on the just and on the unjust." (Matt 5: 43-48)

In the parable of the Good Samaritan (Luke 10: 30-37), Christ teaches us God demands of us the *best* we can give. We must hold nothing back. What most people consider to be a generous act pales in comparison with what the Good Samaritan did. He ministered to one of the Jewish people who despised and looked down upon his people. He put his life at risk by involving himself in the aftermath of a violent confrontation. He not only bound the man's wounds but also treated them with oil and wine. He gave up his own animal and agenda to bring the man to an inn where he continued to care for him. The next day he paid the innkeeper to continue his care committing to pay him whatever more he spent in that care. He held nothing back. I need to do more than intervene. I need to hold nothing back.

Jesus extended the Ten Commandments. "Do good to those who hate you; pray for those who abuse you." (Luke 6: 27-31) "You shall not murder" is extended by the teaching whoever is angry with or insults anyone must ". . . be reconciled to your brother and then come and offer your gift before the altar." (Matt 5: 21-26, Luke 12: 57-59) "You shall not commit adultery" is extended by the teaching ". . . everyone who looks at a woman with lustful intent, has already committed adultery with her in his heart." (Matt 5: 27-30) "An eye for an eye and a tooth for a tooth" is qualified by the teachings "Do not resist the one who is evil"; ". . . if anyone slaps you on the right cheek, turn to him the other also"; ". . . if anyone would sue you and take your tunic, let him have your cloak as well" and ". . . if anyone forces you to go one mile, go with him two miles". (Matt 5: 38-42)

Jesus was specific about avoiding the temptation to be *seen* doing good. "When you give to the needy, do not let your left hand know what your right hand is doing." (Matt 6: 1-4) "When you fast, anoint your head and wash your face, that your fasting may not be seen by others." (Matt 6: 16-18) "When you pray do not heap up empty phrases." (Matt 6: 5-8)

In place of "empty phrases" He gave us the Lord's Prayer (Matt 6: 9-15, Luke 11: 2-4) with the warning ". . . if you do not forgive others their trespasses, neither will your Father forgive your trespasses."

Jesus offered incentives to be humble. When we are invited anywhere we should seek out the lowest place rather than the most sought-after place ". . . so that when your host comes he may say to you, 'Friend, move up higher.'" When it is your turn to invite, invite those who ". . . cannot repay you. For you will be repaid at the resurrection of the just." (Luke 14: 8-14)

I found one of the most difficult to understand of Jesus' parables is that of the Dishonest Manager. (Luke 16: 1-13) Studying Jesus' explanation clarified that we need to use all the gifts we have been given to improve the lot of others. We need to realize everything we have is a gift from God that is intended to be shared. We need to be as shrewd as the dishonest manager in finding ways to use our gifts to benefit others. Jesus concludes with "If you have not been faithful in that which is another's (God's), who will give you (in heaven) that which is your own?" and "You cannot serve God and money."

Twice Jesus warned us not to cause others to sin. (Luke 17: 1-2, Mark 9: 42-48) On both occasions, Jesus illustrated the importance of this warning by describing the severity of the consequences.

Another teaching that puzzled me for a long time was "If your brother sins against you . . . and if he refuses to listen even to the Church let him be to you as a Gentile and a tax collector." (Matt 18: 15-20) For the longest time this teaching seemed contradictory to ". . . if he sins against you seven times in one day and turns to you seven times, saying, 'I repent' you must forgive him." (Luke 17: 3-4) Am I to forgive or shun? I have come to conclude it is up to me to forgive, but up to sinners to repent. If they do not, after my forgiveness, it is their concern rather than mine.

One of the most beautiful items of guidance is Christ's offer "Take my yoke upon you and learn from me, for I am gentle and lowly in heart and you will find rest for your souls. For my yoke is easy and my burden is light." (Matt 11: 28-30) When I reflect on all Christ is demanding of me His yoke appears far from light. However, the more I strive towards the impossible standard He sets for me, the more I feel the lightness of the burden. The more I strive, the more I feel God giving me strength to strive a little more.

I *know* I must continuously strive to approach God's standard of perfection and pray for God's forgiveness and help each time I fall short. I must love my enemies, do good rather than look good and use my gifts to help those who cannot repay me.

So these are the messages I take away on the five most important topics. Before continuing to the ten next most important topics, I'd like to share the last of the case studies offered to me in *Experiential Learning*.

CHAPTER 25

MY FOURTH CASE STUDY

Shortly after Peggy's passing, God sent me a third Roman Catholic. This *Perception* experience had the same effect on me as did that of my second Roman Catholic. I fell deeply in love at first sight. Her deep, dark eyes continue to mesmerize me to this day.

God knows I could not have survived well on my own. Peggy knew that as well. Several times in our marriage she told me she knew she would die before me and she wanted me to find the life partner I would need. I confidently told her she couldn't know when she would die and I would never need or want anyone but her.

As my fiancée and I prepared for marriage, she told me that a few days before her late husband, Bert, passed away, he told her "I don't want you to be alone, Mom. Find another partner." When she later questioned whether she had heard correctly, her sister, who had been present, assured her that was precisely what her late husband had said.

The convictions of her late husband and my late wife made it easier for us to marry and for our children to accept our marriage. As well, Bert and Peggy had both given us a profound lesson in selfless love.

Marcelle is a Francophone who taught grade school throughout her career. After we met I experienced what a great teacher she is. Since high school, I had always wanted to learn French. I counted on the grasp of vocabulary and grammar I had achieved in high school. It never occurred to me until I tried my hand at conversation that all my high school teachers were *English*-speaking. Marcelle's large family speaks French. The bungalow we bought together in Florida is in a gated community in which over 95% of the owners are Québecois. I have my own immersion opportunity. I am fortunate to have "une bonne enseignante."

Marcelle contributed significantly to my *Experiential Learning*. She invited me to say the rosary with her. I had never practiced it, feeling it was not only rote prayer but agonizingly repetitive. Through our discussions and through sharing it with her, I began to appreciate it as a mantra-like prayer. I realized it was a way of closing out mental distraction and focusing on God.

I discovered a way to make the rosary more effective for me. I began to add prayers to my recitation of the rosary for the four families Marcelle and I now had, as well as other people in my life. As you may know, the rosary includes fifty repetitions of the Hail Mary prayer contained in five decades. The leader of each decade recites the first half of the Hail Mary and the participants, the second half. I dedicate two Hail Mary's to each group of people in my life. While the rosary leader is praying the first half of the first of each pair of Hail Mary's, I thank God for His love and protection of each group of people. During the first half of the second of each pair, I ask God to grant them the grace of opening their hearts and minds to His love and to the discernment and accomplishment of His will.

I pray a pair each for my two siblings' families, my two sons and their families, my daughter and her close friends, Marcelle's three children and their partners' families, Marcelle's siblings' families, Peggy's siblings' families, Bert's siblings' families, five groups of my friends and their families, my IBM and post-IBM peers and their families, the parolees and inmates with whom I work, several palliative care patients I visit, those who are mentally, physically and emotionally challenged and all who have lost jobs, homes and hope and who feel unloved. To me, these two prayers – in thanks for God's love and protection of all of them and in request of an opening of all of their hearts and minds to His love and to the discernment and accomplishment of His will – are the most important prayers I could make on behalf of the people in my life.

Marcelle and I became Extraordinary Ministers together, attend retreats together and bring the Eucharist to homebound parishioners together. Like Peggy, she is an excellent listener and has helped me process my doubts, strengthen my thinking and engage my heart. Like Peggy, she doesn't allow my questionings to affect her faith.

All her support and mentoring continue to this day. She accepts when, at times, I am more absorbed in Jesus' teachings than in her. Her unwavering faith is a constant inspiration. Her insight helped me discern Jesus' message on the five most important topics He addressed as well as on nine of the ten next most important topics.

I'll now address the messages I took away from the latter.

CHAPTER 26

THE SAYINGS OF JESUS – 2

Faith

J esus' most-used method of demonstrating the necessity of faith was His approach to many healings. In these cases, He talked with supplicants until they had confessed their faith in His ability to heal them. As you read the following exchanges, is it not clear the faith of the supplicant is a prerequisite of Jesus' healing?

Jesus, at first, refused the Syrophoenician woman a healing leading her to insist ". . . even the dogs under the table eat the children's crumbs." Jesus said her faith in His "crumbs" had healed her daughter. (Mark 7: 27-29, Matt 15: 24-28)

On another occasion, Jesus insisted on "discovering" who had touched His garments. A woman's reply to His question demonstrated her faith in Jesus' physical power. Having connected her faith to His healing, He told her ". . . your faith has made you well." (Luke 8: 45-48, Mark 5: 30-34, Matt 9: 20-22)

When the ruler whose daughter had died demonstrated his faith by saying ". . . come and lay your hand on her and she will live", Jesus went with him to where the dead girl lay. To assure the attention of all those who knew she was dead, He claimed, ". . . she is not dead but sleeping." Knowing this statement would trigger the onlookers' ridicule, He shocked them into belief in Him by saying "Talitha cumi" or "Little girl, I say to you, arise." (Matt 9: 18-19 & 24-26, Mark 5: 22-24 & 35-43, Luke 8: 41-42 & 49-56)

It was obvious what a blind man wanted, but Jesus insisted on asking "What do you want me to do for you?" In so doing, He enabled the blind man to demonstrate his faith in His healing by leading him to reply "Rabbi, let me recover my sight." Jesus capped off the lesson by healing him and saying "Go your way; your faith has made you well." (Mark 10: 51-52, Luke 18: 41-43)

When a group of blind men called out "Have mercy on us, Son of David", Jesus insisted on their answer to the question "Do you believe that I am able to do this?" With their faith established, Jesus said as He healed them "According to your faith be it done to you." (Matt 9: 28-29)

Only after a leper proclaimed, "If You will, You can make me clean", did Jesus heal him with the words "I will, be clean." (Mark 1: 40-44, Matt 8: 2-4, Luke 5: 12-14)

Jesus used the case of the ten lepers to make the point that, in addition to faith in God's mercy, we need to express our thanks to God. When one leper returned to thank Jesus, He said, "Were not ten cleansed? Where are the other nine?" That He added "Rise and go your way; your faith has made *you* well." raises the question, at least for me, whether the cleansing of the other nine resulted in *permanent* healing. (Luke 17: 12-19)

Jesus made the most of the dramatic faith of the centurion who appealed to Him that his servant was ". . . lying paralyzed at home, suffering terribly." When Jesus offered "I will come and heal him", the centurion replied, "Lord, I am not worthy to have You come under my roof, but only say the word and my servant will be healed." Jesus replied, "Truly, I tell you, with no one in Israel have I found such faith." (Matt 8: 6-13, Luke 7: 6-10)

Jesus also used *lack* of faith to demonstrate its necessity. When His disciples were unable to cure a young mute, the father said to Jesus "If You can do anything, have compassion on us and help us." Jesus pointed out the father's lack of faith by repeating his phrase "If you can!" He then made the point "All things are possible for one who believes." After Jesus had cast out the demon, the disciples asked Him "Why could we not cast it out?" Jesus answered, in one account, faith must be accompanied by prayer. (Mark 9: 16-29, Matt 17: 15-20, Luke 9: 38-42)

As well, Jesus used miracles to demonstrate the necessity of faith. The disciples awoke Him from sleep as they crossed a lake in a storm, terrified they would perish. Jesus calmed the storm and asked, "Why are you afraid? Have you still no faith?" (Mark 4: 35-41, Matt 8: 23-27, Luke 8: 22-25)

On another occasion, when the disciples saw Jesus walking towards them on the water, Peter momentarily demonstrated spectacular faith. "Lord, if it is You, command me to come to You on the water." Jesus said, "Come." So Peter got out of the boat and walked on the water towards Jesus. But when he saw the waves, he was afraid and, beginning to sink, cried out "Lord, save me." Jesus immediately reached out His hand and took hold of him saying to him "Oh you of little faith, why did you doubt?" (Matt 14: 25-31) He shows us it is our lack of faith that prevents us from experiencing miracles.

Another time, when some of His disciples had fished all night with no catch, He told them "Put out into the deep and let down your nets for a catch." When they demonstrated their faith by complying, they were rewarded with a huge catch. (Luke 5: 4-6)

Once, while travelling, Jesus found a fig tree with no figs and cursed it. When the tree immediately withered, the disciples' attention was captured. Jesus exhorted them to "Have faith in God. Whoever does not doubt in his heart, but believes what he says will come to pass, it will be done for him." He added, "Whatever you ask in prayer, believe that you have received it and it will be yours." (Mark 11: 12-14 & 20-25, Matt 21: 18-22) I realize what had made it so difficult for me to pray and why, for so long, I had never experienced a miracle. It was my lack of faith in both.

As long as I doubted, my prayers would not be answered and miracles were not going to happen to me. As you read in Chapter 14, I now have faith in prayer and believe it is answered. At this stage of my *Experiential Learning*, I still had difficulty overcoming my doubt in miracles, although I had no valid reason for believing they could not occur. I'm pretty sure it was my doubt that kept them from happening for me. Once I finally accepted the reality of miracles, I experienced one. I'll tell you about that in Chapter 28.

Jesus insisted we have not tested the limits of our faith. "If you had faith like a grain of mustard seed, you could say to this mulberry tree 'Be uprooted and planted in the sea' and it would obey you." (Luke 17: 5-6)

On another occasion, Jesus again made the point we must have faith in prayers. In His parable of the unrighteous judge who finally decides ". . . because this widow keeps bothering me, I will give her justice, so she will not beat me down by her continual coming" He asks ". . . will not God give justice to His elect who cry to Him day and night?" (Luke 18: 2-8) Two things are reinforced for me. Firstly, I must have faith in my prayer.

If I simply pray on the chance my prayer may be answered, it won't be. I have to pray with the faithful assurance it will be answered. Secondly I have to persevere in prayer. It is through my persistence in my prayers that I demonstrate both their importance to me and my faith they will be answered.

Jesus made this clear on another occasion. "Whatever you ask of the Father in my name, He will give it to you. Ask and you will receive, that your joy may be full." (John 16: 23-27). All God demands of us in return for His gift is faith.

I *know* I must grow my faith in my prayers for God's help in accomplishing whatever Jesus demands of me.

Kingdom of God

Jesus began over a dozen of His sayings with words similar to "The kingdom of God is like . . .". I see He offers these teachings because He knows we can't comprehend heaven. He is trying to give us an idea, a concept of what we will find when we finally attain heaven. He is also expressing criteria in a way that is easy to understand but not easy to accept. He is telling us the criteria for our *attainment* of heaven.

Jesus said the kingdom of heaven ". . . is like a grain of mustard seed, which when sown on the ground, is the smallest of all the seeds on earth, yet when it is sown it grows up and becomes larger than all the garden plants and puts out large branches, so that the birds of the air can make nests in its shade." (Matt 13: 31-32, Mark 4: 30-32, Luke 13: 18-19) This says to me the kingdom of heaven is here now to an infinitesimal degree. It was sown by Christ in each of us. It must grow in each of us. When it has fully grown, our lives will be richer than we could have anticipated. We will be an oasis for all those who seek comfort in us.

Jesus said the kingdom of heaven ". . . is like leaven that a woman took and hid in three measures of flour, until it was all leavened." (Luke 13: 20-21, Matt 13: 33) To me, our humanity is the three measures of flour. The leaven is the Word of God that Jesus made available to us. For it to work we must thoroughly mix it into every bit of the flour – our humanity. Once we fully internalize the Word of God, nothing can stop our rising.

Jesus said the kingdom of heaven ". . . is like a treasure hidden in a field, which a man found and covered up. Then in his joy he goes and sells all that he has and buys that field." (Matt 13: 44) From this I conclude the kingdom of heaven is here now but is difficult to discover. Once a person finds it they want to be sure they never lose it. They trade everything they have on Earth for what they have found. They buy into the kingdom of heaven. This is what I was beginning to experience.

Jesus said the kingdom of heaven ". . . is like a merchant in search of fine pearls, who, on finding one pearl of great value, went and sold all that he had and bought it." (Matt 13: 45-46) To me this says to find the one pearl of great value, we need to search. In our search we find many lesser pearls but, with perseverance, we will finally find the pearl of great value. Once we find it, we will see we need to give up all the lesser pearls in order to fully attain the kingdom of God.

Having done His best to convey to us how priceless the kingdom of heaven is, Christ turned to the even more important message. What must *we* do to attain the kingdom of heaven?

In the *Parable of the Great Banquet*, Jesus tells us the master ". . . sent his servants to say to those who had been invited 'Come, for every-thing is now ready.' But they all alike began to make excuses." Enraged, the master said to his servants "Go out quickly . . . and bring in the poor and crippled and blind and lame . . . that my house may be filled." (Luke 14: 16-24)

The first thing this tells me is that a prerequisite for the attainment of heaven is to *accept* the invitation. We accept by choosing to *act* on the Word of God as proclaimed by Christ. Since we have all been given free will whether or not to accept the invitation, the choice is up to us.

The second thing it tells me is those who have not had access to the Word of God, through no fault of their own, will "fill God's house." To me, the poor, crippled, blind and lame include 1) those whose mental challenges keep the Word of God from them, 2) those whose heredity and environment have unavoidably kept the Word of God from them and 3) those whose geography has kept them separated from proclamations of the Word of God. I have none of these excuses. If I do not accept God's invitation, it is my own undoing.

Jesus said the kingdom of heaven ". . . may be compared to a king who gave a wedding feast for his son." Once again, those invited excused themselves and, in this case, killed the servants sent to invite them. The king then sent other servants out to invite everyone ". . . both bad and good." When the wedding hall was filled the king ". . . saw there a man who had no wedding garment." The king told his attendants to ". . . cast him into the outer darkness." Jesus summarized the parable by the warning ". . . many are called, but few are chosen." (Matt 22:

2-14) The message is scarily clear to me. The wedding garment is our preparation of ourselves for the time when we will be called. When we have not adequately prepared, God's correct judgement will be we are not yet ready. Worse, Jesus' summary tells us *few* will have adequately prepared.

Jesus taught the kingdom of heaven ". . . may be compared to a man who sowed good seed in his field." When the plants came up and bore grain then weeds appeared also. So the servants said to their master "Then do you want us to go and gather the weeds?" But the master said, "No, lest in gathering the weeds you root up the wheat along with them. Let both grow together until the harvest and at harvest time I will tell the reapers 'Gather the weeds first and bind them in bundles to be burned, but gather the wheat into my barn.'" (Matt 13: 24-30) This explains to me why for so long I thought, as long as I was as good as most people, I was good enough. I failed to realize I was comparing myself to the other weeds. Blessedly, I have lost my complacency. It also explains why "good things happen to bad people". Both good and bad are given an equal share of *all* life on Earth has to offer. Both exist together until their judgement.

Jesus taught the kingdom of heaven ". . . is like a net that was thrown into the sea and gathered fish of every kind. When it was full, men drew it ashore and sat down and sorted the good into containers but threw away the bad. So it will be at the close of the age. The angels will come out and separate the evil from the righteous." (Matt 13: 47-50) You have already read (and will read more) sayings of Jesus that tell you how high His standards of righteousness are.

Jesus taught the kingdom of heaven ". . . is as if a man should scatter seed on the ground. He sleeps and rises night and day, and the seed sprouts and grows; he knows not how. But when the grain is ripe, at once he puts in the sickle because the harvest has come." (Mark 4: 26-29) I realize I don't know when the sickle will be wielded for me. I had better have produced a full ear of grain by then.

Jesus taught the kingdom of heaven ". . . is like a master of a house who went out early in the morning to hire labourers" at a denarius a day. He continued hiring labourers throughout the day until the last had only an hour's work to do. At the end of the day, each received the same wage. When the first labourers complained, he said, "I choose to give to this last worker as I give to you." (Matt 20: 1-16) This teaches me three things.

Firstly, only the labourers who showed up and *accepted* the master's offer received the denarius. God will grant His grace only when we *pray* (show up) for it. He will not force us to come to Him. He has left the choice to do so up to us. Secondly, it is never too late for us to begin praying to God for that grace. As did the labourers, those who pray for that grace later than others receive equally. Thirdly, we must pray for those who cannot. I have concluded it is our prayers for them that God is awaiting before granting them the grace to open their hearts and minds to the discernment and accomplishment of His will.

Jesus taught the kingdom of heaven ". . . will be like ten virgins who took their lamps and went to meet the bridegroom." Five ran out of oil for their lamps and were away buying more when the bridegroom arrived. When they returned and found the door shut, they said, "Lord, lord, open to us." But He answered, "Truly, I say to you, I do not know you." (Matt 25: 1-13) This says to me it is up to me to have finished preparing for Christ's coming before "the bridegroom arrives". It would be folly for me to not have finished the best preparation of which I am capable before the hour of my death. Christ reminds me "Watch therefore, for you know neither the day nor the hour."

Finally, Christ asks us to share what we know. He asked His disciples "Have you understood all these things?" When they confidently replied affirmatively, He told them (and tells us) "Therefore every scribe who has been trained for the kingdom of heaven is like a master of a house who brings out of his treasure what is new and what is old." (Matt 13: 51-52) A commentary I read helped me to understand this teaching. It suggested our treasure is the knowledge Christ has given us. He has given us what is old, which is the knowledge He has clarified from the Old Testament. He has given us what is new, which is what He has taught in the New Testament. We are to share (bring out) *all* He has given to us.

I *know*, based on Jesus' many sayings, eternal life with God is far beyond what I can imagine and to realize it, I must respond to His invitation and adequately prepare for it in order to be judged ready to attain it.

Laws

Christ wants us to understand the traditions men have made into religious laws are false if they contradict the laws of God. Christ wants us to realize what *He* says *is* God's law. He says, although He is extending the laws of the Old Testament, He is not invalidating them. Finally, He wants us to distinguish between laws of the land and God's laws.

A frequent target was the laws of the Sabbath that prevented doing any work. Facing the Pharisees with a man with a withered hand, He asked them "Is it lawful on the Sabbath to do good or to do harm, to save life or to kill?" When the question silenced them, He healed him saying "Stretch out your hand." (Matt 12: 10-13, Mark 3: 1-5, Luke 6: 6-10) On another occasion, with a bent woman who had not been able to straighten herself for eighteen years, He challenged the Pharisees "Does not each of you on the Sabbath untie his ox or his donkey from the manger and lead it away to water it?" (Luke 13: 11-16) On a third occasion, with a man with dropsy, He put his challenge this way. "Which of you, having a son or an ox that has fallen into a well on a Sabbath day, will not immediately pull him out?" (Luke 14: 2-5) He clearly shows us how ridiculous traditions that religions make into laws can be.

When the Pharisees complained that His disciples, plucking grain to eat on the Sabbath, did what was unlawful to do on the Sabbath, Jesus referred them to King David. "Have you not read what David did when he was hungry and those who were with him: how he entered the house of God and ate the bread of the Presence, which it was not lawful for him to eat nor for those who were with him but only for the priest? And if you had known what this means 'I desire mercy and not sacrifice.' you would not have condemned the guiltless. The Sabbath was made for man, not man for the Sabbath. So the Son of Man is lord even of the Sabbath." (Matt 12: 3-8, Mark 2: 23-28, Luke 6: 1-5) Jesus is clearly insisting *His* Word is the Word of God. We are to *give* things rather than give *up* things. We are to offer mercy rather than self-sacrifice.

Jesus distinguished between God's commandment "Honour your father and your mother" and the priests' law "if anyone tells his father or his mother 'What you would have gained from me is given to God' he need not honour his father. You leave the commandment of God and hold to the tradition of men. And many such things you do." (Matt 15: 1-9, Mark 7: 5-13) I wonder what Jesus would say today about the Roman Catholic *traditions* of 1) banning couples, where either or both were previously married, from receiving the Eucharist without repeated confession of their adultery and 2) ostracising gay and lesbian couples.

The Pharisees complained Jesus' disciples ate without washing their hands as proscribed by tradition. Jesus taught them ". . . it is not what goes into the mouth that defiles a person, but what comes out of the mouth." When the disciples asked Jesus "Do you know that the Pharisees were offended when they heard this saying?" Jesus replied, "Every plant that my heavenly Father has not planted will be rooted up. Let them alone; they are blind guides. And if the blind lead the blind, both will fall into a pit." (Matt 15: 10-20) My understanding of the first part of Jesus' reply is that it refers to those who have not "been planted" by God because it has not yet been asked of Him by them or on their behalf. The second part of Jesus' reply tells me if I blind myself to His teachings, I too will fall into a pit.

He then expanded on His teaching. "Do you not see that whatever goes into a person from outside cannot defile him since it enters not his heart but his stomach and is expelled? What comes out of a person is what defiles him. For from within, out of the heart of man, come evil thoughts, sexual immorality, theft, murder, adultery, coveting, wicked-ness, deceit, sensuality, envy, slander, pride, foolishness. All these evil things come from within and they defile a person." (Mark 7: 14-23) Jesus' point could not have been made more graphically or more powerfully. It is easy for me to *accept* my human nature and to lose track of the laws of God. It is critical for me to *transcend* my human nature and focus on the laws of God.

Jesus stated, ". . . until heaven and earth pass away, not an iota, not one dot will pass from the law." As an example He taught, "Everyone who divorces his wife and marries another commits adultery and he who marries a woman divorced from her husband commits adultery" and ". . . whoever relaxes one of the least of these commandments and teaches others to do the same will be called least in the kingdom of heaven, but whoever does them and teaches them will be called great in the kingdom of heaven. For I tell you, unless your righteousness exceeds that of the scribes and Pharisees, you will never enter the kingdom of heaven." (Luke 16: 15-18, Matt 5: 17-20) For me, being called least in the kingdom of heaven is not good, but at least it happens *in* the kingdom of heaven. Much worse will be my fate if my righteousness does not exceed that of the scribes and Pharisees. I need to worry more about my righteousness than about any single law, such as that of adultery.

Jesus taught a dramatic lesson about judging others. When the Pharisees brought to Him a woman who had been caught in the act of adultery and referred Him to the Mosaic Law that such women should be stoned, Jesus replied, "Let him who is without sin among you be the first to throw a stone at her." When they had all skulked away, Jesus asked, "Woman, where are they? Has no one condemned you? Neither do I condemn you; go and from now on sin no more." (John 8: 3-11) This tells me clearly it is more important to avoid judging others than to avoid a sin (like adultery). Once again, my focus has to be on my righteousness rather than on any single law.

Finally, Jesus supported adherence to worldly laws as well as God's laws. At one point the Pharisees tried to entangle Him in His talk. They asked, "Teacher, we know that You are true and teach the way of God truthfully and You do not care about anyone's opinion, for You are not swayed by appearances. Tell us, then, what You think. Is it lawful to pay taxes to Caesar?" Jesus, aware of their malice, replied, "Why put me to the test, you hypocrites? Show me the coin for the tax. Whose likeness and inscription is this?" When they said, "Caesar's." Jesus said to them "Therefore render to Caesar the things that are Caesar's and to God the things that are God's." (Matt 22: 17-21, Luke 20: 21-25, Mark 12: 14-17)

When they came to Capernaum, the collectors of the half-shekel tax went up to Peter and said, "Does your teacher not pay the tax?" Peter said, "Yes." When he told this to Jesus, He said, "What do you think, Simon? From whom do kings of the earth take toll or tax? From their sons or from others?" When Peter replied, "From others." Jesus said to him "Then the sons are free. However, not to give offense to them, go to the sea and cast a hook and take the first fish that comes up and when you open its mouth you will find a shekel. Take that and give it to them for me and for yourself." (Matt 17: 24-27)

I *know* I must avoid judgement of others and increase *my* righteousness while following God's laws.

Preparedness

The one of Jesus' teachings I find most powerful is also one of the best known. That *The Parable of the Sower* is so well known is its greatest danger, at least for me. I had heard it so often I thought I knew what it taught without having to listen to it again.

Reflecting again on all three accounts of this parable (Matt 13: 3-23, Mark 4: 3-20, Luke 8: 5-15) I realized the teaching is not simply about what happens to the Word of God. It is much more about how *I* have to prepare myself to receive it.

I had blithely visualized some seeds falling on the path and being devoured by birds, some on rocky ground and withering away, some among thorns and being choked and some on the good soil where they produced grain, some a hundredfold. I could see this is what happens to the Word of God when people are exposed to it. It is snatched away from some by the next idea that flies into their minds; it is eagerly embraced by some, but withers as they discover its implications; it is accepted by some until the thorns of day-to-day survival choke it off and it is truly internalized by some and changes their lives.

I have come to understand the parable is about more than what happens to the *seed*. It is about what *I* have to do to prepare myself, by becoming the rich soil, to fully *receive* the Word of God. I need to scare away, from my path, the birds that come to devour the learnings I am being given. That is, I need to assure the worldly ideas that fly into my mind do not snatch away the Word of God before it reaches the rich soil of my full consciousness. I need to move the Word of God from the rocky ground to the rich soil of my full consciousness. The radio, the TV, movies, texting, the Internet, Facebook, Instagram, Twitter and so on and so on are the rocks. When the thorn bushes of family pressures, social pressures, financial concerns, medical concerns, career pressures and similar concerns choke off the Word of God, I need to devote a half hour per day to move the Word of God out of the thorn bushes into the rich soil of my full consciousness. Because I see myself as the rich soil in the parable, I blind myself to the many occasions when I am the path, the rocky ground and the thorn patches.

The next big learning experience for me was to understand Jesus' teaching, in all three of the above accounts ". . . to the one who has, more will be given and he will have an abundance, but from the one who has not, even what he has will be taken away." This not only seemed terribly unfair to me, but it didn't even make sense. It seemed unfair because I read it as the one who has been given many gifts from God has an advantage over the one given fewer. If anything, I thought this should be reversed. However, even that didn't make sense, because I couldn't understand why a loving God would take away *anything* a person had.

Matthew came to the rescue. In his account of the parable, Jesus explains to His disciples "This is why I speak to them in parables, because seeing they do not see and hearing they do not hear, nor do they understand." At first, this explanation didn't help because I failed to realize the *reason* they do not see, do not hear and do not understand. I assumed the reason was the parable was too enigmatic; it was the parable's fault. When I continued to read Matthew's account, I saw the fault was my failure to do my best to fully understand it by opening my eyes, ears, mind and heart to it.

Jesus continued. "For this people's heart has grown dull and with their ears they can barely hear and their eyes they have closed, lest they should see with their eyes and hear with their ears and understand with their heart and turn and I would heal them." I get it. Most of us close our ears, eyes and hearts to any teaching that we need to be *much* better than we are. We don't welcome the teller or the tale into our hearts. We shut our eyes to what we might read of such teachings and we shut our ears to others' interpretations of such teachings.

My difficulty with understanding ". . . even what he has will be taken away" was I thought Jesus was saying *God* will take away even what I have. It's now clear to me. God won't take anything away from me. When I shut out Jesus' teachings, even what the *world* offers will be taken away when I die.

It's clear to me Jesus is telling me in order to prepare myself to understand the Word of God, I must open my heart to it. I must want it more than anything else in my life. I must open my eyes to read and study the Bible, the Roman Catholic Catechism, writings by religious scholars and *THE SAYINGS OF JESUS*. I must continually seek to engage the minds of my priests and others and open my ears to their interpretations of the Word of God. All this takes dedication and perseverance. When I do this, I advance my preparedness. When I don't do this, my preparedness remains inadequate.

It is becoming increasingly clear to me *nothing* is more important to me than to continually seek, in every way I can, to better understand the Word of God. I know the only way I can be judged fit for heaven is to have adequately prepared by *fully* discerning and accomplishing God's will to the best of my ability.

Jesus also addressed our preparedness using the analogy of a lamp. (Mark 4: 21-25, Luke 8: 16-18, Luke 11: 33-36) Jesus is the light that we must not put in a cellar or under a basket. "Pay attention to what you hear: with the measure you use, it will be measured to you and still more will be added." I take this to mean the more effort I put into understanding the Word of God, the more it will be revealed to me. This is indeed what has been happening to me throughout *Experiential Learning*. To be the light of the world, we must ". . . be careful lest the light in you be darkness for the eye is the lamp of the body and when your eye is healthy, your whole body is full of light." I must be diligently observant of all that is presented to my eyes and my ears.

Another teaching escaped me for a long time. Jesus said, "I thank you, Father, Lord of heaven and earth, that You have hidden these things from the wise and understanding and revealed them to little children, yes Father, for such was your gracious will." (Luke 10: 21-23) Why would God hide things from the wise and understanding and reveal them only to little children? As I struggled with this, I was reminded of Jesus' teaching ". . . unless you come as a little child you will never enter the kingdom of heaven." It is now clear to me. Whenever I feel wise and understanding, I don't feel the need of further understanding. I'm OK. It's only when I am reminded of how insignificant I am, how meager my intellect is, how limited my experience has been that I realize how much I need God's revelation. When I realize my limitations and admit my dependency, as all little children do, I am preparing myself to listen so as to receive God's revelation.

Jesus, using a parable of a fig tree, taught it is urgent we double down on our preparedness. (Luke 13: 6-9) When a man discovered no fruit on a fig tree he had planted three years earlier, he told the vinedresser to cut it down. We have only so much time on Earth to bear fruit. The vinedresser answered him "Sir, let it alone this year also, until I dig around it and put on manure. Then if it should bear fruit next year, well and good; but if not, you can cut it down." We need to send out our roots to the vinedresser's fertilizer before our time is up. The vinedresser, Jesus, is begging God to allow more time for the fertilizer of His teachings to feed our prepared-ness. He is fully conscious God will not give us unlimited time on Earth to prepare ourselves.

Jesus taught us to prepare ourselves by *proactively* seeking to under-stand the Word of God so as to discern and accomplish His will. He told us to ". . . *ask* and it will be given to you; *seek* and you will find, *knock* and it will be opened to you." (Luke 11: 5-13, Matt 7: 7-11) and "If you then, who are evil, know how to give good gifts to your children, how much more will the heavenly Father give the Holy Spirit to those who ask Him?" Jesus teaches the Father will give us as much as we ask and more, but *only* if we ask. I understand the Holy Spirit to be the conveyor of God's revelation and we have to ask God to send us the Holy Spirit.

Finally, Jesus told us we must admit we sin (that is, fail to do God's will) and we must repent (that is, pray for forgiveness and commit to better do God's will from now on). When told of some Galileans whose blood Pilate had ". . . mingled with their sacrifices", Jesus answered, "Do you think that these Galileans were worse sinners than all the other Galileans, because they suffered in this way? No, I tell you, but unless you repent, you will all likewise perish." (Luke 13: 2-5) He emphasized our preparedness needs to include continual repentance. I conclude we need to confess so as to more fully *internalize* our failing to do God's will. Our repentance has to include our commitment to do our best to correct our failing. Jesus repeated this teaching in His reference to those on whom the tower of Siloam fell.

I *know* I must open my heart to every insight God sews in me, internalize every teaching Jesus gives me, proactively seek to understand the Word of God and commit to correct each failure to act on it while I still have time on Earth.

Pharisees et al

Jesus saved His most vehement vitriol for Jewish leaders. It makes us cringe and be glad He is not talking about us. However, it doesn't take too much reflection to realize much of what He condemned in them He would also condemn in us. He showed His hatred for what the Pharisees (and we) *do* rather than for what they (and we) *are*. He showed us God hates sin rather than the sinner.

Jesus taught His followers ". . . practice and observe whatever they tell you – but not what they do. For they preach, but do not practice. They tie up heavy burdens, hard to bear, and lay them on people's shoulders, but they themselves are not willing to move them with their finger. They do all their deeds to be seen by others." (Matt 23: 2-7, Luke 20: 46-47, Mark 12: 38-40) It's easy for me to agree with Jesus about the Pharisees, but harder for me to see Jesus is teaching me to focus on what I do rather than what I say and to do good for the *sake* of others rather than for the *impression* I make on others.

Jesus repeatedly called the Pharisees hypocrites. Disturbingly, I find much of what He called out applies to me. The next few quotations provide some colourful similes and metaphors.

"Woe to you, scribes and Pharisees, hypocrites. For you are like whitewashed tombs, which outwardly appear beautiful, but within are full of dead peoples' bones and all uncleanness. So you also outwardly appear righteous to others, but within you are full of hypocrisy and lawlessness." (Matt 23: 25-28) I guard how I *appear* to others pretty carefully. Jesus is telling me I need to focus more on what I *am*.

"You tithe mint and rue and every herb and neglect justice and the love of God. These you ought to have done, without neglecting the others. You blind guides, straining out a gnat and swallowing a camel!" (Luke 11:

39-44, Matt 23: 23-24) I need to focus on treating others justly and on loving God. At the same time, in focusing on these more important things, I cannot ignore one iota, one dot of the law.

"Beware of the leaven of the Pharisees, which is hypocrisy." (Luke 12: 1-3, Mark 8: 15-21, Matt 16: 6-11) I understood *hypocrisy* but *leaven* escaped me. I recently found an explanation that clarified Jesus' reference to leaven. Leaven is hidden, just as hypocrisy is often not seen for what it is. Leaven is spread throughout the dough and once it starts working it doesn't stop until it has affected the whole, just as hypocrisy can spread in me like a virus. The effect of leaven is swelling, just as hypocrisy puffs me up until I believe and suggest to others I am more than I am. I need to beware of such hypocrisy, avoid it and not get caught up in its effect. It can feed complacency.

"For you shut the kingdom of heaven in people's faces. For you neither enter yourselves nor allow those who would enter to go in. You travel to make a single proselyte and make him twice as much a child of hell as yourselves." (Matt 23: 13-15)

"Woe to you, blind guides, who say 'If anyone swears by the temple, it is nothing, but if anyone swears by the gold of the temple he is bound by his oath. If anyone swears by the altar it is nothing, but if anyone swears by the gift that is on the altar, he is bound by his oath.' For which is greater?" (Matt 23: 16-22)

"Woe to you, hypocrites, who say 'if we had lived in the days of our fathers, we would not have taken part in shedding the blood of the prophets.' Therefore, I send you prophets and wise men and scribes, some of whom you will kill and crucify." (Matt 23: 29-36)

Jesus taught us to not subject ourselves to anyone except Him. (Matt 23: 8-12) "You are not to be called rabbi, for you have one teacher and you are all brothers." Rather than trying to teach others, I need to be taught by my brothers' and sisters' understandings of the teachings of Jesus. "Call no man your father on Earth, for you have one Father who is in heaven." I must be wary of self-appointed teachers like TV evangelists, popular authors or any *one* earthly teacher or priest. As a child, the only teacher I can revere as a father, and to whom I can subject my will as to a father, is God. I need to test any teaching by its congruence with the will of God, as proclaimed by Jesus.

I *know* I share hypocrisy with the Jewish leaders. I know I need to discern what, of what I read and hear, is consistent with what I am taught by Jesus.

Rejecting Jesus

For a long time, I rejected Jesus' teachings. I don't mean all His teachings but only the ones I found inconvenient or difficult. Part of my rejection was based on my skepticism. I didn't accept Jesus was the Son of God and the Bible was a reliable source of His teachings. Having read Chapter 16, you know *Experiential Learning* led me to a correction of both errors. Because I know Jesus was God Incarnate, I can reject *nothing* He teaches me.

Jesus taught me the real reason I rejected His teachings is I couldn't or wouldn't accept I needed to be a much better person than I am. I have found no one, myself included, likes to be led to the realization they need to be better than they are. It isn't enough for me to meet *my* standards. I have to avoid rejecting *His* standards.

Jesus taught, ". . . the light has come into the world and people loved the darkness rather than the light because their deeds were evil." (John 3: 16-21) and "You are of your father the devil and your will is to do your father's desires." (John 8: 42-47) Now I readily admit I am not perfect, but I am not so willing to accept my "deeds are evil" and I want to "do the devil's desires." When I look in this mirror Jesus is holding up to me, though, I am forced to reconsider my non-acceptance. I believe Jesus is using evil here to include the sin of not doing God's will. If so, I am guilty as charged. I spend at least as much time putting my will ahead of God's as I do putting God's will ahead of mine. Whenever I deviate from God's will, I am putting the devil's will (that I put myself first) ahead of God's will.

Jesus warned us when we reach out to others, we may experience rejection as He did. "If the world hates you, know that it hated me before it hated you." (John 15: 18-25) I should not get discouraged when my outreach is not appreciated and, in many cases, rejected by others.

Jesus went on to say "If I had not come and spoken to them, they would not have been guilty of sin, but now they have no excuse for their sin." and "Whoever hates me hates my Father also. If I had not done among them the works that no one else did, they would not be guilty of sin, but now they have seen and hated both me and my Father." Now that I have access to Jesus' words, I no longer have any excuse for my sin.

Jesus' use of the word *hate* is foreign to us. We feel He can't mean us because we don't *hate* Him. However, as we observed earlier, He uses *hate* to refer to an absence of love. Seen this way, we can interpret

His teaching as "Whoever does not love me does not love my Father also. If I had not done among them the works that no one else did, they would not be guilty of sin, but now they have seen and did not love both me and my Father." Once again we are told, when we fail to love God and to do His will as taught us by Jesus, we are guilty of sin and have no excuse.

To the Pharisees who suggested He had accused them of being blind, He replied, "If you were blind, you would have no guilt, but now that you say 'We see', your guilt remains." (John 9: 39-41)

These last two teachings – "If I had not done . . ." and "If you were blind, . . ." – terrify me. As long as "I see" and discount Christ's teachings my guilt remains. As long as I allow my skepticism to cause me to reject Jesus' teachings and the content of the Bible my guilt remains. As long as I allow my ignorance to lie fallow and fail to vigorously pursue an understanding of Jesus' teachings my guilt remains. As long as I continue to do less than my best to discern and accomplish the will of God, I remain guilty. I have no excuse. Do those I love?

Jesus told a powerful parable, recounted in three of the gospels, of a master of a house who built a vineyard and leased it to tenants. When he sent servants for the fruits of his vineyard they ended up killing them all so as to inherit the vineyard for themselves. (Matt 21: 33-44, Luke 20: 9-18, Mark 12: 1-11) Jesus quoted the Old Testament passage "The stone that the builders rejected has become the cornerstone; this was the Lord's doing and it is marvelous in our eyes." To me, the master of the house is God, the vineyard is the world and we are the tenants who rejected the servants – the prophets and Christ – who came to urge us to give the fruits of the world to God. I reject Christ, the stone the builders rejected, whenever I insist on using the fruits of the world according to *my* will rather than to the will of God.

Jesus also warned us "A prophet is not without honour, except in his hometown and among his relatives and in his own household." (Mark 6: 1-4, Matt 13: 53-57, Luke 4: 22-28) He tells the people in His home town why He is not doing what He is renowned for doing elsewhere. They need to believe in Him before He can do His works. We need to believe in Him before He can save us.

I *know* I reject Jesus whenever I put my will ahead of God's will. Because Jesus has left no room for doubt about God's will, the guilt is mine and I will have no excuse.

Salvation

Jesus described what we must *do* to inherit eternal life with God in heaven and how unfailingly God will help us prepare every time we ask.

He taught ". . . unless one is born of water and the Spirit, he cannot enter the kingdom of God." (John 3: 3-15) Nicodemus, a teacher of the Israelites, had as difficult a time accepting this as I did. "How can these things be?" Jesus replied, "If I have told you earthly things and you do not believe, how can you believe if I tell you heavenly things?" What does being born of the Spirit mean? Jesus explains. "That which is born of the flesh is flesh and that which is born of the Spirit is spirit." I am born of the flesh with a heredity and environment that is worldly. I need to reject worldly values and accept God's values in order to be born of the Spirit. I am confident being born again is not something that is going to just happen to me, as some Christian sects believe. It is something I must actively choose, ask of God and pursue. I am convinced being born again is the *act* of giving my all to God.

Jesus told us "I have come into the world as light, so that whoever believes in me may not remain in darkness. The one who rejects me and does not receive my words has a judge; the Word that I have spoken will judge him on the last day." (John 12: 44-50) To receive His Word, I have to not only hear it but also understand, internalize and act on it. My salvation will depend on the degree to which I have internalized and acted on God's Word.

Jesus taught a lesson using the word picture of a shepherd who has lost one of his one hundred sheep. "What man of you, having a hundred sheep, if he has lost one of them, does not leave the ninety-nine in the open country and go after the one that is lost until he finds it? And when he has found it, he lays it on his shoulders, rejoicing." (Luke 15: 3-10, Matt 18: 10-14) Jesus illustrates His point again with a story of a woman who has lost one of ten silver coins and then comments on both parables. "There will be more joy in heaven over one sinner who repents than over ninety-nine righteous persons who need no repentance." The well-known *Parable of the Prodigal Son* is the third and most powerful version of this teaching. (Luke 15: 11-32) To me Jesus is saying God is joyful each time a person chooses to do His will. God saves that same joy for *each* one of us no matter *how late* and *how repeatedly* we repent. He makes the point again, saying "So it is not the will of my Father who is in heaven that one of these little ones should perish." God's will is for the salvation of *each* of us. To be saved, I must *accept* His will.

Zacchaeus was a rich tax collector and a sinner in the eyes of Israel. When he climbed a tree so as to see Jesus passing by, Jesus called to him "Zacchaeus, hurry and come down, for I must stay at your house today. Today salvation has come to this house, since he also is a son of Abraham. For the Son of Man came to seek and to save the lost." (Luke 19: 5-10) Jesus *continuously* reaches out to me, a sinner, and waits for me to reach out to Him from time to time.

My sister gave Marcelle and me a picture of Jesus standing outside the door of a house. As you examine it carefully, you see the door has no knob on Jesus' side.

Jesus said, "Truly, truly, I say to you, whoever hears my Word and believes Him who sent me has eternal life. He does not come into judgement, but has passed from death to life." (John 5: 19-24) From what I have learned from His related sayings, I know "hears" my Word means *follows* my Word. I am promised immediate salvation if I follow His Word to the best of my ability. Why do I *not* apply the best of my ability to following His Word? I pray for the grace of God to help me better discern and accomplish His will.

Jesus made it clear *hearing* His Word means *doing* what He says. "Why do you call me, 'Lord, Lord' and not do what I tell you? Everyone who comes to me and hears my words and does them, I will show you what he is like: he is like a man building a house, who dug deep and laid the foundation on the rock." (Luke 6: 46-49)

Jesus made a similar distinction between *committing* to do what He says and *doing* it. "What do you think? A man had two sons. And he went to the first and said, 'Son, go and work in the vineyard today.' And he answered, 'I will not' but afterward he changed his mind and went. And he went to the other son and said the same. And he answered, 'I go sir' but did not go. Which of the two did the will of his father?" (Matt 21: 28-32)

He left no doubt as to whether or not salvation is dependent on *doing* the will of God. "Not everyone who says to me, 'Lord, Lord,' will enter into the kingdom of heaven, but the one who does the will of my Father who is in heaven." (Matt 7: 21-27) I know God wants my salvation. He wants me to live with Him in selfless love for eternity. He wants me to choose to prepare myself by doing His will. Nothing less than my *best* effort to do His will is sufficient.

I *know* salvation requires putting God's values above worldly values. God continuously offers His help but it is up to me to accept it. *Professing* a love of Jesus is not enough. I must *do* what He insists upon.

Riches

I may not feel rich when I learn about those who are hundreds and thousands times richer than I. It takes a bit of reflection to remember they are much less than one tenth of one percent of the world's population. It takes a bit of discipline to redirect my attention to those I don't see who are *much* less rich than I. Who are they? They are retired people without income. They are the people who have lost their jobs or who have lost their savings. They are the mentally, physically and emotionally challenged people who can't support themselves. They are ordinary people who simply haven't been given the gifts God has entrusted to me. Since they are the majority of the population, I am indeed rich.

Being rich is a gift of God, which comes with a catch. I have to use my riches to benefit others. I have to realize my riches are entrusted to me as to a steward. I am rich less because I earned it and more because I was given the gifts to *enable* me to earn it. As you now read of my personal experience, you may agree with me my richness is more *given* than earned.

When I left university, I was *given* a job offer by IBM Canada Ltd. at the dawning of its best years. Early in my career, I was blamed for the unjustified complaints of an activist customer and *given* a time out in what was then known as IBM's penalty box. Scapegoats, like me, were transferred to sales education where they could prove themselves or confirm their incompetence. Today, the penalty box no longer exists and I would likely have been terminated rather than *gifted*. Having achieved considerable recognition in sales education, I was offered a position in a national and highly-visible sales support group. There I was *given* the opportunity to leverage the thinking of its two best experts with whom I built an internationally-recognized enabler of large, complex computer sales. At my 30-year anniversary, I was *given* IBM's golden handshake. Concurrently, I was *given* an offer of an ownership position in a consulting company. Before we sold the company a few years later, a client referred me to a US sales process consulting firm, whose consultants earned considerably more than their counterparts in Canada. I was *given* the opportunity to travel globally on lucrative consulting contracts. I retired with the *gifts* of a fixed benefit pension from IBM and a considerable retirement fund of my own.

These unearned gifts were what provided the many blessings I have experienced throughout my life. It is obvious to me God didn't give *me* those gifts because He liked me more than anyone else. Instead, God made me responsible for *using* His gifts to learn how to selflessly love and support others. It is clear to me it is crucial to my salvation I fully understand all this. To whom much is given, much is expected.

Now back to our regular programming.

Jesus taught us to "... not lay up for yourselves treasures on earth, where moth and rust destroy and where thieves break in and steal, but lay up for yourselves treasures in heaven, where neither moth nor rust destroys and where thieves do not break in and steal. You cannot serve God and money." (Matt 6: 19-24) I know from this I am to *use* my riches rather than preserve them. I am to use them to achieve acts of selfless love so as to prepare myself for heaven.

Jesus told a rich ruler, who sought justification, "If you would be perfect, go, sell what you possess and give to the poor and you will have treasure in heaven; and come, follow me." When the ruler became sad, Jesus observed, "How difficult it is for those who have wealth to enter the kingdom of God. For it is easier for a camel to go through the eye of a needle than for a rich person to enter the kingdom of God." When the disciples asked, "Who, then, can be saved?" Jesus replied, "With man this is impossible, but with God all things are possible." (Matt 19: 17-24, Mark 10: 18-27) I'm pretty sure Jesus knows it is no more possible for me to sell *everything* and give all to the poor than it is for me to achieve perfection. He is telling me I have to *want* with all my heart to approach perfection and to put the welfare of others before my comfort. He is telling me I have to demonstrate my desire by praying to God for the discipline to do *more* for others and keep *less* for myself. I know, in this, He is not asking the impossible of me. He is simply demanding I apply *all* my gifts to *approach* perfection to the very best of my ability.

For many years, I convinced myself it was foolish to give to beggars. I subscribed to the common wisdom they were lazy and would misuse whatever they were given. It was easy to conclude most would simply spend what they got on drugs and alcohol. It was convenient to maintain that giving to them would only encourage them to avoid any effort to look after themselves. It would simply encourage them to continue to take advantage of those who gave to them. The likelihood most of them were emotionally or mentally challenged didn't occur to me. Jesus' words corrected this view.

Christ insisted I give of what has been given to me. He didn't urge me to judge whether or not the recipient is deserving. He asked me to give unconditionally. I will be judged on the degree to which I gave rather than

on the use the recipient made of my gift. I must selflessly and unconditionally love those who beg no matter why they beg.

Another excuse I concocted for not giving to those who approach
me was, because there are so *many* beggars in the world, I could never
make a real difference. This idea was reinforced, some years ago, by
my experience of being overwhelmed by pressing crowds of beggars
during a brief walk in Mumbai. A well-known story cured me of this
misconception.

> A man, walking on a beach saw, in the distance, a small
> boy bending down. As he approached, he saw the boy pick
> up a beached starfish and throw it back into the ocean.
> When he reached the boy, he told him that although his
> initiative was well-meaning, because of the huge number
> of starfish, he could never make a real difference. The
> boy replied, "I made a difference for that one."

Jesus illustrated the folly of amassing wealth in His parable about the
rich man who laid up ample goods for many years. "But God said to him,
'Fool! This night your soul is required of you and the things that you have
prepared, whose will they be?' So is the one who lays up treasure for himself and is not rich toward God." (Luke 12: 14-21) I am reminded of the
French expression "Le coffre-fort ne suit pas le corbillard." (The safe does
not follow the hearse) and the English version "You don't see a U-Haul in
a funeral procession."

Jesus warned us we will have no excuse if we don't act on His
Word while we are alive on Earth. In His parable of *The Rich Man and
Lazarus*, the rich man, who was languishing in hell, asked Abraham
to send Lazarus from heaven to Earth to warn his brothers. Abraham
replied that if his surviving brothers ". . . do not hear Moses and the
Prophets, neither will they be convinced if someone should rise from
the dead." (Luke 16: 19-31) Jesus is saying He has told us everything
we need to know. If we don't take it to heart, even after He has been
crucified and resurrected so we might finally take notice, we have
made our own hell.

Jesus pointed out a widow putting two small copper coins into the
offering box. "Truly, I tell you this poor widow has put in more than all of
them. For they all contributed out of their abundance, but she out of her
poverty put in all she had to live on." (Luke 21: 3-4, Mark 12: 43-44) It is

not enough to give more than others. I must give in proportion to what I have been given.

I *know*, because Jesus' words leave no room for doubt, I must share the gifts of which I am God's steward, not merely more than others do but as much as I am able.

Miracles

At this stage of my *Experiential Learning*, I still did not believe in miracles. I was not ready to study Jesus' sayings on this topic. If *you* are ready, I refer you to the chapter entitled *Miracles* in *THE SAYINGS OF JESUS*[39]. If you are not, Chapter 27, *Miracles*, may lead you to further reflection as it did me. If you are content to keep on reading this chapter, we'll get to Chapter 27 next.

Commandments

Almost everyone is familiar with what Jesus said were the two greatest commandments. You have already read several versions similar to this one. "Hear, O Israel: The Lord our God, the Lord is one. And you shall love the Lord your God with all your heart and with all your soul and with all your mind and with all your strength. The second is this; you shall love your neighbour as yourself. There is no other commandment greater than these." A scribe replied, "You are right, Teacher. You have truly said that He is one and there is no other besides Him. And to love Him with all the heart and with all the understanding and with all the strength and to love one's neighbour as oneself, is much more than all whole burnt offerings and sacrifices." Jesus replied, "You are not far from the kingdom of God." (Mark 12: 29-34, Matt 22: 37-40) As you have read in Chapter 19, it had taken me some time to realize what *all* my heart, mind and strength demands of me.

Jesus used a test put to Him by a lawyer to clarify what He meant by your neighbour. When the lawyer asked, "And who is my neighbour?" Jesus answered with *The Parable of the Good Samaritan*, which we have discussed earlier. (Luke 10: 26-37) As you have read in Chapter 21, it had taken me some time to realize my neighbour includes *all* God's children.

---

[39] Found in the Appendix

As Jesus was preparing people for His departure from Earth, He added more intensity to these commandments, saying "A new commandment I give to you, that you love one another: just as I have loved you, you also are to love one another." (John 13: 34-35) There is no limit to the love Christ is demanding of me.

Jesus featured a vineyard in a powerful parable to show what we must do to be capable of following His commandments. "I am the true vine and my Father is the vinedresser. Every branch of mine that does not bear fruit He takes away and every branch that does bear fruit He prunes, that it may bear more fruit. Abide in me and I in you. As the branch cannot bear fruit by itself, unless it abides in the vine, neither can you, unless you abide in me. I am the vine; you are the branches. Whoever abides in me and I in him, he it is that bears much fruit, for *apart from me you can do nothing*." (Italics mine.)

He describes the alternative to following Him. "If anyone does not abide in me he is thrown away like a branch and withers; and the branches are gathered, thrown into the fire and burned." (John 15: 1-17) I know I will wither if I separate myself from Jesus and the fire represents the pain I will feel from having separated myself from God. The choice is mine.

"If you keep my commandments, you will abide in my love, just as I have kept my Father's commandments and abide in His love. These things I have spoken to you, that my joy may be in you and that your joy may be full." For a long time, I felt following Jesus' commandments would be sacrificial on my part. I am only recently feeling His joy in me. I am beginning to feel the *full joy* of selfless love of others.

Equally well known is *The Golden Rule*. "So whatever you wish that others would do to you, do also to them, for this is the Law and the Prophets." Jesus reminds us once again to "Enter by the narrow gate. For the gate is wide and the way is easy that leads to destruction and those who enter by it are many. For the gate is narrow and the way is hard that leads to life and those who find it are few." (Matt 7: 12-14)

Studying Jesus' Message

What you have just read is what my study of THE SAYINGS OF JESUS has led *me* to discern to be Jesus' teachings on fourteen of the fifteen most important topics He addressed in His three-year ministry on Earth. The most important thing I have learned is I have much more to learn.

Can you see the value of *THE SAYINGS OF JESUS* from what you have just read in PART FIVE?

Have you noticed a teaching you recognize but have been able to ignore when you read it in isolation? When this happened to me, I was able to find a reason to ignore it. I might have felt it didn't apply to me; it didn't apply to our times or I didn't have to take it literally. I found a way to put it aside and dismiss it.

Having studied *THE SAYINGS OF JESUS*, when I see that teaching supported, expanded on and reinforced by *all* He said on that topic, I can no longer dismiss it. I should have realized this as soon as I developed the knowledge Jesus was God Incarnate. I should have realized I cannot dismiss *any* of the Word of God. Instead, I have to immerse myself in *everything* Jesus said in order to fully internalize any one teaching. I cannot afford to fail to fully internalize *all* of the Word of God.

Have you seen any new meanings in any of Jesus' sayings with which you are familiar? Have you discovered any teachings that are new to you? If so, I hope it motivates you to make your own study of *THE SAYINGS OF JESUS*. If you do, you will learn much more than you have learned from following my study of it.

In *your* study of *THE SAYINGS OF JESUS*, you may focus on different topics than those I chose. As well, you may interpret the quotations in the topics you choose differently than I have. This shouldn't surprise or discourage either of us. Jesus' words are incredibly rich and powerful. I am sure He intended what He said would trigger deep thinking in each of us. Wouldn't it be wonderful if we were to share our deep thinking with each other?

Perception **Experiences**	Scientific method	My best friend	Jesus' sayings	The dying
		My late wife	McMaster professor	Blatchford's book
		Pascal's Wager	Two philosophy texts	Abbott's book
		The Catholic Information Centre	Dawson's book	The incarcerated
		My seminarian mentor	Harris' book	Several prisoners
		Bits of the RC Catechism	Sound reasoning	Several parolees
		COR	Much of the Bible	*The Sayings of Jesus*
		Participation House	Religious scholars	My wife
		Marriage Encounter	RC Catechism	
		Daily Mass		
		A bit of the Bible		
		C.S. Lewis' *Mere Christianity*		
Process **Learnings**	There is no proof God exists	I must accept the *possibility* God exists	Atheism is unfounded	I must fully under-stand and carry out Jesus' message to the best of my ability
	Atheism makes sense	The Church establishes a *likelihood* God exists	God created us, loves us and offers us eternal life with Him	Five topics cover over one third of Jesus' message
		The Apostle's Creed is *more likely than not* to be true	God wants us to love Him and all His children as selflessly as we are able	Fifteen topics cover over two thirds of Jesus' message
		I am *capable* of selfless love of others	The Bible *is* the revealed Word of God	
		I am *capable* of selfless love of God	Jesus was human and God Incarnate	
		The Gospels *likely* deliver God's Word	Jesus' words *are* the Word of God	
		I *knew* none of the above	The RC Catechism *is* the revealed Word of God	
Knowledge of **Life's Purpose**	Earthly fulfillment	Live according to Church teaching	Love God and *all* His children as selflessly and unconditionally as we are able	

As you see summarized in my template, at this point in *Experiential Learning*, I had produced my latest (shaded) *Perception* experience, which is entitled *THE SAYINGS OF JESUS*. Its production provided the most comprehensive re-examination of *The Club* that I had accomplished at the time of this writing. It embodied a study of *everything* Jesus was quoted in the Gospels as having said. It covered nearly 400 quotations containing over 40,000 words. As before, this *Perception* experience is the gift that keeps on giving. This part of my re-examination of *The Club* will consume the rest of my days.

The (shaded) *Perception* experience of sharing the results of this study with my wife enriches my internalization of Jesus' overall message.

My production of *THE SAYINGS OF JESUS* established two (shaded) *Process* learnings. I discovered I could study a third of Jesus' overall message by focusing on just the five most important topics, one topic at a time. This produced countless teachings and five topic messages, which we shared in Chapter 24. As well, I could study another third of Jesus' overall message by focusing on the next ten topics alone. The teachings and nine topic *messages* this study produced are detailed in this chapter.

Integrating all fifteen topic messages enabled me to internalize what, for me, is Jesus' overall message.

> Jesus was a man. The miracles Jesus performed were real[40]. Jesus was God Incarnate.
>
> Eternal life with God is far beyond what I can imagine and to realize it, I must respond to His invitation and adequately prepare for it. I need to discern what, of what I read and hear, is consistent with what I am taught by Jesus. *Professing* a love of Jesus is not enough. I must *do* what He insists upon.
>
> I must love my enemies and use my gifts to help those who cannot repay me. I must increase *my* righteousness and avoid judgement of others. I must share the gifts of which I am God's steward, not merely more than others do but as much as I am able.
>
> I must proactively seek to understand the Word of God and commit to correct each failure. I must grow my faith in my prayers for God's help in accomplishing whatever Jesus demands of me. I reject Jesus whenever I put my will ahead of God's will. I will have no excuse. I must love Jesus more than anyone. I am fully accountable. I

---

[40] It was only after completing my study of miracles, described in Chapter 27, that this sentence became part of what I discerned to be Jesus' overall message.

will be judged at the moment of my death as one of the
few sheep or one of the many goats.

The process I used to discern Jesus' overall message from the fifteen topic
messages, is detailed in the Appendix, entitled *THE SAYINGS OF JESUS*.

All this study confirmed my *Knowledge* life's purpose is to love God
and *all* His children as selflessly and unconditionally as we are able.
Christ's teachings soundly support this knowledge. The soundness of my
knowledge has made my membership in *The Club* even more fervent.

At this point, my re-examination of *The Club* was about to take a
major change in direction.

Could I accept *Process* learnings based on sound and supported *belief*
as whole-heartedly as the ones I had accepted based on sound and supported *knowledge*? Up to this point, the answer had been "No".

PART SIX

METANOIA

The Change

Metanoia crept up on me. What is it? Metanoia is defined by Merriam-Webster as a transformative change of heart; *especially* a spiritual conversion. It is different from what is described as being "born again" to which it sounds similar.

The Roman Catholic Catechism states being "born again" is the transformation that God's grace accomplishes in us during baptism. My metanoia did not happen until long after my baptism. Evangelicals claim one is "born again" at the first moment of faith in Christ where one makes a "decision for Christ", says the "sinners' prayer" and is pronounced "saved" by a minister. My metanoia was not dependent on a minister or the result of a single event. Calvinists claim being "born again" is an act of God of which one is unaware. My metanoia was a very *experiential* change.

Now I have to confess I approach this topic with real trepidation. I am pleased you have stayed with me this far in my *Experiential Learning* story. However, I fear you may already be becoming skeptical of where I seem to be claiming it was now taking me. If *I* had read, *before* my metanoia, what you are about to read, I would likely have casually written off the author as a bit delusional at best.

However, I am writing it *after* my metanoia. I am writing it from personal experience. I have been completely open and honest with you to date. I have to continue to be completely open and honest with you.

I believe my metanoia is a miracle. I am convinced this miracle could not have happened to me until I *believed* in miracles. I believe it could not have happened to me without two transforming *Perception* experiences.

The first of these, C.S. Lewis' book entitled *Miracles*[41], was a prerequisite of the second. My study of this book removed the roadblock of my disbelief in miracles. The second of these was my *full* experience of the miracle of the Eucharist. This latter experience continues to sustain my metanoia. What follows is a look at both.

---

[41]   Lewis, C.S. *Miracles*. NY: Harper Collins, 1947

CHAPTER 27

MIRACLES

For most of my life, I had had a great deal of difficulty believing in miracles. My inherent skepticism got in the way. I associated Christian miracles with Andersen's and Grimm's fairy tales. I didn't believe the fairy tales so why would I believe the Christian miracles? Looking back now, I suspect my skepticism was a product of my laziness. It is easier to discount than to try to understand.

Despite my disbelief, I could never get comfortable with my position Christ's miracles were *not* real. On the one hand, if my knowledge Jesus was God Incarnate is correct, nothing could have prevented His miracles. On the other hand, because miracles didn't seem real, I couldn't help *questioning* my knowledge Jesus was God Incarnate and the New Testament content was credible. All the knowledge I had amassed to date was at least somewhat dependent on the knowledge Jesus *was* God Incarnate. To confirm this, I had to resolve my doubt of His miracles. I had completed my initial study of what Jesus *said*. I now needed to resolve my doubts about what He was said to have *done*.

What helped me to try to understand, rather than to discount Jesus' miracles was another of the writings of the self-described skeptic, C.S. Lewis. It is his work simply entitled *Miracles*. In his book, C.S. Lewis limits his discussion to the New Testament miracles performed by Jesus Christ. He states, "A consideration of the Old Testament miracles is beyond the scope of this book and would require many kinds of knowledge which I do not possess."

This satisfied me because my knowledge Jesus was God Incarnate is somewhat dependent on the reality of *His* miracles described in the New Testament. It makes little difference to me whether or not the Old

Testament miracles occurred as described. I feel no need to discount or defend them.

C.S. Lewis classifies the miracles of Christ in two ways.

> The first system yields the classes: 1) Miracles of Fertility, 2) Miracles of Healing, 3) Miracles of Destruction, 4) Miracles of Dominion over the Inorganic, 5) Miracles of Reversal and 6) Miracles of Perfecting or Glorification. The second system, which cuts across the first, yields two classes only: 1) Miracles of the Old Creation and 2) Miracles of the New Creation.

Miracles of the Old Creation	Miracles of Fertility	Miracles of Healing	Miracles of Destruction	Miracles of Dominion over the Inorganic		
Miracles of the New Creation					Miracles of Reversal	Miracles of Perfecting or Glorification

C.S. Lewis articulates his thinking.

> In all these miracles alike the Incarnate God (Jesus) does suddenly and locally something that God *has* done or *will* do in general. Each miracle writes for us in small letters something that God has already written, or will write in letters almost too large to be noticed, across the whole canvas of nature.
>
> They focus at a particular point either God's actual, or His future operations on the universe. When they reproduce operations we have already seen on the large scale they are Miracles of the Old Creation; when they focus on those that are still to come, they are Miracles of the New Creation. Not one of them is isolated or anomalous: each carries the signature of the God whom we know through conscience and from nature. Their authenticity is attested by the *style*.

He is saying the Miracles of the Old Creation are those where Jesus, as God, did what God has *always* done. The Miracles of the New Creation are those where Jesus, as God, showed us what He *will* do.

His first classification focuses on miracles of a specific type. As you will see, exploring them by type helps better understand them.

So I set about looking at each of the Miracles of the Old Creation in light of the position they are simply instances of what God has always done. I began by looking at the **Miracles of Fertility**.

Of these, the first Jesus Christ did was the **Turning of Water into Wine** at the wedding feast in Cana. Is this an instance of what God has always done? I realized God *did* create the grape vine that can turn water, soil and sunlight into a juice that will, under proper conditions, become wine. Looked at this way, God is constantly turning water into wine.

C.S. Lewis puts it this way.

> At Cana, Jesus as God Incarnate, short-circuited the age old process in this one instance. He made water into wine in a specific moment using earthenware jars instead of vegetable fibres to hold the water. The miracle consists in the shortcut but the result is the same as it always has been and will continue to be.

I could see Jesus as God Incarnate simply did differently what God has always done. This miracle produces several lessons for me.

Firstly, God wants us to have good things like wine in abundance. Even if there were as few as four earthenware jars of no more than 20 gallons each, Jesus would have made about 500 bottles of wine for one wedding. To me this is a sign God is my loving Father who wants me to be happy.

Secondly, Jesus pushed back at the implied request of His mother saying His time had not yet come. She ignored His protest and told the stewards to do whatever He said. His deference to His mother shows Jesus was a man as well as God.

Thirdly, God invites us to participate in much of what He does. He is clearly capable of making wine on His own. Still, having created the ingredients and the process, He leaves it up to us to discover and to carry out the process. He invites us to help in His creation of wine by planting and pruning the vines, harvesting the grapes, extracting the juice and managing its fermentation.

I once heard a homily that presented a beautiful analogy of God's invitation. The priest asked us to picture a little child seeing its father making a table. The child asks the father if he or she can help. Of course the father does not need the help of his child and it may require a considerable amount of patience on the father's part to involve the child in what he is doing. However, to not discourage the child, the father says to him or her "Of course you can help" and undertakes to engage the child in whatever aspects of the project of which the child is capable.

The point of the homily was God invites us to help with much more than His creation. He invites us to help Him *care* for each of us, His children. Like the child, we may want to help Him but be incapable unless guided and supported by our loving Father. Like the child, we have to *persevere* in doing our Father's work and *continually* ask for His enablement. Like the father of the child, God waits for *us* to express our desire to help Him care for His children before enabling us. Like the father, God wants us to help Him to the best of our ability. He will help us do this as long as we continually express our desire through prayer and perseverance in action.

The second set of the Miracles of Fertility comprises the two **Miracles of Feeding** of the four thousand and of the five thousand by the miracle of turning a small amount of bread and fish into enough to feed thousands. If Jesus had turned a stone into bread as the Devil tempted Him to do during His forty days in the desert (Matt 4: 1-4), it would not have been what God has always done. However, turning a little wheat (as seed) into much wheat (as crop) *is* what God has always done. Again, the miracle is in the short cut, but the result is the same as what God has always done. Likewise God has always turned one fish (in its spawning) into hundreds of fish. Again, in these two miracles of feeding, the Incarnate God does close and small, under His human hands, what God has always been doing in the fields, the seas, the lakes and the little brooks.

Although God is clearly capable of repeating this miracle, He instead invites us to help in His creation of bread by grinding the grain into flour, mixing the dough and baking the bread. He invites us to help in His provision of fish for a meal by catching the fish, cleaning them and cooking them.

These two miracles are simple, if spectacular reminders of the type of loving Father our God is. He assures we have enough to eat in abundance. These two miracles help me step back from taking this beneficence for granted. They also remind me of His timeless offer to partner with Him. Jesus chose to partner with a small boy by using his lunch to feed the five thousand.

The third Miracle of Fertility is the **Virginal Conception of Jesus**. God impregnated Mary to create His Son. I found this difficult to believe because it seemed to be unnatural and unprecedented. It was indeed unprecedented but was it unnatural?

As I considered this question, I realized God creates *every* living being. No human father or mother ever created a child. It was God who created the first sperm and the first egg and the process by which they produce offspring – each male of which has sperm and each female of which has eggs – and thus every creature created thereafter. God chose to partner with a man and a woman in His creation of each living human being through a process we call procreation. Still, *He* is the creator of each one of us.

God, on one occasion only, acted outside His normal process. He performed the role of the father. It had to be this way for the child of Mary to be God Incarnate. It had to be God who impregnated Mary for her child to be the Son of God. This simply underlines how, on every other occasion, He lovingly partners with the human father and mother in every birth. He allows a man and a woman to take an active part in the creation of each human being. He wants us to be a part of what He does.

Reflecting on all three Miracles of Fertility, I saw each was, indeed, nothing more than a single instance of God doing differently what God always does. Acceptance of the reality of the Miracles of Fertility is supported by our knowledge that God created wheat, grapes and fish as well as the process of combining sperm and egg in the creation of each person.

I next considered whether the same could be said for the **Miracles of Healing**. There are many reports of Jesus healing a person whom he has encountered. Are these, as is commonly held, and as I maintained for most of my life, simply instances of the power of a hypnotic-like suggestion? The miracles of exorcism could be. The miracles where a cripple is told to get up and walk might be. However, the miracles where physical diseases such as blindness, hemorrhaging and leprosy were healed could not be. What could they be?

As I took a broader look at healing, I was reminded the ability of the body to heal itself is built in. That ability was created by God, as was everything else. No doctor ever healed anyone. All a doctor can do is stimulate natural functions or remove what hinders them. When a doctor dresses a wound, sets a broken limb or performs an operation and healing results, we say the doctor cured the patient. When we think through what happened we realize the body healed itself. Put another way, since God created the body's ability to regenerate, He healed every person that ever experienced healing.

God Incarnate frequently acted outside His normal process by instantaneously healing whereas, normally, God lovingly partners with the medical profession in the natural cycle of healings. He allows us to take an active part in the healing of every sick person. He wants us to be a part of what He does.

On these occasions, God Incarnate did, in an instant, what God has always done. As C.S. Lewis sees it "The Power that always was behind all healings put on a face and hands and changed a slow process into an immediate event."

Acceptance of the reality of the Miracles of Healing is supported by our knowledge God created the healing process of every living creature.

Jesus' single **Miracle of Destruction** was the withering of the fig tree. I found it hard to imagine a loving God would destroy anything. However, I recalled Jesus repeatedly warned us we must bear fruit or die. The fig tree did not bear the fruit Jesus sought and He made it die. We don't know whether this was an impetuous act of the human side of Jesus or God Incarnate's way of showing us we must bear fruit. In either case, the question remains, is the miracle believable?

C.S. Lewis explains the miracle.

> Everything that was ever created died. Since it was God's power that created everything and keeps it alive, it follows it is God who withdraws that power at a time of His choosing and allows that specific creation to die. God is always destroying this life in order to create a new life. God destroys everything in its natural cycle – the cycle He created. In this one instance, Jesus, as God Incarnate, destroyed something outside its natural cycle.

I realized this single act was simply a one-time instance of the destruction God has always done and will always do. Acceptance of the reality of the Miracle of Destruction is supported by our knowledge God destroys everything He creates.

What C.S. Lewis calls the **Miracles of Dominion over the Inorganic** includes one that is a Miracle of the Old Creation and one that is a Miracle of the New Creation. As such their pairing helps clarify the distinctions between these two classes of miracle.

The first of the Miracles of Dominion over the Inorganic is the **Miracle of the Calming of the Storm**. Here, as in the miracles we have looked at so far, Jesus, as God Incarnate, is simply doing what God has always done.

God made nature such that there would always be storms and calms. In that sense, God has always and will always create and calm storms. We have seen this so often, over and over again, the process becomes predictable. In this one instance, Jesus did, in a way that was unpredictable, what God has always done in a way that is predictable. Acceptance of the reality of the Miracle of the Calming of the Storm is supported by our knowledge God calms every storm He creates.

The second of the Miracles of Dominion over the Inorganic is the **Miracle of Jesus Walking on Water**. It differs from the Miracle of the Calming of the Storm, which is why it is classified as a Miracle of the New Creation. It is not an instance of God Incarnate doing what God has *always* done, as are the Miracles of the Old Creation. God did not create humans with the power to walk on water. This was a first instance of God Incarnate doing what God *will* do. It initially looked like that miracle would repeat itself. Peter took a few steps on the water before he lost his faith in his new ability and began to sink. For me, this miracle gives a first peek at what God *will* create at the end of the current creation. As He did with Peter, He will give our bodies powers we don't have on Earth.

To a limited degree, we may already *have* powers on Earth of which we remain unaware. Science tells us we are using a somewhat small portion of the capacity of our brains. Jesus tells us if we had faith we could move mountains. We may have power over nature. We may be able to will a control of nature. An example of which we *are* aware is we manipulate nature, by the simple wish to do so, every time we move our limbs or think a thought. As we look at the rest of Jesus' miracles, we will get glimpses of even more spectacular powers that await the end of our earthly lives. These glimpses will suggest the powers that await us may even be limitless.

However, the Miracles of the New Creation, of which this is the first, are easier to question and harder to accept than the Miracles of the Old Creation. Because they are not what we have repeatedly experienced God always doing, they are without precedent. We have to decide whether or not to believe in them not by relating them to what we know of *them*, but by relating them to what we know of *God*. Acceptance of the reality of the Miracles of the New Creation is supported by our knowledge God is all-powerful and capable of everything.

The second of the Miracles of the New Creation is the **Miracle of the Raising of Lazarus**. Once again, this is not something we have experienced God always doing. C.S. Lewis sees it this way.

Once we die, we are buried or cremated – ashes to ashes and dust to dust. Granted some people experience ghosts and claim communication with the spirits of the dead, but these experiences, whether real or hallucinatory are not of the same class. Here people witness a person who has been in a tomb for days, walking out of the tomb, removing the burial clothes and resuming a normal life among them. This is definitely *not* what we have ever experienced.

But it must be something that was once common-place. Creation was, in part, the act of breathing life into the inanimate. There must have been a time when pro-cesses, the reverse of those we now see, were going on: a time of winding up that which is now winding down.

Acceptance of the reality of the Miracle of the Raising of Lazarus is supported by our knowledge God breathed life into every living thing. Thinking further, I found another reason to believe the miracle happened.

God was likely giving us another glimpse of His plan. Before the resurrection of Jesus Christ, the only way we could get a glimpse of our inheritance of eternal life would be to see a human life restored. Even Martha, when told by Jesus her brother would live again, interpreted His statement as referring to eternal life. However, we cannot see eternal life. Before the resurrection the only thing we could witness on Earth was the reversal of the process of death or a process of "undeathing".

It is this aspect of the miracle that caused C.S. Lewis to classify this miracle as a **Miracle of Reversal**. His purpose was to distinguish it from the **Miracle of the Resurrection**. In the case of Lazarus, he returned to the state he was in before he died. He regained his old body and function. In the case of Jesus' resurrection, He gained a new body and function. Could I believe that?

As you read in Chapter 16, I not only believe Jesus was resurrected, but I *know* it. For me, all the arguments presented by C.S. Lewis, Lee Strobel, Norman Geisler, Frank Turek and countless other religious scholars establish Jesus was God Incarnate and His resurrection was real. To these arguments, I added my own. God loves us and wants us to know Him. Because unspoken revelation did not work, the way God chose to help us know Him was to show us Himself in human form. His human body had to die but God could not die. God Incarnate had to be resurrected. What was the nature of His resurrected human body?

As the apostles describe what they saw of the resurrection, it was much more than the empty tomb. The resurrected Jesus talked to Mary Magdalene, talked to two of the apostles on the road to Emmaus, spent time with His apostles together and on another occasion talked with five hundred people. Of these the majority were still alive when St. Paul wrote his First Letter to the Corinthians in about 55 AD. Had Christ simply talked to people, it is conceivable each occasion might have been an illusion, unlikely as it is five hundred people would have had the same illusion simultaneously. However, He did more than that. He had them touch Him and feel His wounds; He ate food with them. Had He simply shown His body the way it had been before He left the tomb, it would have been simply a **Miracle of Reversal** like that of Lazarus. However, He did more than that. He entered a room whose door was locked. He could appear and disappear at will. His resurrected body had new powers His human body did not.

The **Miracles of Perfecting or Glorification** stand in a class by themselves. They give us a first glimpse of what our life after death will be like. They may be best explored in reverse order to that of their occurrence.

The **Miracle of the Ascension** was another one I had a difficult time believing. When I reflect on why this was, I see it was simply because it was unnatural. It was something I had never seen. If I had never seen anything like it, how likely was it that it had actually occurred at one time? On further reflection, I realized it *must* have occurred. Because I *knew* the body of Jesus was resurrected, I had to think about where it could have gone. If after several weeks it was no longer present, alive or dead, it had to have gone somewhere. To have suddenly gone somewhere other than *into* the earth, where every human body has gone at death, it must have gone *away* from Earth. From our point of view, *away* means *up*. To leave Earth, the body of Jesus had to have *ascended.*

I have found no other explanation of where the resurrected body of Jesus went. Since I *know* the resurrection occurred, then I know the ascension must have occurred.

Jesus told His apostles He was ". . . going to prepare a place for *us*". C.S. Lewis interprets Jesus' teaching.

> This must mean He is about to create that whole new nature which will provide the environment or conditions for His glorified humanity and, in Him for *ours*. He goes in His human body into this new environment – this new human nature which He is bringing into existence for us.

This is what C.S. Lewis means by the Miracles of the New Creation.

To me, the metamorphosis of an earth-bound caterpillar into a much more fully endowed, and more beautiful butterfly is God's illustration of what awaits us. The caterpillar in the cocoon must die to enable the creation of a vastly more capable, more beautiful being.

The **Miracle of the Resurrection** gives us a glimpse of what our new human nature will be like. It shows us, like Christ's resurrected body, our new human nature will have new powers. The extent of these new powers is beyond our imagination. They may even transcend time and space. However, the glimpse we have been shown, through the witness of Jesus' resurrected body, includes the inhuman ability to instantaneously be somewhere, to instantaneously leave and to pass through physical objects. Additionally we will have the human functionality of our bodies to touch, eat and interact with one another and with things. That it shows us this makes it one of the Miracles of the New Creation.

The **Miracle of the Transfiguration**, which is the first glimpse of the New Creation, completes its picture for us. We may have the ability to converse with the dead. Jesus was able to converse with Moses and Elijah. The change in His human form was seen as a luminosity or "shining white-ness". He still had all His human characteristics but His human form had new characteristics and powers. Could I believe in the transfiguration?

For me, it was the easiest to accept of the three Miracles of the New Creation. I had come to know the resurrection was real. I knew the reality of the resurrection established the ascension was real. Is it not still less a challenge to accept the transfiguration was real?

However, was my acceptance of the reality of the miracles based on knowledge or simply on belief? I felt the line was blurring. My pursuit of every other question had produced what I had determined to be sound and supported *knowledge*. I felt my pursuit of the Miracles of the Old Creation had as well because the rationale supporting my acceptance of them was based on what I have seen God always doing. However, this was not the case for the Miracles of the New Creation. The only support for our acceptance of them is our knowledge God is all-powerful. I decided my acceptance of them was dependent on soundly supported *belief* rather than on *knowledge*. I accepted I could not *know* everything. I concluded *belief* is as reliable as *knowledge* as long as both enjoy sound and supported rationale.

All this revelation came late in my *Experiential Learning*. However, it did establish a critical link in the body of knowledge I had accumulated to that point. It was important for me to establish the miracles were real because their reality confirmed Jesus was God Incarnate. I had to understand, to the best of my ability, what Jesus *did* as well as what He *said*.

The Miracles as a whole helped establish my *knowledge* Jesus is God. However, they could only do this for someone who *knew* they actually occurred. The Miracles of the Old Creation take the mystery away. They are what God has always done. The Miracles of the New Creation give us glimpses of what God will do. All the miracles in both classes make sense to me and I can find no reason why they could *not* occur. Put another way, of this chapter's many arguments for their reality, all are supported and none are refuted. Until new arguments or flaws in these arguments are established, this alone substantiates my *knowledge* the Miracles of the Old Creation *did* occur, and my soundly supported *belief* the Miracles of the New Creation did as well.

The soundness of the support for the reality of Christ's miracles is a central component of the knowledge I gained from *Experiential Learning*. As well, the soundness of this support takes away the last obstacle to pursuing whether or not the **Miracle of the Eucharist** is real. This miracle is the last of my *Perception* experiences that we'll look at together. It enables my ongoing metanoia.

CHAPTER 28

EUCHARIST

As you likely know, the Eucharist is the Roman Catholic sacrament that the Church claims enables the transubstantiation of properly prepared bread and wine into the body and blood of Jesus Christ. The Church considers this miracle to be an unexplainable mystery. As long as it remained unexplainable how would I substantiate it? How could I establish sound and supported knowledge it is real?

For me, unexplainable equated to unsubstantiated. Since I could not see it or explain it, I concluded it was not real. Later, I realized my human limitations mean this position is equally unsubstantiated. That *I* cannot see or explain something cannot establish it doesn't exist.

For most of my life, I likened the Eucharist to two mysteries – "How many angels can dance on the head of a pin?" (the debate of which is inconsequential) or the doctrine of the Holy Trinity (which is an important description of God, but a mystery that is equally unexplainable). However, I recently realized the Eucharist, unlike the two mysteries with which I had compared it, is not something I can put aside and ignore. If *it* is real, it changes everything.

Let's just accept for a moment the Eucharist might possibly be real. If so, what would be happening during the Eucharist? God would be directly and physically reaching out to us. He would be taking on the form of bread and wine so we can experience a physical relationship with Him. Most startlingly, He would be subjecting Himself to our will. He would be making His desire to be intimate with us dependent on our acceptance of His offer to us. We are talking about a Being, unimaginably more powerful and incomparably better than us, voluntarily subjecting Himself to our will. Is that not staggering?

Recognizing this *could* be true, can you really be comfortable with dismissing the *possibility* of God's outreach? Rather, would you not be better served by pursuing it? I thought *I* would be. However, I found that pursuit very difficult.

Whenever I confront a position that almost everyone I know rejects, I have difficulty accepting the possibility they *all* may be wrong. Non-Christians dismiss it and ignore it without a second thought. Most Protestants consider it an unsubstantiated Roman Catholic teaching. Most Roman Catholics accept their Church's teaching to *some* degree but not fully. Their actions support this observation. If they truly believed the Eucharist is actually the body and blood of Jesus Christ, would they not take *every* available opportunity to experience it? Would they not put participation in Daily Mass at the top of their agenda?

Still, unlike others, I could not be comfortable with ignoring and dismissing the possibility God might be coming to me in the Eucharist. I decided to pursue how I could establish sound and supported knowledge the Eucharist is real. At the time I made this decision, I didn't realize I can never possess that knowledge. Following my pursuit, you will see why.

Before I launch into my pursuit, let me reiterate why I think this is the most important question of all. If the Eucharist is real, most people are missing the most beautiful, powerful and empowering experience available to them. Their God is reaching out to them every day and they are ignoring Him most, if not all days. By rejecting God's physical outreach, they may inadvertently miss much of God's spiritual outreach. Put another way, if the Eucharist is not real, ignoring it risks nothing. However, if the Eucharist is real, ignoring it risks everything. Once one realizes how high the stakes are, is it not folly to fail to pursue whether or not the Eucharist is real?

For most of my life, I was a victim of this folly. I had not pursued my doubt thoroughly enough to determine whether or not the Eucharist is the body and blood of Jesus Christ. I had simply put the question aside. It was now long past time to pursue it.

I started my pursuit with a review of the reasons for my skepticism about its reality. Firstly, I knew of no process where something is changed into something completely different, for example, alchemy. Secondly, I was unaware of the consecrated bread and wine ever having passed a scientific test that confirmed any change in its composition. Thirdly, I was skeptical of the motive behind the Church's teaching. I felt, since only a priest can accomplish transubstantiation, the teaching might have been motivated by a desire to draw people into the Church.

On the first doubt, I realized, while it's true we *know* of no process where a physical substance is changed into another physical substance, it's not true this means no process exists.

Because we have never observed alchemy, we can't know whether or not it exists. We can suspect it doesn't exist but we can't be sure. We can't know it is impossible it exists simply because we have seen no evidence of its existence. Take another example. We can't know whether or not a time dimension exists. We can form our own opinion of whether or not it is likely one exists. However, all we can *know* is we can see no evidence of it. Must this not apply to transubstantiation as well? The fact we can see no evidence of transubstantiation does not establish it doesn't exist.

On the second doubt, I had already established the lack of scientific proof something occurred was not proof it did not occur.

When science is looking for proof the transubstantiated wafer and wine are really the body and blood of Jesus Christ, does it even know what it is looking for? We know the composition of our body and blood when we scientifically analyze it but do we really know the composition of Christ's body and blood? Having been fathered by God and mothered by Mary, Christ is different from us. We know, while He was alive on Earth, His body had our human bodies' characteristics. However, we don't know what other characteristics it had or the nature of His resurrected body. We can't know the composition of the resurrected Christ's body and blood based solely on our knowledge of our own. Science can't prove whether or not transubstantiation occurs because it can't recognize the evidence. It doesn't know the characteristics of the transubstantiated substances.

On the third doubt, my thinking was the fact we can only physically experience God's presence in the Eucharist in a Church-led sacrament gives the Church a pretty powerful monopoly.

However, I realized, although it may be true some leaders of some churches may see the Eucharist as a way of establishing their power, it doesn't mean that is all there is to it. It doesn't mean God wants this to be the case. It simply means we are looking at some instances of a human failing. I couldn't dismiss transubstantiation simply because of the unsubstantiated feeling some might use others' belief in it for their own purposes.

Having discounted my doubts, I pursued reasons why it might possibly be true.

I decided it all came down to determining whether it was *more likely than not* God would want to give us the experience of His presence in the Eucharist. If God *wanted* us to experience it, He would make that experience real. Nothing is impossible for God.

The first indication God wants the experience of the Eucharist to be real for us is God Incarnate's words themselves. Jesus said explicitly the Eucharist is most definitely His body and blood. He said He will be in us when we eat His body and drink His blood in remembrance of Him.

> And He took bread and when He had given thanks, He broke it and gave it to them, saying "This is my body, which is given for you. Do this in remembrance of me." And likewise the cup after they had eaten, saying "This cup that is poured out for you is the new covenant in my blood." (Luke 22: 17-20)

> Truly, truly, I say to you, unless you eat the flesh of the Son of Man and drink His blood, you have no life in you. Whoever feeds on my flesh and drinks my blood has eternal life and I will raise him up on the last day. Whoever feeds on my flesh and drinks my blood abides in me and I in him. (John 6: 53-56)

As you read in Chapter 16, I know Jesus was God Incarnate and the Bible accurately reports what He said. It might seem to you, based on this alone, I would have to accept what He said was true.

Ah, but the mind is a marvelous machine. My skepticism delivered an escape hatch. Maybe Jesus meant what He said to be taken figuratively rather than literally. As you continue to read, you'll learn my reasoning mind soon slammed that escape hatch shut.

The next indication God wants the experience of the Eucharist to be real for us is Church teaching. Much Christian teaching insists the Eucharist most definitely is the body and blood of Jesus Christ. The Roman Catholic, Eastern Orthodox, Oriental Orthodox, High Anglican and Lutheran Churches teach when they follow Christ's institution and command in the Lord's Supper and say, "This is my body," then it *is* His body, not on their authority, but because of *His* command and deed that He has attached to their speaking as He instructed them to speak. The only difference in these Churches' teachings is *how* it is accomplished. Some claim it is done through transubstantiation, others, spiritually and still others, through sacramental union. Does it matter *how* it is done?

What matters is if it is *real*. Sadly, I found Church teaching, lacking sub-stantiation, failed to satisfy me.

I next turned to common sense. What can common sense tell us about whether or not God *would* want the experience of the Eucharist to be real for us? Firstly I realized God knows we physically experience things only through our five senses, of which sight, touch and taste figure prom-inently. Secondly, I reflected God knows we experience physical intimacy most strongly when we feel a presence within our bodies. Finally, God knows we know our bodies. We know when we take something into our mouths it goes into our digestive system, from there into our circulatory system and then to every cell of our bodies. It seemed God would want us to know His presence was in the totality of our being. Let's look at each of these observations a bit more thoroughly.

Firstly, God knows we are unable to *physically* experience His *spiritual* presence within us. We can only physically experience His *physical* presence. Reflecting on this, I could see the only way God could enable us to sensually experience Him, after God Incarnate was no longer with us, would be by coming to us through something physical like bread and wine. The only way we can physically experience Him is through our senses of sight, touch and taste. The choice of bread and wine may be arbitrary, but the choice of something we can see, touch and taste is necessary for us to sensually experience God.

Secondly, the greatest intimacy we can experience is when we feel inside each other. When we kiss and make love we are as much inside each other as we can be. It made sense to me God would enable us to take Him into our bodies. To do so, He must come to us through some-thing we can ingest and digest. Again, that He chose bread and wine to make into His body and blood might be arbitrary. However, it does seem to me there is some suggestive symbolism there. Bread is a solid as we feel our bodies to be. Wine is a red liquid, as we know our blood to be. I decided by coming to us in the physical form of bread and wine, He is making Himself, in the absence of God Incarnate, as much like us as we can experience. By coming inside us He is enabling the greatest intimacy with Him we can *physically* experience.

Finally, it seemed to me, by taking the form of something we can eat and drink, God is enabling us to experience His physical presence *throughout* our bodies. We can taste Him on our tongue and palate. We can feel Him on our lips, in our mouth and in our throat. When we swallow we can sense Him descending to our stomach. In our stomach, we know His physical presence will experience our digestive system and, through it, enter our circulatory system. We know our circulatory system will take His physical presence into every cell of our body. It made sense to me God would choose a way for us to experience Him throughout every fibre of our being.

In summary, common sense *indicates* the Eucharist is real; Church teaching *claims* it is real and Jesus, Himself, *says* it is real. I found all my doubts about the reality of the Eucharist to be unsubstantiated. I had sound support for a *belief* God Incarnate meant His teaching, that the bread and wine are His body and blood, to be taken literally rather than symbolically. The escape hatch had been slammed shut.

I had to stop wishing I could *know* the reality of the Eucharist as well as I had determined I know all the other aspects of life's purpose. Just as science could not prove it was not the body and blood of Jesus Christ, I could not prove it was. I realized I would have to accept or reject the reality of the Eucharist based solely on my sound and supported *belief* it was something God would want us to experience. I had to *believe* what I could not *know*.

It was only when I realized *why* I could not know this that I finally accepted I could do no better than establish a sound and supported *belief* in it. I realize it is God's will I do *not* know it. I should have known this a long time ago. As you have read in Chapters 12, 14, 15, 16 and 21, I had known for some time God wants us to *choose* intimacy with Him. He cannot reveal Himself to us without taking away our free will to *choose* to love Him. If God allowed us to *know* He was in the Eucharist, we would be left with no *real* choice. We would be unable to choose to ignore Him. God intends the Eucharist remains unknowable. He intentionally leaves us vulnerable to doubt. I have to put the desire to *know* behind me and accept soundly supported *belief*.

I found this to be a very important realization. I can't let my inability, to know *how* God can be in the wafer and wine, justify an unsupported insistence He is not, and prevent me from gratefully experiencing His presence in my body. I now see, as long as I fail to accept Jesus' presence in the Eucharist, I remain as blind as the scribes and Pharisees who failed to see God in Jesus. I conclude sound and supported *belief* in His presence is as reliable as knowledge when the rationale supporting that belief removes all reasonable doubt.

My belief was a major factor in my metanoia. Daily Mass became an essential to me. I made every effort to daily be where God presents Himself physically to me. I am overwhelmed each day as I receive the Eucharist. On the rare occasions when I don't attend Daily Mass, I miss the experience of Jesus entering my body. Each time I experience His physical presence, I am reminded of His spiritual omnipresence. Because He is always in me, I am always in Him. No day is complete without the experience of the Eucharist. Now that no reasonable doubt remains I can finally *fully* experience the Mass.

My Experience of the Eucharist

What follows is a very brief description of my *full* experience of the Eucharist. Roman Catholics may wonder why I would describe what I experience. Each of their experiences is their own. Those of you, other than members of the Roman Catholic, Eastern Orthodox, Oriental Orthodox, High Anglican and Lutheran Churches, may wonder why I would describe something you are not even *able* to experience. I offer this description because I can find no other way to convey the life-changing, overwhelming experience of *feeling* God within one's body, which the *full* experience of the Eucharist provides.

I begin Mass with my preparation for the Eucharist. During the *Penitential Rite*, I reflect on the occasions where *I* have sinned in my thoughts, in my words, in what I have *done* and in what I have *failed* to do. During the *Preparation of the Gifts*, I intersperse *my* offerings of my *life* and my *gifts* with the priest's offerings of the bread and the wine. "Blessed are You, Lord, God of all creation, for through Your goodness I have received the *life* I offer You – my longevity, my soundness of body, my health and my energy. Help me to use these attributes of my life in pursuit of Your purpose for it." and "Blessed are You, Lord, God of all creation, for through Your goodness I have received the *gifts* I offer You, which I discern, enrich with Your revelation and apply in the world. Help me to use these gifts in pursuit of Your purpose for my life."

Recently, a picture came to mind that made the *Preparation of the Gifts* more impactful for me. It happened as I focused on the phrase "through Your goodness, I have received the gifts that I offer You." It hit me that, in the Mass, we are simply offering to God what we make from what He has given us. It reminded me of my children giving me a birthday card they had made from our gifts to them of paper, scissors and crayons. I thought of them buying me a gift with the allowance we had given them. We are truly like little children when we offer God nothing more than what we make from the gifts we have received through His goodness. Because my children's gifts were dear to me, I conclude our gifts to God are dear to Him.

Having prepared, I can now *fully* experience the *transubstantiation*. During the *Eucharistic Prayer*, I twice thank God for the Eucharist. As the bread is transubstantiated into Jesus' body, I thank God for His presence. "Thank-You God for coming into this church, onto this altar and into my body in the physical form of bread and wine so, when I feel Your physical presence enter my body, I become more aware of Your spiritual omni-presence, Your love and Your revelation. "Thank-You for opening my mind, heart, eyes and ears to Your omnipresence, Your love and Your rev-elation." As the wine is transubstantiated, I thank God for calling me back to Him. "When I am careless with this gift, when I wander aimlessly and distractedly through life, self-centred, self-absorbed and self-indulgent, I thank You, God, for calling me back to You as You come across my lips in a form I can see, touch and taste, so my senses refocus me on You. Never let me be separated from You." As the priest lifts the body and then the blood, I twice say, "My Lord, my saviour and my God."

After taking communion, I thank God for the experience of His presence. "Thank-You for coming 'under my roof', across my lips, into my mouth, onto my tongue, against my palette, into my throat, descending to my stomach, experiencing my digestive system, entering my circulatory system and, through it, flowing to every fibre of my being. Increase my awareness of Your presence in me, mine in You and You beside me this day in everything I say and do."

A small, but effective part of my metanoia is adding gesture to my words. In the past, when I would see people doing this, I judged them as being demonstrative and as wanting to be seen as being "holier than thou". Because I have now experienced how gestures help me focus on my words, I realize how foolish and unsubstantiated that judgement was.

During the *Penitential Rite*, as I say, ". . . in my thoughts, in my words, in what I have done and what I have failed to do", I respectively touch my forehead, my lips, my body and open my arms in emptiness. As I say, ". . . and so I ask you, my brothers and sisters, to pray for me to the Lord our God", I briefly turn towards my brothers and sisters in the congregation.

During the *Eucharistic Prayer*, as I say, "Thank-You God for coming into this church, onto this altar and into my body in the physical form of bread and wine", I touch my body. As I say, ". . . so that when I feel Your physical presence entering my body, I can become more aware of Your spiritual omnipresence, Your love and Your revelation" I point firstly to my mouth and secondly to my mind (the source of my awareness).

As I say, "Thank-You for opening my mind, heart, eyes and ears to Your omnipresence, Your love and Your revelation." I point, respectively, to my forehead, heart, left eye and right ear, which together resemble a (sideways) sign of the cross. As I say, "Thank-You, God, for calling me back to You as You come across my lips in a form I can see, touch and taste, so that my senses refocus me on You" I touch respectively my lips, eyes, fingers and tongue.

After I say, "I am not worthy that You should come under my roof, but only say the word and my soul shall be healed" and accept the Eucharist, I thank God for coming "under my roof". I *feel* God on my lips, entering under the roof of my mouth, onto my tongue, against my palate and in my throat. I imagine Him in my stomach, experiencing my digestive system, entering my circulatory system and flowing to every fibre of my being.

I find I am much more intimately connected with the Eucharist and with God as I say my personal prayers and make the accompanying gestures. That feeling often lasts all day. This *full*, daily experience of the Eucharist is a major part of my metanoia.

The Effect

My metanoia is the crowning result of my *Experiential Learning*. Over a period of a couple of years, I went from an intellectual, experiential relationship with God to an intimate, spiritual relationship. I went from an occasional connection with God to what is almost a continual connection with God. I relate everything I experience to the Word of God. I can't (and don't want to) ignore God for more than a few minutes or at most a few hours. I am completely absorbed in God. I am mesmerized, enthralled and captivated by God. My metanoia took me far beyond any other part of my *Experiential Learning*. That it took place is a mystery to me. It is my own personal miracle.

My metanoia established my respect for belief. I finally understand how peoples' faith can be supported by *belief* in the absence of *knowledge*. Belief demands the use of my heart as well as my mind. When that belief is supported by facts and rationale, it is as sound as knowledge. I can *prove* nothing and will never know everything, but I can (and must) know enough to allow my heart to make the leap of faith of *knowing* life's purpose.

Before my metanoia, I hadn't realized I had imprisoned my heart within my mind. Due to my inherent scepticism and my scientific discipline, I had discounted anything for which my heart cried out. From my very early years, I had put aside anything I could not determine I knew. I had put my heart on a starvation diet.

221

Perception **Experiences**	Scientific method	My best friend	Jesus' sayings	The dying
		My late wife	McMaster professor	Blatchford's book
		Pascal's Wager	Two philosophy texts	Abbott's book
		The Catholic Information Centre	Dawson's book	The incarcerated
		My seminarian mentor	Harris' book	Several prisoners
		Bits of the RC Catechism	Sound reasoning	Several parolees
		COR	Much of the Bible	*The Sayings of Jesus*
		Participation House	Religious scholars	My wife
		Marriage Encounter	RC Catechism	C.S. Lewis' *Miracles*
		Daily Mass		The Eucharist
		A bit of the Bible		
		C.S. Lewis' *Mere Christianity*		
Process **Learnings**	There is no proof God exists	I must accept the *possibility* God exists	Atheism is unfounded	I must fully understand and carry out Jesus' message to the best of my ability
	Atheism makes sense	The Church establishes a *likelihood* God exists	God created us, loves us and offers us eternal life with Him	Five topics cover over one third of Jesus' message
		The Apostle's Creed is *more likely than not* to be true	God wants us to love Him and all His children as selflessly as we are able	Fifteen topics cover over two thirds of Jesus' message
		I am *capable* of selfless love of others	The Bible *is* the revealed Word of God	Jesus' miracles are *real*
		I am *capable* of selfless love of God	Jesus was human and God Incarnate	The Eucharist *is* Jesus' body and blood
		The Gospels *likely* deliver God's Word	Jesus' words *are* the Word of God	Metanoia is my own personal miracle
		I *knew* none of the above	The RC Catechism *is* the revealed Word of God	
***Knowledge* of Life's Purpose**	**Earthly fulfillment**	**Live according to Church teaching**	**Love God and *all* His children as selflessly and unconditionally as we are able**	

You have read how, as my *Perception* set expanded, it started to feed my heart. As you can see on my template, it now had included the (shaded) *Perception* experiences of C.S. Lewis' *Miracles* and the Eucharist.

My (shaded) *Process* learnings were the product of my heart breaking out of the fetters with which I had bound it. I now had established sound and supported *belief* Jesus' miracles were real, the Eucharist is real and my metanoia was my own personal miracle.

My metanoia is the triumph of my heart. It is a heady feeling. It amplifies the experiences in which I find myself absorbed. My active prayers are as much from my heart as from my mind. My connection with God is very much driven by my heart. It's not surprising that, in hindsight, I am now puzzled at how long it took for this to happen. I don't let my puzzlement bother me though. I just enjoy the ride.

As I suspected, a miracle couldn't happen to me until I *believed* it could. I conclude my belief in miracles was a prerequisite of my metanoia. Arriving at my sound and supported belief the Eucharist is real enabled my metanoia. It is a miracle I never anticipated. My *Knowledge* of life's purpose was now confirmed by my heart *and* my mind. I had now become a permanently fervent member of *The Club*.

At this point, you may very well be saying what does all this have to do with me? Despite your perseverance in reading Chapters 27 and 28, you may remain convinced a metanoia could not happen to you. You may remain like I was. If I had read a description of metanoia, like the one you just read, I am very fearful I would have discounted it. Now that you have read mine, I hope you are less inclined to do so.

Fortunately, a metanoia is *not* a prerequisite of discovering life's purpose. *Experiential Learning* can lead you to your discovery of life's purpose whether or not it leads you to a metanoia.

I certainly never expected my metanoia. You may not expect one either. Then again, you may experience a big surprise!

Are you now ready to consider how you might undertake *Experiential Learning*?

PART SEVEN

EXPERIENTIAL LEARNING

CHAPTER 29

EXPERIENCING EXPERIENTIAL LEARNING

B efore launching into how you might undertake *Experiential Learning*, let's review what my experience with it reveals to be important for you to keep in mind.

Perception **Experiences**	Scientific method	My best friend	Jesus' sayings	The dying
		My late wife	McMaster professor	Blatchford's book
		Pascal's Wager	Two philosophy texts	Abbott's book
		The Catholic Information Centre	Dawson's book	The incarcerated
		My seminarian mentor	Harris' book	Several prisoners
		Bits of the RC Catechism	Sound reasoning	Several parolees
		COR	Much of the Bible	*The Sayings of Jesus*
		Participation House	Religious scholars	My wife
		Marriage Encounter	RC Catechism	C.S. Lewis' *Miracles*
		Daily Mass		The Eucharist
		A bit of the Bible		
		C.S. Lewis' *Mere Christianity*		
Process **Learnings**	There is no proof God exists	I must accept the *possibility* God exists	Atheism is unfounded	I must fully understand and carry out Jesus' message to the best of my ability
	Atheism makes sense	The Church establishes a *likelihood* God exists	God created us, loves us and offers us eternal life with Him	Five topics cover over one third of Jesus' message
		The Apostle's Creed is *more likely than not* to be true	God wants us to love Him and all His children as selflessly as we are able	Fifteen topics cover over two thirds of Jesus' message
		I am *capable* of selfless love of others	The Bible *is* the revealed Word of God	Jesus' miracles are *real*
		I am *capable* of selfless love of God	Jesus was human and God Incarnate	The Eucharist *is* Jesus' body and blood
		The Gospels *likely* deliver God's Word	Jesus' words *are* the Word of God	Metanoia is my own personal miracle
		I *knew* none of the above	The RC Catechism *is* the revealed Word of God	
Knowledge of **Life's Purpose**	**Earthly fulfillment**	**Live according to Church teaching**	**Love God and *all* His children as selflessly and unconditionally as we are able**	

1. Aggressively pursue your *Perception* set. As you see in my template, in the columns from left to right, my *Perception* set grew from one experience to a dozen more and later to nineteen more. In all, it totalled thirty-two *Perception* experiences.
2. Take every opportunity to strengthen *Process* learnings. I first learned the scientific method. I next learned to trust my heart, apply inductive and deductive reasoning and comparative analysis of arguments. Full pursuit of *Process* learnings benefits from all four.
3. Accept necessary corrections to your *Knowledge*. Knowledge, limited to what I could prove, was corrected by what I discovered was *likely* and corrected again by sound and supported rationale.

As you consider whether or not to undertake *Experiential Learning*, it might help to reflect on one of Jesus' most encouraging teachings. "Ask and it will be given to you; seek and you will find; knock and it will be opened to you." If you feel *Experiential Learning* may be too difficult and/or too much work, try to at least knock. Make the decision to begin ". . . and it will be opened to you".

Jesus will give you the insight and strength to continue. Once underway, ". . . seek and you will find". The more thoroughly you seek *Perception* experiences, the more "you will find". "Ask and it will be given to you". The more thoroughly you question doubts and pursue *Process* learnings, the more likely it is sound and supported *Knowledge* "will be given to you".

Perception **Experiences**			
Process **Learnings**			
Knowledge of **Life's Purpose**			

The template that I used and offer you allows you to capture what you have experienced to date in the left-hand column and what you will continue to experience in the right-hand column. If your knowledge of life's purpose evolved throughout your life (as mine did) you may want to divide the leftmost column.

What led to your initial knowledge goes to the left of the dotted line and what led to your later knowledge goes to its right (as you see in my completed template).

To fill the columns, you reminisce and reflect. You recall your significant *Perception* experiences and reflect on the *Process* learnings to which they led. Probe your memory for *all* the most impactful people, events and readings that make up your *Perception* set. The more *Perception* experiences you recall and the more you reflect on them, the more likely *Knowledge* will result (and sometimes be corrected). For example, limiting my *Perception* experience to the scientific method produced my *Knowledge* life's purpose was earthly fulfillment. Opening myself to additional *Perception* experiences and removing that limit, produced two corrections to that knowledge.

This ability to *correct*, as well as *confirm* knowledge is the most powerful aspect of *Experiential Learning*. Your ongoing reminiscence can lead to discovery of new *Perception* experiences and *Process* learnings that call into question the *Knowledge* of life's purpose at which you had previously arrived. These you will want to place in the rightmost column where they may lead to a correction of your *Knowledge* of life's purpose. For example, my *Perception* experience of sound reasoning uncovered new *Process* learnings and corrected my *Knowledge* life's purpose was *likely* to live according to Church teaching. The correction established my much richer and sounder *Knowledge* life's purpose is to love God and *all* His children as selflessly and unconditionally as we are able.

To complete your *Perception* set, you will need to focus on *Perception* experiences that your predominant strength may have caused you to overlook in the past. For example because my predominant strength was my mind, for some time I overlooked some people and events in my life. If your predominant strength is your heart, you may similarly be in danger of overlooking some readings to which you were exposed.

To complete your *Process* learnings, think of what you learned (or could learn) from each person, event or reading and capture that *Process* learning in a few words in the appropriate column. As you capture each *Process* learning, reflect on the *Perception* experience (person, event or reading) that produced it. Is there anything else you can learn from that *Perception* experience? Lastly look at each person, event or reading that did *not* produce a *Process* learning. Re-experience it. Can you discover a *Process* learning you may have missed?

Sometimes you will do so. For example, for a considerable time I failed to learn from a very important *Perception* experience. As I re-thought the little reading of the Bible I had undertaken, I realized I had ignored most of the Old Testament and discounted most of the New Testament. The inconsistencies in the former and perceived questionability of the latter led me to move on from both. As I reminisced about my exposure to the Bible, I began to wonder if the inconsistencies could be resolved and the validity soundly established. As you'll recall from Chapters 14 through 16, my reflection not only achieved both but also led to several new *Process* learnings.

You may need to be patient and persevering to arrive at *Knowledge* of life's purpose. All your *Perception* experiences and *Process* learnings may not yet lead to *Knowledge*. However, you can continue to pursue *Perception* experiences and *Process* learnings as your life on Earth continues to play out. My experience indicates your continued pursuit will eventually lead you to *Knowledge* of life's purpose.

You may find it difficult to capture all your *Perception* experiences and *Process* learnings on this book's blank one-page template. People who have experienced this problem have found, by reproducing the template on a large flipchart page (or even several taped together), they can produce a more usable template.

As you recollect what you have read in this book of my *Experiential Learning* and review its results in my template, you will have an example of this process. You may get the impression the process is too difficult. It is demanding but not difficult. Its demands on you are rewarded by the enjoyment of your reminiscing and your acquisition of new knowledge. Almost everyone enjoys reminiscing and learning.

I am sure you will find your pursuit of your *Experiential Learning* as rewarding as I found mine. It will almost assuredly lead you to sound and supported knowledge of life's purpose. *Knowing* your position on life's purpose will help you to commit yourself more fully to better accomplishing it.

What could be more important than accomplishing your life's purpose during your short lifetime on Earth?

The reward of my *Experiential Learning* is *my* knowledge of life's purpose. It is not knowledge that can be proven. It is God's intent that it will *never* be provable. Instead, God gives us the mind and heart we need to *choose* to discern and accomplish His will. Our minds enable the capture of facts and rationale that establish sound and supported belief. Our hearts enable the leap of faith to which our belief leads. Both produce sound and supported knowledge of life's purpose.

CHAPTER 30

THE DOZEN THINGS I KNOW

1) **I know** I (and each one of us) was created by a loving God to live with Him for eternity. I know this by philosophic argument. We must have a creator because we couldn't exist without one. In all we experience of creation (our parental procreation) we consistently observe that *all* capable creators (parents), who create with intent, love the children they create and intend their children not predecease them. Since our Creator is capable, created with intent and is *eternal*, I *know* He loves us and intends that we have *eternal* life. These three findings comprise the first part of my *foundational knowledge*.

2) **I know** life's purpose is to love God and *all* His children as selflessly and unconditionally as we are able. I know this by philosophic argument. In all we experience of creation (our parental procreation) we consistently observe that *all* capable creators (parents), who create with intent, want their children to choose to love *all* their siblings and them as they love, and want them to achieve their *best*. Since God is capable, created with intent and loves us selflessly and unconditionally, I *know* God wants us to choose to love Him and *all* His children as He loves – selflessly and unconditionally – and wants us to do this to the *best* of our ability. The will of our creator must be life's purpose. This is the second part of my *foundational knowledge*.

3) **I know** the Bible reveals the Word of God. I know this because it logically follows from my *foundational knowledge* – God wants us to *choose* to love Him and to do His will. To preserve our *choice*, He must *reveal* His will rather than dictate it. The Bible is the first

vehicle to have claimed to be the revealed Word of God. God's *need* of such a vehicle substantiates this claim. Until I find an argument that refutes this claim or flaws in the many arguments that support it, I know the Bible is the revealed Word of God.

4) **I know** Jesus Christ was God Incarnate, the Son of God and His words are the Word of God. I know this because it logically follows from my *foundational knowledge* – God wants us to *choose* to love Him and to do His will. Revealing His will spiritually was insufficient. God needed a vehicle to speak to us *directly*. To *speak* to us, God would have to become a person. One way to become a person would be to father a Son, as Jesus Christ uniquely and consistently claimed Himself to be. God's *need* of such a vehicle substantiates His claim. Until I find an argument that refutes this knowledge or flaws in the many arguments that support it, I know Christ was God Incarnate, the Son of God and His words are the Word of God.

5) **I know** the Roman Catholic Catechism reveals the Word of God. I know this because it logically follows from my *foundational knowledge* – God wants us to *choose* to love Him and to do His will. Jesus' three year ministry was insufficient to teach us the will of God. God needed a vehicle to *continue* to reveal His will. Jesus, as God Incarnate, committed to send the Holy Spirit to His Church led by Peter and his successors. His Church's leaders capture the Holy Spirit's revelations in the Roman Catholic Catechism. Despite the human fallibility of its authors' *interpretations* of some of what is revealed to them, where the Roman Catholic Catechism is consistent with Christ's teachings, it is the best record we have of the Holy Spirit's *revelations* of the Word of God. Until I find an argument that refutes this knowledge or flaws in the many arguments that support it, I know the Roman Catholic Catechism is the revealed Word of God.

6) **I know** God wants me to love Him with *all* my heart, with *all* my strength, with *all* my mind and with *all* my soul. I know this because it logically follows from my *foundational knowledge* – God wants me to selflessly love Him as He loves me to the *best* of my ability. For me to become as capable of selfless love as I am able, I must give my *all* to loving Him. It must be *all* of which I am capable. I know this because my three sources of the Word of God (the Bible, *THE SAYINGS OF JESUS* and the Roman Catholic Catechism) support this knowledge.

7) **I know** God wants me to love *all* His children as selflessly and unconditionally as I am able. I know this because it logically follows from my *foundational knowledge* – God's will is I do my best to love *all* His children as He does. I know this because my three sources of the Word of God (the Bible, *THE SAYINGS OF JESUS* and the Roman Catholic Catechism) support this knowledge.

8) **I know** I must use *all* my gifts to selflessly love *every* day of my life. I know this because it logically follows from my *foundational knowledge* – God wants me to *do my best* to love Him and all His children selflessly and unconditionally. To *do my best* I must *fully* use *all* my gifts. I must be *all* my gifts enable – all I *can* be. I know this because my three sources of the Word of God (the Bible, *THE SAYINGS OF JESUS* and the Roman Catholic Catechism) support this knowledge.

9) **I know** I *will* be judged as to whether I have adequately or inadequately prepared for eternal life in heaven. I know this because of what Jesus taught in the Lord's Prayer. "Thy will be done as *it is* in heaven." He didn't add "by some of the people there some of the time." Clearly, in heaven, *everyone* does God's will. It follows God must separate those who *have* done their *best* to do His will from those who have *not*. Secondly, Jesus insisted *few* are chosen. To be one of the few my preparation must be the *best* I can accomplish. I know this because my three sources of the Word of God (the Bible, *THE SAYINGS OF JESUS* and the Roman Catholic Catechism) support this knowledge.

10) **I know** at my judgement, I will have *no* excuse for my failures. I know this because I have been given the opportunity to learn *everything* about how to do God's will from the Word of God as delivered through the Bible, the words of Jesus and the Roman Catholic Catechism. God would not blame any of those who have had *no* opportunity to learn these things. However, I am certain He will hold *everyone* accountable who *has* had an opportunity to learn these things. I know this because my three sources of the Word of God (the Bible, *THE SAYINGS OF JESUS* and the Roman Catholic Catechism) support this knowledge.

11) **I know** I must pray for God's help to achieve selfless, unconditional love. I know this because I am fully aware I am self-centred, self-absorbed and self-indulgent. Because God knows this and loves me, He *continuously* offers His help to me as does a father. I know *God* will not change me but He gave me the free will

to *choose* His help and to change *myself*. I must pray for God's help and then *use* His help to the *best* of my ability. I know this because my three sources of the Word of God (the Bible, *THE SAYINGS OF JESUS* and the Roman Catholic Catechism) support this knowledge.

12) **I know** I must do my *best* to share everything I have learned in *Experiential Learning* with everyone whom I encounter. I know this because it logically follows from my *foundational knowledge*. As an essential part of loving *all* God's children as well as I am *able*, I must illustrate, to as many of them as I am able, a route to the most important knowledge of all. I must pray they all receive the grace of God to open their hearts and their minds to His love and to the discernment and accomplishment of His will. I know this because my three sources of the Word of God (the Bible, *THE SAYINGS OF JESUS* and the Roman Catholic Catechism) support this knowledge.

I do not claim to have *proven* the dozen things I know. However, I do maintain that the combined weight of the facts that I have cited and the soundness of the arguments I have discovered establish what I know as sound and supported.

I am convinced no one can prove that my knowledge is correct or incorrect. I can know nothing absolutely. I will never have sufficient facts to *prove* what I know. However, I do have sufficient facts and arguments to lead to my *acceptance* of what I *must* know.

CONCLUSION

*E*xperiential Learning developed my knowledge of life's purpose – to love God and *all* His children as selflessly and unconditionally as we are able. It continues to give me a deeper understanding of life's purpose. It has taught me that to gain this deeper understanding, I must *fully* internalize and *live* Jesus' message.

To *selflessly* love God, I must love Him before all else. I must learn to love God with *all* my heart, strength, mind, and soul. I must learn to love Him not for Him but for me. I need to *choose* God. To learn to love God, I need to continue to better *know* Him, to *discern* and *accomplish* His will and to *ask* Him to help me whenever I repeatedly fall short.

To *selflessly* love *all* God's children, I need to learn to love those I dislike and those I have difficulty not hating. I need to love others more than I love myself. I need to *act* on that love by using my gifts to support the needs of others rather than to support my selfish indulgences. I need to get out of myself.

Because these are the attributes of God's love, I need to fully develop my ability to selflessly love in order to belong where "His will is done." I must *choose* eternal life with Him and put my *all* into preparing myself.

Many Christian readers will not accept what I have come to know. They believe we are ". . . not saved by works". They believe we are saved by faith *alone*. They believe the experience of being born again will save them. They correctly conclude we cannot *earn* heaven. We can't feel we've earned it by being better than others. It is only by the grace of God we will live with Him for eternity.

However, I also know it is up to us to *choose* Him and to *adequately prepare* ourselves. Saint James was clear. "Faith without works is dead." (James 2: 14-18) Jesus was adamant. "Why do you call me Lord, Lord and not *do* what I tell you." (Luke 6: 46-49) and "Not everyone who says to me, 'Lord, Lord' will enter the kingdom of heaven, but the one who does the will of my Father who is in heaven." (Matt 7: 21-27) To *believe* in Jesus is to *do* what He says, not in order to earn heaven but out of love. When I was "born again" at my baptism God cleansed me but, ever since, it has been up to *me* to *do* His will.

Many non-Christian readers will not accept what I have come to know. They will see what I know is largely (but not wholly) dependent on knowing Jesus is the Son of God and what He says is the Word of God. It is true my knowledge Jesus is the Son of God is the *soundest* foundation of all I know but, as you have read, it is not its only foundation.

Where does that leave the non-Christian part of the world? Jewish people base what they know on the Tanach (Hebrew Bible), which contains the Torah (comprising the first five books of the Old Testament and the 613 commandments – mitzvot), their prophets and their prayerful relationship with God. Muslims base what they know on the Koran as well as on their prayerful relationship with Allah. Others are given their own knowledge of God in different ways. I don't disparage or despair of any of these ways. I simply feel access to the spoken Word of God is the best foundation of *my* knowledge.

I am reminded, once again, of my earlier reference to Rumi, and where it led my thinking.

> The truth was a mirror in the hands of God. It fell and broke into pieces. Everybody took a piece of it and they looked at it and thought they had the truth.

This book is my attempt to share my piece of glass. I find it is easier to write about it than to discuss it in conversation. I have a tendency in conversation of falling into the trap of defending my idea rather than pursuing another's idea. This inevitably leads to some degree of confrontation, which quickly shuts down the communication. I find others fall into this same trap. If instead I present my thinking in writing, others can read it privately. They don't have to respond. There is no pressure to defend their differing view. It is a more effective presentation of my piece of glass.

However, sadly, it doesn't give me access to *others'* pieces of glass. I have to hope my readers will reach out to me. I heartily invite you to share your thinking with me at delsmith@rogers.com whenever you feel you'd like to do so.

My piece of glass is my knowledge every word Jesus uttered *is* the Word of God. It doesn't matter whether I agree with Him on any teaching or not. My opinion is no longer pertinent. My only sane course is to apply every capability I have to more fully understand every word He uttered. I can't pick and choose. Any ideas I get that are counter to Jesus' teachings are false.

What encourages me to *continue* to pursue every word Jesus said? It is when I read His words over and over again, I more fully understand His teaching. When I find a scholarly interpretation of His teaching, I am often able to see it in a fuller light. When I read the parts of the Old Testament that I had put aside in my full focus on Jesus' teachings, I understand better the foundation of knowledge upon which He built. When I read the rest of the New Testament, I learn from how His followers interpreted His teaching. I increase my understanding of Jesus' message.

Despite all this, the soundness of my knowledge does not protect me from *unreasonable* doubt. For example, at times, I become uncertain of the dozen things I claim to know. This *unreasonable* doubt creeps in whenever I reflect that most people I know do not accept *some* (or all) of what I know.

I am reminded of the story about the proud mother who remarked her Johnny was the only soldier who was in step. If I am the only person (at least of those with whom I am connected) who *knows* the dozen things I know, isn't there some doubt *I* do?

I then have to remind myself that in my early years I, like René Descartes, could not claim to *know* anything I could not know *absolutely*. Later in life, I realized it is precisely because I *can't* know anything absolutely that I must act on what I *can* know based on sound and supported reasoning.

Most of the time when *unreasonable* doubt returns, I am able to banish it by reflecting that my knowledge is sound because it is rigorously supported by deductive and inductive reasoning and/or comparative analysis of arguments. However, sometimes, even after reminding myself of this, I still need a crutch. I turn to my trusty *Pascal's Wager*. Paraphrased for this situation, it goes like this.

Either the dozen things I know are correct or they are flawed. If they are flawed and I live my life according to them as best as I am able, I risk little. It definitely pushes and challenges me but, worst case, it helps me to be a better person. Conversely if they *are* true and I do *not* live my life according to what I *know*, I risk everything. If they are true, I cannot ignore them and be adequately prepared at my death for eternal life with God.

When *unreasonable* doubt plagues me, *Pascal's Wager* brings back my confidence in my sound and supported knowledge.

On occasion, I have been asked if I would recommend *Experiential Learning* to others. My answer is a definite "Yes". I give this unqualified answer for several reasons and with a few unavoidable caveats.

I would recommend it because it is free, there is no pressure from mentors or professors, there are no assignments or annual examinations and it is self-paced. I would recommend it because it is one of the most rewarding experiences of one's life, if not *the* most rewarding.

The caveats are few. The first is you have to die to take the final exam. The second is no one on Earth will know if you passed. The third is there are no mid-term tests along the way to show you how well you are prepared for the final exam. The final caveat is, because it is self-paced, it demands a great deal of application, perseverance and dedication.

I pray you have benefited a bit from tracing my *Experiential Learning* and that you will undertake yours.

On the other hand, I am aware you may not want to commit yourself to a full course of study. I think back to the suggestion made to me early in my *Experiential Learning*. I was told I needed to understand what philosophers had written before writing about philosophy myself.

As you have read, I was not prepared to commit myself to even a first year course much less a full course of study. You may feel the same way about *Experiential Learning*.

What I *did* find valuable, though, was a study of a couple of philosophy textbooks. This is why this book includes a copy of the *Experiential Learning* textbook – *THE SAYINGS OF JESUS* – in the Appendix.

I pray, if you are as unwilling to fully pursue *Experiential Learning* as I was to fully pursue philosophy, you will entertain the idea (as I did) of studying a textbook.

I offer you *THE SAYINGS OF JESUS*. It starts on the next couple of pages.

BIBLIOGRAPHY

Abbott, Edwin A. *Flatland – A Romance of Many Dimensions*. Mineola NY: Dover Publications Inc., 1884

Baker, Ann and Bonjour, Lawrence. *Philosophical Problems – An Annotated Anthology*. NY: Pearson Education Inc., 2005

Blatchford, Robert. *Not Guilty – A Defense of the Bottom Dog*. New York: Boni and Liveright, 1918

Dawkins, Richard. *The GOD Delusion*. NY: Houghton Mifflin Company, 2006

Geisler, Norman L. and Turek, Frank. *I Don't Have Enough Faith to Be an Atheist*. Wheaton, Illinois: Crossway Books, 2004

Harris, Sam. *A Letter to a Christian Nation*. Toronto, Ontario: Random House of Canada Ltd., 2008

John Paul II. *Man and Woman He Created Them: Theology of the Body*. Boston: Pauline Books and Media, 2006

Kolb, David A. *Experiential Learning*. Upper Saddle River, NJ: Prentice Hall Inc., 1984

Lewis, C.S. *Mere Christianity*. NY: Harper Collins, 1952

Lewis, C.S. *Miracles*. NY: Harper Collins, 1947

Morris, Thomas V. *Philosophy for Dummies*. St. Louis, Missouri: Sierra Nevada Books, 1999

Strobel, Lee. *The Case for Christ*. Grand Rapids, Michigan: Zondervan Publishing House, 1997

The Holy Bible – English Standard Version. Wheaton, Illinois: Crossway Bibles, 2001

Vaticana, Liberia Editrice. *Catechism of the Catholic Church*. Bentonville AR: Enterprises Books, 2000

West, Christopher. *Fill These Hearts: God, Sex, and the Universal Longing*. New York: Image, an imprint of the Crown Publishing Group, 2012

APPENDIX

THE SAYINGS OF JESUS

THE SAYINGS OF JESUS

DEL H. SMITH

Contents

INTRODUCTION

My purpose in preparing this textbook is to help you understand Jesus' message. For those of you who know (or whose faith is unshakeable) Jesus Christ is the Son of God, understanding what *He* says is understanding what *God* says. The more fully we understand God's Word, the better we are able to discern and accomplish His will. For you, what could be more important? For those of you who believe Jesus is merely a good teacher, this book provides unique and powerful access to His teachings.

Other books have done an excellent job of helping the reader understand individual parables. Still others help the reader understand specific things Jesus is quoted to have said. However, I have not found one that succeeds in helping the reader discover Jesus' *overall* message from the hundreds of things He said.[42]

Undoubtedly, one could eventually discern Jesus' *overall* message by simply re-reading the Bible as many times as one needed. However, for me, it didn't work. I had read and listened to all four Gospels so many times, I thought I knew all I had to know about what Jesus said. I had essentially boiled down His message to "Play nice". I had taken away no overall message on any individual topic.

One problem, with relying on the Bible alone, is I read it as I do any book. I start at the beginning of a Gospel and read each page in sequence until I get to the end. Each Gospel tells Jesus' story as a narrative. As a result when I come across something He said on a topic of interest, I don't have access to what else He said on that topic. As I continue in the Bible narrative my attention is diverted to something He said on another topic.

---

[42] If you have read PART FIVE of *Discovering* LIFE'S PURPOSE you will have already read much of the content of the following paragraphs and of the section entitled *Preparing the Textbook*

When later He again addresses the earlier topic, I have forgotten (and can no longer even locate) His earlier commentary. I find each Gospel to be a compelling story of Jesus' ministry, but a scattered portrayal of His message on any given topic.

I have a second problem. When I'm reading Mark, I can't relate what I'm reading to Matthew, Luke or John. I have to read all four Gospels to see *everything* Jesus is quoted as saying on any given topic. I can't keep track of a topic while reading *one* Gospel, let alone *four*. I am unable to see all His teachings on any one topic together. As a result, I cannot see how they support, expand on and reinforce each other to produce an overall message on that topic.

A third problem is trying to cope with the volume of Jesus' sayings. In the four Gospels, Jesus is quoted almost 400 times. He addresses almost five dozen topics. I can't internalize five dozen topics at the same time. I need to be able to pick a topic and focus on it before tackling a second topic. Like many of us, I can only do one thing at a time.

Finally, I need to be able to focus my attention on the most *important* topics Jesus addressed. Ideally, I would like to start with *the* most important topic. I could focus on it until I had discerned its overall message. Only then would I be ready to tackle the second most important topic. However, using the Bible alone, how could I know the order of importance of 55 topics?

THE SAYINGS OF JESUS solves these problems. It assembles everything Jesus is quoted as having said on each topic in a separate chapter, determines the relative importance of topics and sequences its chapters in order of importance. This allows readers to *complete* their study of a topic before adding another topic to their study. How was this textbook prepared in a way that produced these benefits?

Preparing the Textbook

The first step was to assign each of Jesus' almost-400 quotations in the four gospels to a topic. For example, when I read the following quotation, I assigned it to a topic I named *Discipleship*.

> If anyone would come after me, let him deny himself and take up his cross daily and follow me. For whoever would save his life will lose it, but whoever loses his life for my sake will save it. For what does it profit a man if he gains the whole world and loses or forfeits himself?

> For whoever is ashamed of me and of my words, of him will the Son of Man be ashamed when He comes in His glory and the glory of the Father and of the holy angels. But I tell you truly, there are some standing here who will not taste death until they see the kingdom of God. (Luke 9: 23-27)

On reading this quotation, it seemed to me it is what Jesus demands of each of us in order for us to be one of His disciples. The body of this textbook assigns every one of Jesus' teachings to its topic and cites its Bible book/chapter/verse.

The second step was to establish criteria for the relative importance of each topic and rank topics accordingly. It seemed to me the more often Jesus is quoted as addressing a topic, the more important that topic is. It further seemed the more Jesus said on a topic, the more important it is. I combined these two criteria to produce a *topic rank*. The chapters of *THE SAYINGS OF JESUS* are sequenced by *topic rank*.

The final step was to identify the *focus* of Jesus' message. To do this, I simply divided the almost-400 quotations into three equal groups. I discovered all the quotes in the first third were devoted solely to the five most-important topics. Those in the second third were devoted solely to the next ten most-important topics. The remaining 40 topics made up the final third of the quotes. It became clear to me that the first fifteen topics must have been those that Jesus determined were most important. For me, that the 40 remaining topics represent less than a third of *everything* He said and less than a third of the total number of His sayings further supports the contention His focus was on the first fifteen.[43]

Now you know how the textbook was produced. Let me now share with you some of my experience in using this textbook – *THE SAYINGS OF JESUS*.

Using the Textbook

From my study of the textbook, a couple of approaches emerge. You might consider starting with the most important topic. When you have completed your study of it, you could move to the next most important

---

[43] A more detailed description of the analysis that produced these conclusions can be found at the end of this book on the two pages prior to Figure 1 under a heading entitled *The Research that Produced THE SAYINGS OF JESUS (for nerds only)*.

topic and then continue at your own pace with as many of the remaining topics as you choose, in order of their importance. Alternatively you might select any one of the topics that most puzzles *you*, or is most important to *you* and then continue with the topic you find to be the next most puzzling or important to you. Probably about a dozen or dozen and a half topics will suffice for your initial study.

Once you've selected a topic, you might read each quote in turn. You'll discover where the same quote is reported in more than one passage in the four gospels, I've generally placed those passages together.[44]

As you read each passage of the same quote, you may find how the quote is reported in one passage helps you to better understand how it is reported in another passage. For example, in Matthew Jesus is quoted as saying "Whoever loves father or mother more than me is not worthy of me . . ." (Matt 10: 37) while in Luke, the same quotation reads "If anyone comes to me and does not hate his own father and mother . . ." (Luke 14: 26) Luke's quotation uses the word *hate* while Matthew's does not. Reading both we can see Jesus is using *hate* as *love less*.

As you read each quote, you may discover what Jesus says in one quote helps you to better understand what He is saying in another quote. You may even discover, taken as a group, the quotes reinforce each other and/or elaborate on each other.

Before moving to the next topic, I would suggest you reflect on the overall message you discern from *all* the quotes on the topic you are currently studying. In each chapter you will find a suggestion to create (and then add to) a journal containing what you conclude to be Jesus' overall message on that topic. Below it, you will also find what *I* conclude to be Jesus' topic message. You may want to underline, as I have done, key words in what you have determined to be Jesus' overall message.

For example, on the topic *Discipleship* the overall message for me was this.

> <u>I must love Jesus more than anyone</u>, emulate Him daily and proclaim God's Word zealously despite rejection. <u>I am fully accountable</u> for dutifully following all His teachings.

When you're ready to move to the next topic, you might follow the same approach, or any modification of my suggested approach you find helpful.

---

[44] Wherever this duplication occurs, the number of quotes will be lower than the number of passages.

iv

When you've completed your study of all the topics that currently interest you, but at most a dozen and a half, I expect you will be ready to discern what, for you, is Jesus' overall message. As you did for the quotes in each topic, you may discover what you determined to be Jesus' message on one topic helps you to better understand that of another topic. You may even discover, taken as a group, the topic messages reinforce each other and/or elaborate on each other.

At the conclusion of this textbook, you will find an example showing how I arrived at what I concluded was Jesus' overall message. As you read this example, you'll see I copied the underlined words in the overall messages of the fifteen topics onto a single page. This enabled me to see, in one place, all fifteen topics' messages expressed in a few words. My final step was to place the message of each topic where I concluded it fitted in with that of the others. The end result was what I concluded to be Jesus' overall message expressed in four short paragraphs.

As you study the messages you take from the topics you choose to pursue, you might find a similar process works for you. If so, in the Conclusion of this book, you'll find two reminders to try it out. Seeing what you have determined to be Jesus' topic messages on a single page may enable you to discover what, for you, is Jesus' overall message.

Of course, the value of all this study is dependent upon how *accurately* the Bible quotes Jesus' teachings. It is true there is much scholarly debate about the Bible's accuracy. I am not qualified to even participate in such debate. However, it is clear to me, even if *some* passages are misquoted, it is extremely unlikely they *all* are. Any error in a single passage would stand out by its inconsistency with the rest of the quotations on that topic when they are all viewed together. *THE SAYINGS OF JESUS* provides such a view.

Even after all this study, you may find determining Jesus' overall message is still a daunting exercise. *I* certainly did. However, I discovered it was much more doable with a study of my textbook than without it.

Jesus said a great deal in a few words. He was trying to teach our limited intellects something unfathomable and unimaginable. It is not surprising we didn't get it. It is not surprising it takes a lot of study of *THE SAYINGS OF JESUS* to begin to get it. It would not even be surprising that, if you were to repeat the whole exercise in a year or two, you might discover meanings that had eluded you on your first study.

Experiential Learning[45] taught me I can *know* Jesus is the Son of God. Because Jesus is the Son of God, what He *says* is the Word of God. It's clear to me I have to devote all the energy and intellect I am able to summon up to discerning the Word of God so as to better accomplish, to the *best* of my capability, the will of God.

If you were to conclude Jesus is the Son of God, would you not be equally compelled?

If you doubt Jesus is the Son of God, you may find this book's sister book – *Discovering* LIFE'S PURPOSE - RE-EXAMINING *THE CLUB* – helps you further pursue your doubt.

In either case, I offer you my textbook, *THE SAYINGS OF JESUS*, and trust it will be of value to you in your study. Is it time to hit the books?

---

[45]   The book of which this book is an Appendix – *Discovering* LIFE'S PURPOSE – RE-EXAMINING *THE CLUB* – describes *Experiential Learning*.

CHAPTER 1

PASSION AND DEATH

My Overall Message:

Please consider adding to your journal what you determine to be Jesus' overall message on this topic.

Author's Overall Message:

<u>Jesus was a man</u> who loved us beyond measure. His lament to God "Why have You forsaken me?" shows me the pain He endured for us. The fact Jesus was a human made His acceptance of God's will over His own something I, a child of God, must emulate.

Luke 13: 32-35 Go and tell that fox "Behold, I cast out demons and perform cures today and tomorrow and the third day I finish my course. Nevertheless, I must go on my way today and tomorrow and the day following, for it cannot be that a prophet should perish away from Jerusalem." O Jerusalem, Jerusalem, the city that kills the prophets and stones those who are sent to it! How often would I have gathered your children together as a hen gathers her brood under her wings and you would not! Behold, your house is forsaken. And I tell you, you will not see me until you say, "Blessed is He who comes in the name of the Lord!"

Mark 9: 2-13 {Peter seeing Jesus intensely white, with Elijah and Moses: Rabbi, it is good that we are here. Let us make three tents, one for You and one for Moses and one for Elijah.} {voice from the cloud: This is my beloved Son; listen to Him. And suddenly, looking around, they no longer saw anyone with them but Jesus only.} {Disciples: Why do the scribes say that first Elijah must come?} Elijah does come first to restore all things. And how is it written of the Son of Man that He should suffer many things and be treated with contempt? But I tell you that Elijah has come and they did to him whatever they pleased, as it is written of him.

Matt 17: 7-12 Rise and have no fear. Tell no one the vision, until the Son of Man is raised from the dead. Elijah does come and He will restore all things. But I tell you that Elijah has already come and they did not recognize him, but did to him whatever they pleased. So also the Son of Man will certainly suffer at their hands.

Matt 23: 37-39 O Jerusalem, Jerusalem, the city that kills the prophets and stones those who are sent to it! How often would I have gathered your children together as a hen gathers her brood under her wings and you would not! See, your house is left to you desolate. For I tell you, you will not see me again, until you say, "Blessed is He who comes in the name of the Lord."

Luke 19: 42-44 Would that you, even you, had known on this day the things that make for peace! But now they are hidden from your eyes. For the days will come upon you, when your enemies will set up a barricade around you and surround you and hem you in on every side and tear you down to the ground, you and your children within you. And they will not leave one stone upon another in you, because you did not know the time of your visitation.

Mark 11: 2-3 Go into the village in front of you and immediately as you enter it you will find a colt tied, on which no one has ever sat. Untie it and bring it. If anyone says to you "Why are you doing this?" say, "The Lord has need of it and will send it back here immediately."

Luke 19: 30-31 Go into the village in front of you, where on entering you will find a colt tied, on which no one has ever yet sat. Untie it and bring it here. If anyone asks you "Why are you untying it?" you shall say this: "The Lord has need of it."

Matt 21: 2-3 Go into the village in front of you and immediately you will find a donkey tied and a colt with her. Untie them and bring them to me. If anyone says anything to you, you shall say, "The Lord needs them," and he will send them at once.

John 12: 23-28 The hour has come for the Son of Man to be glorified. Truly, truly, I say to you, unless a grain of wheat falls into the earth and dies, it remains alone; but if it dies, it bears much fruit. Whoever loves his life loses it and whoever hates his life in this world will keep it for eternal life. If anyone serves me, he must follow me; and where I am, there will my servant be also. If anyone serves me, the Father will honour him. Now is my soul troubled. And what shall I say? "Father, save me from this hour?" But for this purpose I have come to this hour. Father, glorify Your name. {voice from heaven: I have glorified it and I will glorify it again.}

John 12: 30-36 This voice has come for your sake, not mine. Now is the judgement of this world; now will the ruler of this world be cast out. And I, when I am lifted up from the earth, will draw all people to myself. The light is among you for a little while longer. Walk while you have the light, lest darkness overtake you. The one who walks in the darkness does not know where he is going. While you have the light, believe in the light, that you may become sons of light.

Luke 22: 8-12 Go and prepare the Passover for us, that we may eat it. Behold, when you have entered the city, a man carrying a jar of water will meet you. Follow him into the house that he enters and tell the master of the house "The Teacher says to you, where is the guest room where I may eat the Passover with my disciples?" And he will show you a large upper room furnished; prepare it there.

Matt 26: 18 Go into the city to a certain man and say to him "The Teacher says, My time is at hand. I will keep the Passover at your house with my disciples."

Mark 14: 12-15 {Disciples: Where will You have us go and prepare for You to eat the Passover?} Go into the city and a man carrying a jar of water will meet you. Follow him and wherever he enters, say to the master of the house "The Teacher says, Where is my guest room, where I may eat the Passover with my disciples?" And he will show you a large upper room furnished and ready; there prepare for us.

Luke 22: 15-22 I have earnestly desired to eat this Passover with you before I suffer. For I tell you I will not eat it until it is fulfilled in the kingdom of God. Take this and divide it among yourselves. For I tell you that from now on I will not drink of the fruit of the vine until the kingdom of God comes. This is my body, which is given for you. Do this in remembrance of me. This cup that is poured out for you is the new covenant in my blood. But behold, the hand of him who betrays me is with me on the table. For the Son of Man goes as it has been determined, but woe to that man by whom He is betrayed!

Matt 26: 26-29 Take, eat; this is my body. Drink of it, all of you, for this is my blood of the covenant, which is poured out for many for the forgiveness of sins. I tell you I will not drink again of this fruit of the vine until that day when I drink it new with you in my Father's kingdom.

Mark 14: 22-25 Take; this is my body. This is my blood of the covenant, which is poured out for many. Truly, I say to you, I will not drink again of the fruit of the vine until that day when I drink it new in the kingdom of God.

Matt 26: 21-25 Truly, I say to you, one of you will betray me. {Disciples: Is it I Lord?} He who has dipped his hand in the dish with me will betray me. The Son of Man goes as it is written of Him, but woe to that man by whom the Son of Man is betrayed! It would have been better for that man if he had not been born. {Judas: Is it I, Rabbi?} You have said so.

John 13: 21-27 Truly, truly, I say to you, one of you will betray me. {Disciple: Lord, who is it?} It is he to whom I will give this morsel of bread when I have dipped it. {to Judas} What you are going to do, do quickly.

Mark 14: 18-21 Truly, I say to you, one of you will betray me, one who is eating with me. {to one another: Is it I?} It is one of the twelve, one who is dipping bread into the dish with me. For the Son of Man goes as it is written of Him, but woe to that man by whom the Son of Man is betrayed! It would have been better for that man if he had not been born.

John 14: 1-7 Let not your hearts be troubled. Believe in God; believe also in me. In my Father's house are many rooms. If it were not so would I have told you that I go to prepare a place for you? And if I go and prepare a place for you, I will come again and will take you to myself, that where I am you may be also. And you know the way to where I am going. {Thomas: Lord, we do not know where You are going. How can we know the way?} I am the way and the truth and the life. No one comes to the Father except through me. If you had known me, you would have known my Father also. From now on you do know Him and have seen Him.

Mark 14: 32-42 Sit here while I pray. My soul is very sorrowful, even to death. Remain here and watch. Abba, Father, all things are possible for You. Remove this cup from me. Yet not what I will, but what You will. Simon, are you asleep? Could you not watch one hour? Watch and pray that you may not enter into temptation. The spirit indeed is willing, but the flesh is weak. Are you still sleeping and taking your rest? It is enough; the hour has come. The Son of Man is betrayed into the hands of sinners. Rise, let us be going; see my betrayer is at hand.

Matt 26: 36-46 Sit here, while I go over there and pray. My soul is very sorrowful, even to death; remain here and watch with me. My Father, if it be possible, let this cup pass from me; nevertheless, not as I will but as You will. So, could you not watch with me one hour? Watch and pray that you may not enter into temptation. The spirit indeed is willing, but the flesh is weak. My Father, if this cannot pass unless I drink it, Your will be done. Sleep and take your rest later on. See, the hour is at hand and the Son of Man is betrayed into the hands of sinners. Rise, let us be going; see, my betrayer is at hand.

Luke 22: 40-46 Pray that you may not enter into temptation. Father, if You are willing, remove this cup from me. Nevertheless, not my will, but Yours, be done. Why are you sleeping? Rise and pray that you may not enter into temptation.

Mark 14: 27-31 You will all fall away, for it is written "I will strike the shepherd and the sheep will be scattered." But after I am raised up, I will go before you to Galilee. {Peter: Even though they all fall away, I will not.} Truly, I tell you, this very night, before the rooster crows twice, you will deny me three times. {Peter: If I must die with You, I will not deny You.}

Matt 26: 31-35 You will all fall away because of me this night. For it is written "I will strike the shepherd and the sheep of the flock will be scattered." But after I am raised up I will go before you to Galilee. {Peter: Though they all fall away because of You, I will never fall away.} Truly, I tell you, this very night, before the rooster crows, you will deny me three times. {Peter: Even if I must die with You, I will not deny You!}

Luke 22: 31-34 Simon, Simon, behold, Satan demanded to have you, so that he might sift you like wheat, but I have prayed for you that your faith may not fail. And when you have turned again, strengthen your brothers. {Peter: Lord, I am ready to go with you both to prison and to death.} I tell you, Peter, the rooster will not crow this day, until you deny three times that you know me.

Matt 26: 49-56 {kissing Jesus, Judas: Greetings, Rabbi!} Friend, do what you came to do. {at the cutting off of the high priest's ear} Put your sword back into its place. For all who take the sword will perish by the sword. Do you think that I cannot appeal to my Father and He will at once send me more than twelve legions of angels? But how then should the Scriptures be fulfilled, that it must be so? Have you come out as against a robber, with swords and clubs to capture me? Day after day I sat in the temple teaching and you did not seize me. But all this has taken place that the Scriptures of the prophets might be fulfilled.

Mark 14: 45-49 {Judas to Jesus: Rabbi!} Have you come out as against a robber, with swords and clubs to capture me? Day after day I was with you in the temple teaching and you did not seize me. But let the Scriptures be fulfilled.

Luke 22: 48-53 Judas, would you betray the Son of Man with a kiss? No more of this! Have you come out as against a robber, with swords and clubs? When I was with you day after day in the temple, you did not lay hands on me. But this is your hour and the power of darkness.

John 18: 4-11 Whom do you seek? {Pharisees: Jesus of Nazareth.} I am he. {silence} Whom do you seek? {Pharisees: Jesus of Nazareth.} I told you that I am he. So, if you seek me, let these men go. {after Peter cut off the ear of Malchus, the high priest's servant} Put your sword into its sheath; shall I not drink the cup that the Father has given me?

John 18: 17-27 {Servant girl to Peter: You also are not one of this man's disciples, are you?} {Peter: I am not.} {to the high priest} I have spoken openly to the world. I have always taught in synagogues and in the temple, where all Jews come together. I have said nothing in secret. Why do you ask me? Ask those who have heard me what I said to them; they know what I said. {Soldier: Is that how You answer the high priest?} If what I said is wrong, bear witness about the wrong; but if what I said is right, why do you strike me? {by the charcoal fire: You also are not one of His disciples, are you?} {Peter: I am not.} {Relative of Malchus: Did I not see you in the garden with Him?} {Peter denied it and at once a rooster crowed.}

Luke 22: 67-70 {If You are the Christ, tell us.} If I tell you, you will not believe and if I ask you, you will not answer. But from now on the Son of Man shall be seated at the right hand of the power of God. {Are You the Son of God then?} You say that I am.

Mark 14: 61-62 {Are You the Christ, the Son of the Blessed?} I am and you will see the Son of Man seated at the right hand of Power and coming with the clouds of heaven.

Matt 26: 63-64 {High priest: I adjure You by the living God, tell us if You are the Christ, the Son of God.} You have said so. But I tell you, from now on you will see the Son of Man seated at the right hand of Power and coming on the clouds of heaven.

Mark 15: 2 {Pilate: Are You the King of the Jews?} You have said so.

Matt 27: 11 {Pilate: Are You the King of the Jews?} You have said so.

John 19: 11 You would have no authority over me at all unless it had been given you from above. Therefore he who delivered me over to you has the greater sin.

Luke 23: 28-31 Daughters of Jerusalem, do not weep for me, but weep for yourselves and for your children. For behold, the days are coming when they will say, "Blessed are the barren and the wombs that never bore and the breasts that never nursed!" Then they will begin to say to the mountains "Fall on us," and to the hills "Cover us." For if they do these things when the wood is green, what will happen when it is dry?

John 19: 21-22 {Chief priests: Do not write "The King of the Jews," rather "This man said, I am King of the Jews."} {Pilate: What I have written I have written.}

John 19: 26-30 {to His mother, her sister, Mary the wife of Clopus and Mary Magdalene} Woman, behold, your son! {to the disciple} Behold, your mother! I thirst. It is finished.

Luke 23: 34-43 Father, forgive them, for they know not what they do. {Rulers: He saved others; let Him save Himself if He is the Christ of God, His Chosen One!} {Soldiers: If you are the King of the Jews, save yourself!} {The other criminal: Do you not fear God, since you are under the same sentence of condemnation? And we indeed justly, for we are receiving the due reward of our deeds; but this man has done nothing wrong. Jesus remember me when you come into your kingdom} Truly, I say to you, today you will be with me in Paradise.

Mark 15: 34-39 Eloi, Eloi, lema sabachthani? - My God, My God, why have You forsaken me? {Bystanders: Behold, He is calling Elijah. Wait, let us see whether Elijah will come to take Him down.} {Centurion: Truly, this man was the Son of God.}

Matt 27: 46 Eli, Eli, lema sabachthani? My God, my God, why have You forsaken me?

CHAPTER 2

DISCIPLESHIP

My Overall Message:

Please consider adding to your journal what you determine to be Jesus' overall message on this topic.

Author's Overall Message:

I must love Jesus more than anyone, emulate Him daily and proclaim God's Word zealously despite rejection. I am fully accountable for dutifully following all His teachings.

Luke 9: 23-27   If anyone would come after me, let him deny himself and take up his cross daily and follow me. For whoever would save his life will lose it, but whoever loses his life for my sake will save it. For what does it profit a man if he gains the whole world and loses or forfeits himself? For whoever is ashamed of me and of my words, of him will the Son of Man be ashamed when He comes in His glory and the glory of the Father and of the holy angels. But I tell you truly, there are some standing here who will not taste death until they see the kingdom of God.

Matt 16: 24-28   If anyone would come after me, let him deny himself and take up his cross and follow me. For whoever would save his life will lose it, but whoever loses his life for my sake will find it. For what will it profit a man if he gains the whole world and forfeits his life? Or what shall a man give in return for his life? For the Son of Man is going to come with His angels in the glory of his Father and then He will repay each person according to what He has done. Truly, I say to you, there are some standing here who will not taste death until they see the Son of Man coming in His kingdom.

Matt 10: 34-39 Do not think that I have come to bring peace to the earth. I have not come to bring peace, but a sword. For I have come to set a man against his father and a daughter against her mother and a daughter-in-law against her mother-in-law. And a person's enemies will be those of his own household. Whoever loves father or mother more than me is not worthy of me and whoever loves son or daughter more than me is not worthy of me. And whoever does not take his cross and follow me is not worthy of me. Whoever finds his life will lose it and whoever loses his life for my sake will find it.

Luke 14: 26-33 If anyone comes to me and does not hate his own father and mother and wife and children and brothers and sisters, yes and even his own life, he cannot be my disciple. Whoever does not bear his own cross and come after me cannot be my disciple. For which of you, desiring to build a tower, does not first sit down and count the cost, whether he has enough to complete it? Otherwise, when he has laid a foundation and is not able to finish, all who see it begin to mock Him, saying "This man began to build and was not able to finish." Or what king, going out to encounter another king in war, will not sit down first and deliberate whether he is able with ten thousand to meet him who comes against him with twenty thousand? And if not, while the other is yet a great way off, he sends a delegation and asks for terms of peace. So therefore, any one of you who does not renounce all that he has cannot be my disciple.

Matt 19: 27-30 {Peter: See, we have left everything and followed You. What then will we have?} Truly I say to you, in the new world, when the Son of Man will sit on His glorious throne, you who have followed me will also sit on twelve thrones, judging the twelve tribes of Israel. And everyone who has left houses or brothers or sisters or father or mother or children or lands, for my name's sake, will receive a hundredfold and will inherit eternal life. But many who are first will be last and the last first.

Matt 12: 48-50 Who is my mother and who are my brothers? Here are my mother and my brothers! For whoever does the will of my Father in heaven is my brother and sister and mother.

Matt 28: 18-20 All authority in heaven and on earth has been given to me. Go therefore and make disciples of all nations, baptizing them in the name of the Father and of the Son and of the Holy Spirit, teaching them to observe all that I have commanded you. And behold, I am with you always, to the end of the age.

Mark 16: 15-18 Go into all the world and proclaim the gospel to the whole creation. Whoever believes and is baptized will be saved, but whoever does not believe will be condemned. And these signs will accompany those who believe: in my name they will cast out demons; they will speak in new tongues; they will pick up serpents with their hands; and if they drink any deadly poison, it will not hurt them; they will lay their hands on the sick and they will recover.

Matt 5: 13-16 You are the salt of the earth, but if salt has lost its taste, how shall its saltiness be restored? It is no longer good for anything except to be thrown out and trampled under people's feet. You are the light of the world. A city set on a hill cannot be hidden. Nor do people light a lamp and put it under a basket, but on a stand and it gives light to all in the house. In the same way, let your light shine before others, so that they may see your good works and give glory to your Father who is in heaven.

Luke 14: 34-35 Salt is good, but if salt has lost its taste, how shall its saltiness be restored? It is of no use either for the soil or for the manure pile. It is thrown away. He who has ears to hear, let him hear.

Luke 10: 2-12 The harvest is plentiful, but the labourers are few. Therefore pray earnestly to the Lord of the harvest to send out labourers into His harvest. Go your way; behold, I am sending you out as lambs in the midst of wolves. Carry no moneybag, no knapsack, no sandals and greet no one on the road. Whatever house you enter, first say "Peace be to this house!" And if a son of peace is there, your peace will rest upon him. But if not, it will return to you. And remain in the same house, eating and drinking what they provide, for the labourer deserves his wages. Do not go from house to house. Whenever you enter a town and they receive you, eat what is set before you. Heal the sick in it and say to them "The kingdom of God has come near to you". But whenever you enter a town and they don't receive you, go into its streets and say "Even the dust of your town that clings to our feet we wipe off against you. Nevertheless know this that the kingdom of God has come near." I tell you, it will be more bearable on that day for Sodom than for that town.

Matt 9: 37-38 The harvest is plentiful, but the labourers are few; therefore pray earnestly to the Lord of the harvest to send out labourers into His harvest.

Luke 17: 7-10 Will any one of you who has a servant plowing or keeping sheep say to him when he has come in from the field "Come at once and recline at table"? Will he not rather say to him "Prepare supper for me and dress properly and serve me while I eat and drink and afterward you will eat and drink"? Does he thank the servant because he did what was commanded? So you also, when you have done all that you were commanded, say "We are unworthy servants; we have only done what was our duty."

Matt 20: 21-28 {to the mother of two sons of Zebedee} What do you want? You do not know what you are asking. Are you able to drink the cup that I am to drink? You will drink my cup, but to sit at my right hand and at my left is not mine to grant, but it is for those for whom it has been prepared by my Father. You know that the rulers of the Gentiles lord it over them and their great ones exercise authority over them. It shall not be so among you. But whoever would be great among you must be your servant and whoever would be first among you must be your slave, even as the Son of Man came not to be served but to serve and to give His life as a ransom for many.

Mark 10: 35-45 {James and John, the sons of Zebedee: Teacher, we want You to do for us whatever we ask of You.} What do you want me to do for you? {Grant us to sit, one at Your right hand and one at Your left, in Your glory.} You do not know what you are asking. Are you able to drink the cup that I drink, or to be baptised with the baptism with which I am baptized? {We are able.} The cup that I drink you will drink and with the baptism with which I am baptized you will be baptized, but to sit at my right hand or at my left is not mine to grant, but it is for those for whom it has been prepared. {to the other indignant disciples} You know that those who are considered rulers of the Gentiles lord it over them and their great ones exercise authority over them. But it shall not be so among you. But whoever would be great among you must be your servant and whoever would be first among you must be slave of all. For even the Son of Man came not to be served but to serve and to give His life as a ransom for many.

Luke 10: 17-20 {Disciples: Lord, even the demons are subject to us in Your name.} I saw Satan fall like lightning from heaven. Behold, I have given you authority to tread on serpents and scorpions and over all the power of the enemy and nothing shall hurt you. Nevertheless, do not rejoice in this, that the spirits are subject to you, but rejoice that your names are written in heaven.

Luke 10: 10-16 But whenever you enter a town and they do not receive you, go into its streets and say "Even the dust of your town that clings to our feet we wipe off against you. Nevertheless know this that the kingdom of God has come near." I tell you it will be more bearable on that day for Sodom than for that town. Woe to you Chorazin! Woe to you, Bethsaida! For if the mighty works done in you had been done in Tyre and Sidon, they would have repented long ago, sitting in sackcloth and ashes. But it will be more bearable in the judgement for Tyre and Sidon than for you. And you, Capernaum, will you be exalted to heaven? You shall be brought down to Hades. The one who hears you hears me and the one who rejects you rejects me and the one who rejects me rejects Him who sent me.

Matt 11: 21-24 Woe to you, Chorazin! Woe to you, Bethsaida! For if the mighty works done in you had been done in Tyre and Sidon, they would have repented long ago in sackcloth and ashes. But I tell you, it will be more bearable on the day of judgement for Tyre and Sidon than for you. And you, Capernaum, will you be exalted to heaven? You will be brought down to Hades. For if the mighty works done in you had been done in Sodom, it would have remained until this day. But I tell you that it will be more tolerable on the day of judgement for the land of Sodom than for you.

Luke 9: 3-5 Take nothing for your journey, no staff, nor bag, nor bread, nor money; and do not have two tunics. And whatever house you enter, stay there and from there depart. And wherever they do not receive you, when you leave that town shake off the dust from your feet as a testimony against them.

Mark 6: 10-11 Whenever you enter a house, stay there until you depart from there. And if any place will not receive you and they will not listen to you, when you leave, shake off the dust that is on your feet as a testimony against them.

Matt 10: 5-15 Go nowhere among the Gentiles and enter no town of the Samaritans, but go rather to the lost sheep of the house of Israel. And proclaim as you go, saying "The kingdom of heaven is at hand." Heal the sick, raise the dead, cleanse lepers, cast out demons. You received without paying; give without pay. Acquire no gold nor silver nor copper for your belts, no bag for your journey, nor two tunics nor sandals nor a staff, for the labourer deserves his food. And whatever town or village you enter, find out who is worthy in it and stay there until you depart. As you enter the house, greet it. And if the house is worthy, let your peace come upon it, but if it is not worthy, let your peace return to you. And if anyone will not receive you or listen to your words, shake off the dust from your feet when you leave that house or town. Truly, I say to you, it will be more bearable for the land of Sodom and Gomorrah than for that town.

Luke 21: 10-19 Nation will rise against nation and kingdom against kingdom. There will be great earthquakes and in various places famines and pestilences. And there will be terrors and great signs from heaven. But before all this they will lay their hands on you and persecute you, delivering you up to the synagogues and prisons and you will be brought before kings and governors for my name's sake. This will be your opportunity to bear witness. Settle it therefore in your minds not to meditate beforehand how to answer, for I will give you a mouth and wisdom, which none of your adversaries will be able to withstand or contradict. You will be delivered up even by parents and brothers and relatives and friends and some of you they will put to death. You will be hated by all for my name's sakes. But not a hair of your head will perish. By your endurance you will gain your lives.

Matt 10: 16-23 Behold, I am sending you out as sheep in the midst of wolves, so be wise as serpents and innocent as doves. Beware of men, for they will deliver you over to courts and flog you in their synagogues and you will be dragged before governors and kings for my sake, to bear witness before them and the Gentiles. When they deliver you over, do not be anxious how you are to speak or what you are to say, for what you are to say will be given to you in that hour. For it is not you who speak but the Spirit of your Father speaking through you. Brother will deliver brother over to death and the father his child and children will rise against parents and have them put to death and you will be hated by all for my name's sake. But the one who endures to the end will be saved. When they persecute you in one town, flee to the next, for truly, I say to you, you will not have gone through all the towns of Israel before the Son of Man comes.

Mark 13: 9-13 But be on your guard. For they will deliver you over to councils and you will be beaten in synagogues and you will stand before governors and kings for my sake, to bear witness before them. And the gospel must first be proclaimed to all nations. And when they bring you to trial and deliver you over, do not be anxious beforehand what you are to say, but say whatever is given you in that hour, for it is not you who speak, but the Holy Spirit. And brother will deliver brother over to death and the father his child and children will rise against parents and have them put to death. And you will be hated by all for my name's sake. But the one who endures to the end will be saved.

Matt 8: 19-22 {Scribe: Teacher, I will follow You wherever You go.} Foxes have holes and birds of the air have nests, but the Son of Man has nowhere to lay His head. {Another disciple: Lord, let me go first and bury my father.} Follow me and leave the dead to bury their own dead.

Luke 9: 58-62 Foxes have holes and birds of the air have nests, but the Son of Man has nowhere to lay His head. Follow me. Leave the dead to bury their own dead. But as for you, go and proclaim the kingdom of God. No one who puts his hand to the plow and looks back is fit for the kingdom of God.

Luke 22: 35-38 When I sent you out with no moneybag or knapsack or sandals, did you lack anything? But now let the one who has a moneybag take it and likewise a knapsack. And let the one who has no sword sell his cloak and buy one. For I tell you that this Scripture must be fulfilled in me: "And He was numbered with the transgressors." For what is written about me has its fulfillment. It is enough.

John 21: 15-19 Simon, son of John, do you love me more than these? {Peter: Yes, Lord; You know that I love You.} Feed my lambs. Simon, son of John, do you love me? {Yes, Lord;

You know that I love You.} Tend my sheep. Simon, son of John, do you love me? {Lord, You know everything; You know that I love You.} Feed my sheep. Truly, truly, I say to you, when you were young, you used to dress yourself and walk wherever you wanted, but when you are old, you will stretch out your hands and another will dress you and carry you where you do not want to go. Follow me.

John 21: 21-22 {Peter, about another disciple: Lord, what about this man?} If it is my will that he remain until I come, what is that to you? You follow me!

CHAPTER 3

AUTHORITY

My Overall Message:

Please consider adding to your journal what you determine to be Jesus' overall message on this topic.

Author's Overall Message:

Jesus was God Incarnate.

Luke 7: 22-23   {to John's disciples} Go and tell John what you have seen and heard: the blind receive their sight, the lame walk, lepers are cleansed and the deaf hear, the dead are raised up, the poor have good news preached to them. And blessed is the one who is not offended by me.

Matt 11: 3-6   {John's disciples: Are You the one who is to come, or shall we look for another?} Go and tell John what you hear and see: the blind receive their sight and the lame walk, lepers are cleansed and the deaf hear and the dead are raised up and the poor have good news preached to them. And blessed is the one who is not offended by me.

Luke 11: 17-23 Every kingdom divided against itself is laid waste and a divided household falls. And if Satan also is divided against himself, how will his kingdom stand? For you say that I cast out demons by Beelzebul. And if I cast out demons by Beelzebul, by whom do your sons cast them out? Therefore they will be your judges. But if it is by the finger of God that I cast out demons, then the kingdom of God has come upon you. When a strong man, fully armed, guards his own palace, his goods are safe; but when one stronger than he attacks him and overcomes him, he takes away his armour in which he trusted and divides his spoil. Whoever is not with me is against me and whoever does not gather with me scatters.

Matt 12: 25-32 Every kingdom divided against itself is laid waste and no city or house divided against itself will stand. And if Satan casts out Satan, he is divided against himself. How then will his kingdom stand? And if I cast out demons by Beelzebul, by whom do your sons cast them out? Therefore they will be your judges. But if it is by the Spirit of God that I cast out demons, then the kingdom of God has come upon you. Or how can someone enter a strong man's house and plunder his goods, unless he first binds up the strong man? Then indeed he may plunder his house. Whoever is not with me is against me and whoever does not gather with me scatters. Therefore I tell you, every sin and blasphemy will be forgiven people, but the blasphemy against the Spirit will not be forgiven. And whoever speaks a word against the Son of Man will be forgiven, but whoever speaks against the Holy Spirit will not be forgiven, either in this age of in the age to come.

Mark 3: 23-30 How can Satan cast out Satan? If a kingdom is divided against itself, that kingdom cannot stand. And if a house is divided against itself, that house will not be able to stand. And if Satan has risen up against himself and is divided, he cannot stand, but is coming to an end. But no one can enter a strong man's house and plunder his goods, unless he first binds the strong man. Then indeed he may plunder his house. Truly, I say to you, all sins will be forgiven the children of man and whatever blasphemies they utter, but whoever blasphemes against the Holy Spirit never has forgiveness, but is guilty of an eternal sin. {for they had said, "He has an unclean spirit."}

Mark 2: 5-11 My son, your sins are forgiven. Why do you question these things in your hearts? Which is easier, to say to the paralytic "Your sins are forgiven," or to say "Rise, take up your bed and walk"? But that you may know that the Son of Man has authority on earth to forgive sins - I say to you, rise, pick up your bed and go home.

Matt 9: 2-6 Take heart, my son; your sins are forgiven. Why do you think evil in your hearts? For which is easier, to say "Your sins are forgiven" or to say "Rise and walk"? But that you may know that the Son of Man has authority on earth to forgive sins – Rise, pick up your bed and go home.

Luke 5: 20-24 Man, your sins are forgiven you. Why do you question in your hearts? Which is easier, to say "Your sins are forgiven you" or to say "Rise and walk"? But that you may know that the Son of Man has authority on earth to forgive sins, I say to, rise, pick up your bed and go home.

John 14: 8-14 {Philip: Lord, show us the Father and it is enough for us.} Have I been with you so long and you still do not know me, Philip? Whoever has seen me has seen the Father. How can you say "Show us the Father"? Do you not believe that I am in the Father and the Father is in me? The words that I say to you I do not speak on my own authority, but the Father who dwells in me does His works. Believe me that I am in the Father and the Father is in me, or else believe on account of the works themselves. Truly, truly, I say to you, whoever believes in me will also do the works that I do; and greater works than these will he do, because I am going to the Father. Whatever you ask in my name, this I will do, that the Father may be glorified in the Son. If you ask me anything in my name, I will do it.

Mark 11: 29-33 I will ask you one question; answer me and I will tell you by what authority I do these things. Was the baptism of John from heaven or from man? Answer me. {If we say "From heaven." He will say "Why then did you not believe him?" But shall we say "From man."? – they were afraid of the people, for they all held that John really was a prophet. So they answered Jesus: "We do not know."} Neither will I tell you by what authority I do these things.

Luke 20: 3-8   I also will ask you a question. Now tell me, was the baptism of John from heaven or from man? {If we say "From heaven." He will say "Why did you not believe him?" But if we say "From man." all the people will stone us to death, for they are convinced that John was a prophet. So they answered that they did not know where it came from.} Neither will I tell you by what authority I do these things.

Matt 21: 24-27 I also will ask you one question and if you tell me the answer, then I also will tell you by what authority I do these things. The baptism of John, from where did it come? From heaven or from man? {Chief priests and elders: If we say "From heaven." He will say to us "Why then did you not believe him?" But if we say "From man." we are afraid of the crowd, for they all hold that John was a prophet. We do not know.} Neither will I tell you by what authority I do these things.

John 7: 16-24   My teaching is not mine, but His who sent me. If anyone's will is to do God's will, he will know whether the teaching is from God or whether I am speaking on my own authority. The one who speaks on his own authority seeks his own glory, but the one who seeks the glory of Him who sent Him is true and in Him there is no falsehood. Has not Moses given you the law? Yet none of you keeps the law. Why do you seek to kill me? {Crowd: You have a demon! Who is seeking to kill You?} I did one deed and you all marvel at it. Moses gave you circumcision (not that it is from Moses, but from the fathers) and you circumcise a man on the Sabbath. If on the Sabbath a man receives circumcision, so that the law of Moses may not be broken, are you angry with me because on the Sabbath I made a man's whole body well? Do not judge by appearances, but judge with right judgement.

John 5: 30-36   I can do nothing on my own. As I hear, I judge and my judgement is just, because I seek not my own will but the will of Him who sent me. If I alone bear witness about myself, my testimony is not deemed true. There is another who bears witness about me and I know that the testimony that He bears about me is true. You sent to John and he has borne witness to the truth. Not that the testimony that I receive is from man, but I say these things so that you may be saved. He was a burning and shining lamp and you were willing to rejoice for a while in his light. But the testimony that I have is greater than that of John. For the works that the Father has given me to accomplish, the very works that I am doing, bear witness about me that the Father has sent me.

John 9: 2-7   {Disciples: Rabbi, who sinned, this man or his parents, that he was born blind?} It was not that this man sinned or his parents, but that the works of God might be displayed in him. We must work the works of Him who sent me while it is day; night is coming when no one can work. As long as I am in the world, I am the light of the world. Go wash in the pool of Siloam.

John 4: 7-15   {to woman, drawing water} Give me a drink. {Woman: How is it that You, a Jew, ask for a drink from me, a woman of Samaria?} If you knew the gift of God and who it is that is saying to you "Give me a drink." you would have asked Him and He would have given you living water. {Woman: Sir, You have nothing to draw water with and the well is deep. Where do You get that living water? Are You greater than our father Jacob? He gave us the well and drank from it himself, as did his sons and his livestock.} Everyone who drinks of this water will be thirsty again, but whoever drinks of the water that I will give him will never be thirsty forever. The water that I will give him will become in him a spring of water welling up to eternal life. {Woman: Sir, give me this water, so that I will not be thirsty or have to come here to draw water.}

John 4: 16-26 Go, call your husband and come here. {Woman: I have no husband.} You are right in saying "I have no husband"; for you have had five husbands and the one you now have is not your husband. What you have said is true. {Woman: Sir, I perceive that You are a prophet. Our fathers worshiped on this mountain, but You say that in Jerusalem is the place where people ought to worship.} Woman, believe me, the hour is coming when neither on the mountain nor in Jerusalem will you worship the Father. You worship what you do not know; we worship what we know, for salvation is from the Jews. But the hour is coming and is now here, when the true worshipers will worship the Father in spirit and truth, for the Father is seeking such people to worship Him. God is spirit and those who worship Him must worship in spirit and truth. {Woman: I know that Messiah is coming (he who is called Christ). When He comes, He will tell us all things.} I who speak to you am He.

John 9: 35-38   Do you believe in the Son of Man? {Man who was blind: And who is he, sir that I may believe in him?} You have seen Him and it is He who is speaking to you. {Lord, I believe.}

John 5: 25-29   Truly, truly, I say to you, an hour is coming and is now here, when the dead will hear the voice of the Son of God and those who hear will live. For as the Father has life in Himself, so He has granted the Son also to have life in Himself. And He has given Him authority to execute judgement, because He is the Son of Man. Do not marvel at this, for an hour is coming when all who are in the tombs will hear His voice and come out, those who have done good to the resurrection of life and those who have done evil to the resurrection of judgement.

John 7: 25- 29   {People of Jerusalem: Is not this the man whom they seek to kill? And here He is, speaking openly and they say nothing to Him! Can it be that the authorities really know that this is the Christ? But we know where this man comes from and when the Christ appears, no one will know where He comes from.} You know me and you know where I come from? But I have not come of my own accord. He who sent me is true and Him you do not know. I know Him, for I come from Him and He sent me.

John 8: 12-19   I am the light of the world. Whoever follows me will not walk in darkness, but will have the light of life. {Pharisees: You are bearing witness about Yourself; Your testimony is not true.} Even if I do bear witness about myself, my testimony is true, for I know where I came from and where I am going, but you do not know where I come from or where I am going. You judge according to the flesh; I judge no one. Yet even if I do judge, my judgement is true, for it is not I alone who judge, but I and the Father who sent me. In your Law it is written that the testimony of two men is true. I am the one who bears witness about myself and the Father who sent me bears witness about me. {Pharisees: Where is Your Father?} You know neither me nor my Father. If you knew me, you would know my Father also.

John 8: 21-29   I am going away and you will seek me and you will die in your sin. Where I am going, you cannot come. {Jews: Will He kill Himself, since He says "Where I am going, you cannot come"?} You are from below; I am from above. You are of this world; I am not of this world. I told you that you would die in your sins, for unless you believe that I am He you will die in your sins. {Jews: Who are You?} Just what I have been telling you from the beginning. I have much to say about you and much to judge, but He who sent me is true and I declare to the world what I have heard from Him. When you have lifted up the Son of Man, then you will know that I am He and that I do nothing on my own authority, but speak just as the Father taught me. And He who sent me is with me. He has not left me alone, for I always do the things that are pleasing to Him.

John 8: 31-38   If you abide in my Word, you are truly my disciples and you will know the truth and truth will set you free. {Jews: We are offspring of Abraham and have never been enslaved to anyone. How is it that You say "You will become free."?} Truly, truly, I say to you, everyone who commits sin is a slave to sin. The slave does not remain in the house forever; the son remains forever. So if the Son sets you free, you will be free indeed. I know that you are offspring of Abraham; yet you seek to kill me because my Word finds no place in you. I speak of what I have seen with my Father and you do what you have heard from your father.

John 8: 48-58 {Jews: Are we not right in saying that You are a Samaritan and have a demon?} I do not have a demon, but I honour my Father and you dishonour me. Yet I do not seek my own glory, there is One who seeks it and He is the judge. Truly, truly, I say to you, if anyone keeps my Word, he will never see death. {Jews: Now we know that You have a demon! Abraham died, as did the prophets, yet You say "If anyone keeps my Word, he will never taste death." Are You greater than our father Abraham, who died? And the prophets died! Who do You make Yourself out to be?} If I glorify myself, my glory is nothing. It is my Father who glorifies me, of whom you say "He is our God." But you have not known Him. I know Him. If I were to say that I do not know Him, I would be a liar like you, but I do know Him and I keep His Word. Your father Abraham rejoiced that he would see my day. He saw it and was glad. {Jews: You are not yet fifty years old and have You seen Abraham?} Truly, truly, I say to you, before Abraham was, I AM.

John 18: 33-37 {Pilate: Are You the King of the Jews?} Do you say this of your own accord, or did others say it to you about me? {Pilate: Am I a Jew? Your own nation and the chief priests have delivered You over to me. What have You done?} My kingdom is not of the world. If my kingdom were of this world, my servants would have been fighting, that I might not be delivered over to the Jews. But my kingdom is not from the world. {Pilate: So You are a king?} You say that I am a king. For this purpose I was born and for this purpose I have come into the world - to bear witness to the truth. Everyone who is of the truth listens to my voice.

Luke 23: 3 {Are You the King of the Jews?} You have said so.

CHAPTER 4

CLOSE OF THE AGE

My Overall Message:

Please consider adding to your journal what you determine to be Jesus' overall message on this topic.

Author's Overall Message:

<u>I will be judged at the moment of my death as one of the few sheep or one of the many goats</u>. Because my death may occur at any moment, I must prepare now. To avoid being led astray I must test every idea against a *full* understanding of Jesus' teaching.

Matt 25: 31-36 When the Son of Man comes in His glory and all the angels with Him then He will sit on his glorious throne. Before Him will be gathered all the nations and He will separate people one from another as a shepherd separates the sheep from the goats. And He will place the sheep on His right, but the goats on the left. Then the King will say to those on His right "Come, you who are blessed by my Father, inherit the kingdom prepared for you from the foundation of the world. For I was hungry and you gave me food, I was thirsty and you gave me drink, I was a stranger and you welcomed me, I was naked and you clothed me, I was sick and you visited me, I was in prison and you came to me."

Matt 25: 37-40 Then the righteous will answer Him, saying "Lord, when did we see You hungry and feed You, or thirsty and give You drink? And when did we see You a stranger and welcome You, or naked and clothe You? And when did we see You sick or in prison and visit You?" And the King will answer them "Truly I say to you, as you did it to one of the least of these my brothers, you did it to me."

Matt 25: 41-46 Then He will say to those on His left "Depart from me, you cursed, into the eternal fire prepared for the devil and his angels, for I was hungry and you gave me no food, I was thirsty and you gave me no drink, I was a stranger and you did not welcome me, naked and you did not clothe me, sick and in prison and you did not visit me." Then they also will answer saying "Lord, when did we see You hungry or thirsty or a stranger or naked or sick or in prison and did not minister to You?" Then He will answer them, saying "Truly, I say to you, as you did not do it to one of the least of these, you did not do it to me." And they will go away into eternal punishment, but the righteous into eternal life.

Luke 13: 24-30 Strive to enter through the narrow door. For many, I tell you, will seek to enter and will not be able. When once the master of the house has risen and shut the door and you begin to stand outside and to knock at the door, saying "Lord, open to us," then He will answer you "I do not know where you come from." Then you will begin to say "We ate and drank in Your presence and You taught in our streets." But He will say "I tell you, I do not know where you come from. Depart from me, all you workers of evil!" In that place there will be weeping and gnashing of teeth, when you see Abraham and Isaac and Jacob and all the prophets in the kingdom of God but you yourselves cast out. And people will come from east and west and from north and south and recline at table in the kingdom of God. And behold, some are last who will be first and some are first who will be last.

Luke 21: 8-9 See that you are not led astray. For many will come in my name, saying "I am he!" and "The time is at hand!" Do not go after them. And when you hear of wars and tumults, do not be terrified, for these things must first take place, but the end will not be at once.

Matt 24: 36-44 But concerning that day and hour no one knows, not even the angels of heaven, nor the Son, but the Father only. As were the days of Noah, so will be the coming of the Son of Man. For as in those days before the flood they were eating and drinking, marrying and giving in marriage, until the day when Noah entered the ark and they were unaware until the flood came and swept them all away, so will be the coming of the Son of Man. Then two men will be in the field; one will be taken and one left. Two women will be grinding at the mill; one will be taken and one left. Therefore, stay awake, for you do not know on what day your Lord is coming. But know this that, if the master of the house had known in what part of the night the thief was coming, he would have stayed awake and would not have let his house be broken into. Therefore you also must be ready, for the Son of Man is coming at an hour you do not expect.

Mark 13: 32-37 But concerning that day or that hour, no one knows, not even the angels in heaven, nor the Son, but only the Father. Be on guard, keep awake. For you do not know when the time will come. It is like a man going on a journey, when he leaves home and puts his servants in charge, each with his work and commands the door-keeper to stay awake. Therefore stay awake - for you do not know when the master of the house will come, in the evening, or at midnight, or when the cock crows, or in the morning - lest he come suddenly and find you asleep. And what I say to you I say to all: Stay awake.

Matt 24: 3-14 {Disciples: Tell us, when will these things be, and what will be the sign of Your coming and of the close of the age?} See that no one leads you astray. For many will come in my name, saying "I am the Christ," and they will lead many astray. And you will hear of wars and rumours of wars. See that you are not alarmed, for this must take place, but the end is not yet. For nation will rise against nation and kingdom against kingdom and there will be famines and earthquakes in various places. All these are but the beginning of the birth pains. Then they will deliver you up to tribulation and put you to death and you will be hated by all nations for my name's sake. And then many will fall away and betray one another and hate one another. And many false prophets will arise and lead many astray. And because lawlessness will be increased the love of many will grow cold. But the one who endures to the end will be saved. And this gospel of the kingdom will be proclaimed throughout the whole world as a testimony to all nations and then the end will come.

Matt 24: 23-28 Then if anyone says to you "Look, here is the Christ!" or "There he is!" do not believe it. For false christs and false prophets will arise and perform great signs and wonders, so as to lead astray, if possible, even the elect. See, I have told you beforehand. So, if they say to you "Look, he is in the wilderness," do not go out. If they say "Look, he is in the inner rooms," do not believe it. For as the lightning comes from the east and shines as far as the west, so will be the coming of the Son of Man. Wherever the corpse is, there the vultures will gather.

Mark 13: 5-8 See that no one leads you astray. Many will come in my name, saying "I am he!" and they will lead many astray. And when you hear of wars and rumours of wars, do not be alarmed. This must take place, but the end is not yet. For nation will rise against nation and kingdom against kingdom. There will be earthquakes in various places; there will be famines. These are but the beginning of the birth pains.

Luke 12: 35-40 Stay dressed for action and keep your lamps burning and be like men who are waiting for their master to come home from the wedding feast, so that they may open the door to him at once when he comes and knocks. Blessed are those servants whom the master finds awake when he comes. Truly, I say to you, he will dress himself for service and have them recline at table and he will come and serve them. If he comes in the second watch, or in the third and finds them awake, blessed are those servants! But know this, that if the master of the house had known at what hour the thief was coming, he would not have left his house to be broken into. You also must be ready, for the Son of Man is coming at an hour you do not expect.

Luke 17: 20-27 The kingdom of God is not coming with signs to be observed nor will they say "Look, here it is!" or "There!" for behold, the kingdom of God is in the midst of you. The days are coming when you will desire to see one of the days of the Son of Man and you will not see it. And they will say to you "Look, there!" or "Look here!" Do not go out or follow them. For as the lightning flashes and lights up the sky from one side to the other so will the Son of Man be in His day. But first He must suffer many things and be rejected by this generation. Just as it was in the days of Noah, so will it be in the days of the Son of Man. They were eating and drinking and marrying and being given in marriage, until the day when Noah entered the ark and the flood came and destroyed them all.

Luke 17: 28-37 Likewise, just as it was in the days of Lot - they were eating and drinking, buying and selling, planting and building, but on the day when Lot went out from Sodom, fire and sulfur rained from heaven and destroyed them all – so will it be on the day when the Son of Man is revealed. On that day, let the one who is on the housetop, with his goods in the house, not come down to take them away and likewise let the one who is in the field not turn back. Remember Lot's wife. Whoever seeks to preserve his life will lose it, but whoever loses his life will keep it. I tell you, in that night there will be two in one bed. One will be taken and the other left. There will be two women grinding together. One will be taken and the other left. {Disciples: Where Lord?} Where the corpse is, there the vultures will gather.

Mark 13: 24-27 But in those days, after that tribulation, the sun will be darkened and the moon will not give its light and the stars will be falling from heaven and the powers in the heavens will be shaken. And then they will see the Son of Man coming in clouds with great power and glory. And then He will send out the angels and gather His elect from the four winds, from the ends of the earth to the ends of heaven.

Luke 21: 20-24 But when you see Jerusalem surrounded by armies, then know that its desolation has come near. Then let those who are in Judea flee to the mountains and let those who are inside the city depart and let not those who are out in the country enter it, for these are days of vengeance, to fulfill all that is written. Alas for women who are pregnant and for those who are nursing infants in those days! For there will be great distress upon the earth and wrath against this people. They will fall by the edge of the sword and be led captive among all nations and Jerusalem will be trampled underfoot by the Gentiles, until the times of the Gentiles are fulfilled.

Luke 21: 25-28 And there will be signs in sun and moon and stars and on the earth distress of nations in perplexity because of the roaring of the sea and the waves, people fainting with fear and with foreboding of what is coming on the world. For the powers of the heavens will be shaken. And then they will see the Son of Man coming in a cloud with power and great glory. Now when these things begin to take place, straighten up and raise your heads, because your redemption is drawing near.

Mark 13: 14-23 But when you see the abomination of desolation standing where it ought not to be (let the reader understand), then let those who are in Judea flee to the mountains. Let the one who is on the housetop not go down, nor enter his house, to take anything out and let the one who is in the field not turn back to take his cloak. And alas for women who are pregnant and for those who are nursing infants in those days! Pray that it may not happen in winter. For in those days there will be such tribulation as has not been from the beginning of the creation that God created until now and never will be. And if the Lord had not cut short the days, no human being would be saved. But for the sake of the elect, whom He chose, He shortened the days. And then if anyone says to you "Look, here is the Christ!" or "Look, there he is!" do not believe it. False christs and false prophets will arise and perform signs and wonders, to lead astray, if possible, the elect. But be on guard; I have told you all things beforehand.

Matt 24: 15-31 So when you see the abomination of desolation spoken of by the prophet Daniel, standing in the holy place (let the reader understand), then let those who are in Judea flee to the mountains. Let the one who is on the house top not go down to take what is in his house and let the one who is in the field not run back to take his cloak. And alas for women who are pregnant and for those who are nursing infants in those days! Pray that your flight may not be in winter or on a Sabbath. For then there will be great tribulation, such as has not been from the beginning of the world until now, no and never will be. And if those days had not been cut short, no human being would be saved. But for the sake of the elect those days will be cut short. Then if anyone says to you "Look, here is the Christ!" or "There he is!" do not believe it. For false christs and false prophets will arise and perform great signs and wonders so as to lead astray, if possible, even the elect. See, I have told you beforehand. So, if they say to you "Look, he is in the wilderness", do not go out. If they say "Look he is in the inner rooms" do not believe it. For as the lightning comes from the east and shines as far as the west, so will be the coming of the Son of Man. Wherever the corpse is, there the vultures will gather. Immediately after the tribulation of those days the sun will be darkened, and the moon will not give its light, and the stars will fall from heaven, and the powers of the heavens will be shaken. Then will appear in heaven the sign of the Son of Man, and then all the tribes of the earth will mourn, and they will see the Son of Man coming on the clouds of heaven with power and great glory. And he will send out his angels with a loud trumpet call, and they will gather his elect from the four winds, from one end of heaven to the other.

Luke 21: 29-36 Look at the fig tree and all the trees. As soon as they come out in leaf, you see for yourselves and know that the summer is already near. So also, when you see these things taking place, you know that the kingdom of God is near. Truly, I say to you, this generation will not pass away until all has taken place. Heaven and earth will pass away, but my words will not pass away. But watch yourselves lest your hearts be weighed down with dissipation and drunkenness and cares of this life and that day come upon you suddenly like a trap. For it will come upon all who dwell on the face of the whole earth. But stay awake at all times, praying that you may have strength to escape all these things that are going to take place, and to stand before the Son of Man.

Matt 24: 32-35 From the fig tree learn its lesson: as soon as its branch becomes tender and puts out its leaves, you know that summer is near. So also, when you see all these things, you know that He is near, at the very gates. Truly, I say to you, this generation will not pass away until all these things take place. Heaven and earth will pass away, but my words will not pass away.

Mark 13: 28-31 From the fig tree learn its lesson: as soon as its branch becomes tender and puts out its leaves, you know that summer is near. So also, when you see all these things taking place, you know that He is near, at the very gates. Truly, I say to you, this generation will not pass away until all these things take place. Heaven and earth will pass away, but my words will not pass away.

Matt 24: 45-51 Who then is the faithful and wise servant, whom his master has set over his household, to give them their food at the proper time? Blessed is that servant whom his master will find so doing when he comes. Truly, I say to you, he will set him over all his possessions. But if that wicked servant says to himself "My master is delayed," and begins to beat his fellow servants and eats and drinks with drunkards, the master of that servant will come on a day when he does not expect him and at an hour he does not know and will cut him in pieces and put him with the hypocrites. In that place, there will be weeping and gnashing of teeth.

Luke 12: 42-46 Who then is the faithful and wise manager, whom his master will set over his household, to give them their portion of food at the proper time? Blessed is that servant whom his master will find so doing when he comes. Truly, I say to you, he will set him over all his possessions. But if that servant says to himself "My master is delayed in coming," and begins to beat the male and female servants and to eat and drink and get drunk, the master of that servant will come on a day when he does not expect him and at an hour he does not know and will cut him in pieces and put him with the unfaithful.

Luke 12: 47-48 And that servant who knew his master's will but did not get ready or act according to his will, will receive a severe beating. But the one who did not know and did what deserved a beating, will receive a light beating. Everyone to whom much is given, of him much will be required and from him to whom they entrusted much, they will demand the more.

Matt 24: 2 {to his disciples, pointing out the buildings of the temple} You see all these, do you not? Truly, I say to you, there will not be left here one stone upon another that will not be thrown down.

CHAPTER 5

GUIDANCE

My Overall Message:

Please consider adding to your journal what you determine to be Jesus' overall message on this topic.

Author's Overall Message:

I must continuously strive to approach God's standard of perfection and pray for God's forgiveness and help each time I fall short. <u>I must love my enemies</u>, do good rather than look good <u>and use my gifts to help those who cannot repay me</u>.

Matt 5: 43-48 You have heard that it was said "You shall love your neighbor and hate your enemy." But I say to you, Love your enemies and pray for those who persecute you, so that you may be sons of your Father who is in heaven. For He makes His sun rise on the evil and on the good and sends rain on the just and on the unjust. For if you love those who love you, what reward do you have? Do not even the tax collectors do the same? And if you greet only your brothers, what more are you doing than others? Do not even the Gentiles do the same? You therefore must be perfect, as your heavenly Father is perfect.

Luke 18: 10-14 Two men went up into the temple to pray, one a Pharisee and the other a tax collector. The Pharisee, standing by himself, prayed thus: "God, I thank you that I am not like other men, extortioners, unjust, adulterers, or even like this tax collector. I fast twice a week, I give tithes of all that I get." But the tax collector, standing far off, would not even lift up his eyes to heaven, but beat his breast, saying "God, be merciful to me, a sinner!" I tell you, this man went down to his house justified, rather than the other. For everyone who exalts himself will be humbled, but the one who humbles himself will be exalted.

Luke 6: 32-36 If you love those who love you, what benefit is that to you? For even sinners love those who love them. And if you do good to those who do good to you, what benefit is that to you? For even sinners do the same. And if you lend to those from whom you expect to receive, what credit is that to you? Even sinners lend to sinners, to get back the same amount. But love your enemies and do good and lend, expecting nothing in return and your reward will be great and you will be sons of the Most High, for He is kind to the ungrateful and the evil. Be merciful, even as your Father is merciful.

Luke 10: 30-37 A man was going down from Jerusalem to Jericho and he fell among robbers, who stripped him and beat him and departed, leaving him half dead. Now by chance a priest was going down that road, and when he saw him he passed by on the other side. So likewise a Levite, when he came to the place and saw him, passed by on the other side. But a Samaritan, as he journeyed, came to where he was, and when he saw him, he had compassion. He went to him and bound up his wounds, pouring on oil and wine. Then he set him on his own animal and brought him to an inn and took care of him. And the next day he took out two denarii and gave them to the innkeeper, saying "Take care of him and whatever more you spend, I will repay you when I come back." Which of these three, do you think proved to be a neighbour to the man who fell among the robbers? {The one who showed him mercy.} You go and do likewise.

Luke 6: 27-31 But I say to you who hear, Love your enemies, do good to those who hate you, bless those who curse you, pray for those who abuse you. To one who strikes you on the cheek, offer the other also. And from one who takes away your cloak do not withhold your tunic either. Give to everyone who begs from you and from one who takes away your goods do not demand them back. And as you wish that others would do to you, do so to them.

Matt 5: 21-26 You have heard that it was said to those of old "You shall not murder; and whoever murders will be liable to judgement." But I say to you that everyone who is angry with his brother will be liable to judgement; whoever insults his brother will be liable to the council and whoever says "You fool!" will be liable to the hell of fire. So if you are offering your gift at the altar and there remember that your brother has something against you, leave your gift there before the altar and go. First be reconciled to your brother and then come and offer your gift. Come to terms quickly with your accuser while you are going with him to court, lest your accuser hand you over to the judge and the judge to the guard and you be put in prison. Truly, I say to you, you will never get out until you have paid the last penny.

Luke 12: 57-59 And why do you not judge for yourselves what is right? As you go with your accuser before the magistrate, make an effort to settle with him on the way, lest he drag you to the judge and the judge hand you over to the officer and the officer put you in prison. I tell you, you will never get out until you have paid the very last penny.

Matt 5: 27-30 You have heard that it was said "You shall not commit adultery." But I say to you that everyone who looks at a woman with lustful intent has already committed adultery with her in his heart. If your right eye causes you to sin, tear it out and throw it away. For it is better that you lose one of your members than that your whole body be thrown into hell. And if your right hand causes you to sin, cut it off and throw it away. For it is better that you lose one of your members than that your whole body go into hell.

Matt 5: 38-42 You have heard that it was said "An eye for an eye and a tooth for a tooth." But I say to you, Do not resist the one who is evil. But if anyone slaps you on the right cheek, turn to him the other also. And if anyone would sue you and take your tunic, let him have your cloak as well. And if anyone forces you to go one mile, go with him two miles. Give to the one who begs from you and do not refuse the one who would borrow from you.

Matt 6: 1-4   Beware of practicing your righteousness before other people in order to be seen by them, for then you will have no reward from your Father who is in heaven. Thus, when you give to the needy, sound no trumpet before you, as the hypocrites do in the synagogues and in the streets, that they may be praised by others. Truly, I say to you, they have received their reward. But when you give to the needy, do not let your left hand know what your right hand is doing, so that your giving may be in secret. And your Father who sees in secret will reward you.

Matt 6: 16-18   And when you fast, do not look gloomy like the hypocrites, for they disfigure their faces that their fasting may be seen by others. Truly, I say to you, they have received their reward. But when you fast, anoint your head and wash your face that your fasting may not be seen by others but by your Father who is in secret. And your Father who sees in secret will reward you.

Matt 6: 5-8   And when you pray, you must not be like the hypocrites. For they love to stand and pray in the synagogues and at the street corners, that they may be seen by others. Truly, I say to you, they have received their reward. But when you pray, go into your room and shut the door and pray to your Father who is in secret. And your Father who sees in secret will reward you. And when you pray, do not heap up empty phrases as the Gentiles do, for they think that they will be heard for their many words. Do not be like them, for your Father knows what you need before you ask Him.

Matt 6: 9-15   Pray then like this "Our Father in heaven, hallowed be Your name. Your kingdom come, Your will be done, on earth as it is in heaven. Give us this day our daily bread and forgive us our debts, as we also have forgiven our debtors. And lead us not into temptation, but deliver us from evil." For if you forgive others their trespasses, your heavenly Father will also forgive you, but if you do not forgive others their trespasses, neither will your Father forgive your trespasses.

Luke 11: 2-4   When you pray, say: "Father, hallowed be Your name. Your kingdom come. Give us each day our daily bread and forgive us our sins, for we ourselves forgive everyone who is indebted to us. And lead us not into temptation."

Luke 14: 8-11 When you are invited by someone to a wedding feast, do not sit down in a place of honour, lest someone more distinguished than you be invited by him and he who invited you both will come and say to you "Give your place to this person" and then you will begin with shame to take the lowest place. But when you are invited, go and sit in the lowest place, so that when your host comes he may say to you "Friend, move up higher." Then you will be honoured in the presence of all who sit at table with you. For everyone who exalts himself will be humbled and he who humbles himself will be exalted.

Luke 14: 12-14 When you give a dinner or a banquet, do not invite your friends or your brothers or your relatives or rich neighbours, lest they also invite you in return and you be repaid. But when you give a feast, invite the poor, the crippled, the lame, the blind and you will be blessed, because they cannot repay you. You will be repaid at the resurrection of the just.

Luke 16: 1-8 There was a rich man who had a manager and charges were brought to him that this man was wasting his possessions. And he called him and said to him "What is this that I hear about you? Turn in the account of your management, for you can no longer be my manager." And the manager said to himself "What shall I do, since my master is taking the management away from me? I am not strong enough to dig and I am ashamed to beg. I have decided what to do, so that when I am removed from management, people may receive me into their houses." So, summoning his master's debtors one by one, he said to the first "How much do you owe my master?" He said, "A hundred measures of oil." He said to him "Take your bill and sit down quickly and write fifty." Then he said to another "And how much do you owe?" He said, "A hundred measures of wheat." He said to him "Take your bill and write eighty." The master commended the dishonest manager for his shrewdness. For the sons of this world are more shrewd in dealing with their own generation than the sons of light.

Luke 16: 9-13 And I tell you, make friends for yourselves by means of unrighteous wealth, so that when it fails they may receive you into the eternal dwellings. One who is faithful in a very little is also faithful in much and one who is dishonest in a very little is also dishonest in much. If then you have not been faithful in the unrighteous wealth, who will entrust to you the true riches? And if you have not been faithful in that which is another's who will give you that which is your own? No servant can serve two masters, for either he will hate the one and love the other, or he will be devoted to the one and despise the other. You cannot serve God and money.

Luke 17: 1-2 Temptations to sin are sure to come, but woe to the one through whom they come! It would be better for him if a millstone were hung around his neck and he were cast into the sea than that he should cause one of these little ones to sin.

Mark 9: 42-50 Whoever causes one of these little ones who believe in me to sin, it would be better for him if a great millstone were hung around his neck and he were thrown into the sea. And if your hand causes you to sin, cut it off. It is better for you to enter life crippled than with two hands to go to hell, to the unquenchable fire. And if your foot causes you to sin, cut it off. It is better for you to enter life lame than with two feet to be thrown into hell. And if your eye causes you to sin, tear it out. It is better for you to enter the kingdom of God with one eye than with two eyes to be thrown into hell ". . . where the worm does not die and the fire is not quenched." For everyone will be salted with fire. Salt is good, but if the salt has lost its saltiness, how will you make it salty again? Have salt in yourselves and be at peace with one another.

Matt 18: 15-20 If your brother sins against you, go and tell him his fault, between you and him alone. If he listens to you, you have gained your brother. But if he does not listen, take one or two others along with you, that every charge may be established by the evidence of two or three witnesses. If he refuses to listen to them, tell it to the church. And if he refuses to listen even to the church let him be to you as a Gentile and a tax collector. Truly, I say to you, whatever

41

you bind on earth shall be bound in heaven and whatever you loose on earth shall be loosed in heaven. Again I say to you, if two of you agree on earth about anything they ask, it will be done for them by my Father in heaven. For where two or three are gathered in my name, there am I among them.

Luke 17: 3-4 Pay attention to yourselves! If your brother sins, rebuke him and if he repents, forgive him and if he sins against you seven times in one day and turns to you seven times, saying "I repent," you must forgive him.

Matt 11: 25-30 I thank You, Father, Lord of heaven and earth, that You have hidden these things from the wise and understanding and revealed them to little children; yes, Father, for such was Your gracious will. All things have been handed over to me by my Father and no one knows the Son except the Father and no one knows the Father except the Son and anyone to whom the Son chooses to reveal Him. Come to me, all who labour and are heavy laden and I will give you rest. Take my yoke upon you and learn from me, for I am gentle and lowly in heart and you will find rest for your souls. For my yoke is easy and my burden is light.

CHAPTER 6

FAITH

My Overall Message:

Please consider adding to your journal what you determine to be Jesus' overall message on this topic.

Author's Overall Message:

I must grow my faith in my prayers for God's help in accomplishing whatever Jesus demands of me.

Mark 7: 27-29   {to the Syrophoenician woman begging to have the demon cast out of her daughter} Let the children be fed first, for it is not right to take the children's bread and throw it to the dogs. {Woman: Yes, Lord; yet even the dogs under the table eat the children's crumbs.} For this statement you may go your way; the demon has left your daughter.

Matt 15: 24-28   I was sent only to the lost sheep of the house of Israel. It is not right to take the children's bread and throw it to the dogs. O, woman, great is your faith! Be it done for you as you desire.

Luke 8: 45-48   Who was it that touched me? Someone touched me for I perceive that power has gone out from me. Daughter, your faith has made you well; go in peace.

Mark 5: 30-34   Who touched my garments? Daughter, your faith has made you well; go in peace and be healed of your disease.

Matt 9: 21-22   {Woman: If I only touch His garment, I will be made well.} Take heart, daughter; your faith has made you well.

Matt 9: 18-24   {Ruler: My daughter has just died, but come and lay Your hand on her and she will live.} Go away, for the girl is not dead, but sleeping.

Mark 5: 36-41   Do not fear, only believe. Why are you making a commotion and weeping? The child is not dead but sleeping. Talitha cumi (Little girl, I say to you, arise).

Luke 8: 50-54   Do not fear; only believe and she will be well. Do not weep, for she is not dead but sleeping. Child arise.

Mark 10: 51-52 What do you want me to do for you? {Rabbi, let me recover my sight.} Go your way; your faith has made you well.

Luke 18: 41-42   What do you want me to do for you? Recover your sight; your faith has made you well.

Matt 9: 28-30   {Blind men: Have mercy on us, Son of David.} Do you believe that I am able to do this? According to your faith be it done to you. See that no one knows about it.

Mark 1: 40-44   {Leper: If You will, You can make me clean.} I will; be clean. See that you say nothing to anyone, but go, show yourself to the priest and offer for your cleansing what Moses commanded, for a proof to them.

Matt 8: 2-4   {Leper: Lord, if You will, You can make me clean.} I will; be clean. See that you say nothing to anyone, but go, show yourself to the priest and offer the gift that Moses commanded, for a proof to them.

Luke 9: 41   {when disciples could not heal} O faithless and twisted generation, how long am I to be with you and bear with you? Bring your son here.

Mark 4: 35-40   Let us go across to the other side. {Disciples, after waking Him during a storm: Teacher, do You not care that we are perishing?} Peace! Be still! Why are you so afraid? Have you still no faith?

Matt 8: 25-26 {Save us, Lord; we are perishing.} Why are you afraid, O you of little faith?

Luke 8: 25 {as the boat was being swamped} Where is your faith?

Luke 5: 4-5 Put out into the deep and let down your nets for a catch. {Simon: Master, we toiled all night and took nothing! But at Your word I will let down the nets.}

Mark 11: 14-25 {finding a fig tree with nothing but leaves} May no one ever eat fruit from you again. {Peter, remembering next day: Rabbi, look! The fig tree that You cursed has withered.} Have faith in God. Truly, I say to you, whoever says to this mountain "Be taken up and thrown into the sea," and does not doubt in his heart, but believes that what he says will come to pass, it will be done for him. Therefore I tell you, whatever you ask in prayer, believe that you have received it and it will be yours. And whenever you stand praying, forgive, if you have anything against anyone, so that your Father also who is in heaven may forgive you your trespasses.

Matt 21: 19-22 {Jesus, hungry and finding a tree with no figs} May no fruit ever come from you again! {Disciples: How did the fig tree wither at once?} Truly I say to you, if you have faith and do not doubt, you will not only do what has been done to the fig tree, but even if you say to this mountain "Be taken up and thrown into the sea," it will happen. And whatever you ask in prayer, you will receive, if you have faith.

Luke 17: 6 If you had faith like a grain of mustard seed, you could say to this mulberry tree "Be uprooted and planted in the sea," and it would obey you.

Luke 18: 2-8 In a certain city there was a judge who neither feared God nor respected man. And there was a widow in that city who kept coming to him and saying "Give me justice against my adversary." For a while he refused, but afterward he said to himself "Though I neither fear God nor respect man, yet because this widow keeps bothering me, I will give her justice, so that she will not beat me down by her continual coming." Hear what the unrighteous judge says. And will not God give justice to His elect, who cry to Him day and night? Will He delay long over them? I tell you, He will give justice to them speedily. Nevertheless, when the Son of Man comes, will He find faith on earth?

John 16: 23-27 Truly, truly, I say to you, whatever you ask of the Father in my name, He will give it to you. Until now you have asked nothing in my name. Ask and you will receive, that your joy may be full. I have said these things to you in figures of speech. The hour is coming when I will no longer speak to you in figures of speech but will tell you plainly about the Father. In that day you will ask in my name, and I do not say to you that I will ask the Father on your behalf; for the Father Himself loves you, because you have loved me and have believed that I came from God.

CHAPTER 7

KINGDOM OF GOD

My Overall Message:

Please consider adding to your journal what you determine to be Jesus' overall message on this topic.

Author's Overall Message:

<u>Eternal life with God is far beyond what I can imagine and to realize it, I must respond to His invitation and adequately prepare for it</u> in order to be judged ready to attain it.

Matt 13: 31-32 The kingdom of heaven is like a grain of mustard seed that a man took and sowed in his field. It is the smallest of all seeds, but when it has grown it is larger than all the garden plants and becomes a tree, so that the birds of the air come and make nests in its branches.

Mark 4: 30-32 With what can we compare the kingdom of God, or what parable shall we use for it? It is like a grain of mustard seed, which, when sown on the ground, is the smallest of all the seeds on earth, yet when it is sown it grows up and becomes larger than all the garden plants and puts out large branches, so that the birds of the air can make nests in its shade.

Luke 13: 18-20 What is the kingdom of God like? And to what shall I compare it? It is like a grain of mustard seed that a man took and sowed in his garden and it grew and became a tree and the birds of the air made nests in its branches. To what shall I compare the kingdom of God? It is like leaven that a woman took and hid in three measures of flour, until it was all leavened.

Matt 13: 33   The kingdom of heaven is like leaven that a woman took and hid in three measures of flour, till it was all leavened.

Matt 13: 44   The kingdom of heaven is like treasure hidden in a field, which a man found and covered up. Then in his joy he goes and sells all that he has and buys that field.

Matt 13: 45-46   Again, the kingdom of heaven is like a merchant in search of fine pearls, who, on finding one pearl of great value, went and sold all that he had and bought it.

Luke 14: 16-24   A man once gave a great banquet and invited many. And at the time for the banquet he sent his servants to say to those who had been invited "Come, for everything is now ready." But they all alike began to make excuses. The first said to him "I have bought a field and I must go out and see it. Please have me excused." And another said, "I have bought five yoke of oxen and I go to examine them. Please have me excused." And another said, "I have married a wife and therefore I cannot come." So the servant came and reported these things to his master. Then the master of the house became angry and said to his servant "Go out quickly to the streets and lanes of the city and bring in the poor and crippled and blind and lame." And the servant said, "Sir, what you commanded has been done and still there is room." And the master said to the servant "Go out to the highways and hedges and compel people to come in, that my house may be filled. For I tell you, none of those men who were invited shall taste my banquet."

Matt 22: 2-7   The kingdom of heaven may be compared to a king who gave a wedding feast for his son and sent his servants to call those who were invited to the wedding feast, but they would not come. Again he sent other servants, saying "Tell those who are invited, See, I have prepared my dinner, my oxen and my fat calves have been slaughtered and everything is ready. Come to the wedding feast." But they paid no attention and went off, one to his farm another to his business, while the rest seized his servants, treated them shamefully and killed them. The king was angry and he sent his troops and destroyed those murderers and burned their city.

Matt 22: 8-14 Then he said to his servants "The wedding feast is ready, but those invited were not worthy. Go therefore to the main roads and invite to the wedding feast as many as you find." And those servants went out into the roads and gathered all whom they found, both bad and good. So the wedding hall was filled with guests. But when the king came in to look at the guests, he saw there a man who had no wedding garment. And he said to him "Friend, how did you get in here without a wedding garment?" And he was speechless. Then the king said to the attendants "Bind him hand and foot and cast him into the outer darkness. In that place there will be weeping and gnashing of teeth." For many are called, but few are chosen.

Matt 13: 24-30 The kingdom of heaven may be compared to a man who sowed good seed in his field, but while his men were sleeping, his enemy came and sowed weeds among the wheat and went away. So when the plants came up and bore grain then the weeds appeared also. And the servants of the master of the house came and said to him "Master, did you not sow good seed in your field? How then does it have weeds?" He said to them "An enemy has done this." So the servants said to him "Then do you want us to go and gather them?" But he said, "No, lest in gathering the weeds you root up the wheat along with them. Let both grow together until the harvest and at harvest time I will tell the reapers, Gather the weeds first and bind them in bundles to be burned, but gather the wheat into my barn."

Matt 13: 37-43 The one who sows the good seed is the Son of Man. The field is the world and the good seed is the children of the kingdom. The weeds are the sons of the evil one and the enemy who sowed them is the devil. The harvest is the close of the age and the reapers are angels. Just as the weeds are gathered and burned with fire, so will it be at the close of the age. The Son of Man will send His angels and they will gather out of His kingdom all causes of sin and all law-breakers and throw them into the fiery furnace. In that place there will be weeping and gnashing of teeth. Then the righteous will shine like the sun in the kingdom of their Father. He who has ears, let him hear.

Matt 13: 47-50 Again, the kingdom of heaven is like a net that was thrown into the sea and gathered fish of every kind. When it was full, men drew it ashore and sat down and sorted the good into containers but threw away the bad. So it will be at the close of the age. The angels will come out and separate the evil from the righteous and throw them into the fiery furnace. In that place there will be weeping and gnashing of teeth.

Mark 4: 26-29 The kingdom of God is as if a man should scatter seed on the ground. He sleeps and rises night and day and the seed sprouts and grows; he knows not how. The earth produces by itself, first the blade, then the ear, then the full grain in the ear. But when the grain is ripe, at once he puts in the sickle, because the harvest has come.

Matt 20: 1-8 For the kingdom of heaven is like a master of a house who went out early in the morning to hire labourers for his vineyard. After agreeing with the labourers for a denarius a day, he sent them into his vineyard. And going out about the third hour he saw others standing idle in the market place and to them he said, "You go into the vineyard too and whatever is right I will give you." So they went. Going out again about the sixth hour and the ninth hour, he did the same. And about the eleventh hour he went out and found others standing. And he said to them "Why do you stand here idle all day?" They said to him "Because no one has hired us." He said to them "You go into the vineyard too." And when evening came, the owner of the vineyard said to his foreman "Call the labourers and pay them their wages, beginning with the last, up to the first."

Matt 20: 9-16   And when those hired about the eleventh hour came, each of them received a denarius. Now when those hired first came, they thought they would receive more but each of them also received a denarius. And on receiving it they grumbled at the master of the house, saying "These last worked only one hour and you have made them equal to us who have borne the burden of the day and the scorching heat." But he replied to one of them "Friend, I am doing you no wrong. Did you not agree with me for a denarius? Take what belongs to you and go. I choose to give to this last worker as I give to you. Am I not allowed to do what I choose with what belongs to me? Or do you begrudge my generosity?" So the last will be first and the first last.

Matt 25: 1-13   Then the kingdom of heaven will be like ten virgins who took their lamps and went to meet the bridegroom. Five of them were foolish and five were wise. For when the foolish took their lamps, they took no oil with them, but the wise took flasks of oil with their lamps. As the bridegroom was delayed, they all became drowsy and slept. But at midnight there was a cry "Here is the bridegroom! Come out to meet him." Then all those virgins rose and trimmed their lamps. And the foolish said to the wise "Give us some of your oil, for our lamps are going out." But the wise answered, saying "Since there will not be enough for us and for you, go rather to the dealers and buy for yourselves." And while they were going to buy, the bridegroom came and those who were ready went in with him to the marriage feast and the door was shut. Afterward the other virgins came also, saying "Lord, lord, open to us." But he answered, "Truly, I say to you, I do not know you." Watch therefore, for you know neither the day nor the hour.

Matt 13: 51-52 Have you understood all these things? Therefore every scribe who has been trained for the kingdom of heaven is like a master of a house who brings out of his treasure what is new and what is old.

CHAPTER 8

LAWS

My Overall Message:

Please consider adding to your journal what you determine to be Jesus' overall message on this topic.

Author's Overall Message:

I must increase _my_ righteousness by following God's laws and avoid judgement of others.

Matt 12: 11-13   Which one of you who has a sheep, if it falls into a pit on the Sabbath, will not take hold of it and lift it out? Of how much more value is a man than a sheep! So it is lawful to do good on the Sabbath. Stretch out your hand.

Mark 3: 3-5   {to a man with a withered hand} Come here. {to the Pharisees} Is it lawful on the Sabbath to do good or to do harm, to save life or to kill? {angry at their hardness of heart} Stretch out your hand.

Luke 6: 8-10   Come and stand here. {to the Pharisees} I ask you, is it lawful on the Sabbath to do good or to do harm, to save life or to destroy it? Stretch out your hand.

Luke 13: 15-16   You hypocrites! Does not each of you on the Sabbath untie his ox or his donkey from the manger and lead it away to water it? And ought not this woman, a daughter of Abraham whom Satan bound for eighteen years, be loosed from this bond on the Sabbath day?

Luke 14: 3-5   Is it lawful to heal on the Sabbath or not? Which of you, having a son or an ox that has fallen into a well on a Sabbath day, will not immediately pull him out?

Matt 12: 3-8   Have you not read what David did when he was hungry and those who were with him: how he entered the house of God and ate the bread of the Presence, which it was not lawful for him to eat nor for those who were with him, but only for the priests? Or have you not read in the Law how on the Sabbath the priests in the temple profane the Sabbath and are guiltless? I tell you, something greater than the temple is here. And if you had known what this means "I desire mercy and not sacrifice," you would not have condemned the guiltless. For the Son of Man is lord of the Sabbath.

Mark 2: 25-28   Have you never read what David did, when he was in need and was hungry, he and those who were with him: how he entered the house of God, in the time of Abiathar the high priest and ate the bread of the Presence, which it is not lawful for any but the priests to eat and also gave it to those who were with him? The Sabbath was made for man, not man for the Sabbath. So the Son of Man is lord even of the Sabbath.

Luke 6: 3-5   Have you not read what David did when he was hungry, he and those who were with him: how he entered the house of God and took and ate the bread of the Presence, which is not lawful for any but the priests to eat and also gave it to those with him? The Son of man is lord of the Sabbath.

Matt 15: 3-9   And why do you break the commandment of God for the sake of your tradition? For God commanded "Honour your father and your mother," and "Whoever reviles father or mother must surely die." But you say "If anyone tells his father or his mother, what you would have gained from me is given to God, he need not honour his father." So for the sake of your tradition you have made void the Word of God. You hypocrites! Well did Isaiah prophesy of you, when he said: "This people honours me with their lips, but their heart is far from me; in vain do they worship me, teaching as doctrines the commandments of men."

Mark 7: 5-13 {Pharisees: Why do Your disciples not walk according to the tradition of the elders, but eat with defiled hands?} Well did Isaiah prophesy of you hypocrites, as it is written "This people honours me with their lips, but their heart is far from me; in vain do they worship me, teaching as doctrines the commandments of men." You leave the commandment of God and hold to the tradition of men. You have a fine way of rejecting the commandment of God in order to establish your tradition! For Moses said "Honour your father and your mother," and "Whoever reviles father or mother must surely die." But you say "If a man tells his father or his mother, Whatever you would have gained from me is Corban" (that is, given to God) - then you no longer permit him to do anything for his father or mother, thus making void the Word of God by your tradition that you have handed down. And many such things you do.

Matt 15: 10-20 Hear and understand: it is not what goes into the mouth that defiles a person, but what comes out of the mouth; this defiles a person. Every plant that my heavenly Father has not planted will be rooted up. Let them alone; they are blind guides. And if the blind lead the blind, both will fall into a pit. Are you also still without understanding? Do you not see that whatever goes into the mouth passes into the stomach and is expelled? But what comes out of the mouth proceeds from the heart and this defiles a person. For out of the heart come evil thoughts, murder, adultery, sexual immorality, theft, false witness, slander. These are what defile a person. But to eat with unwashed hands does not defile anyone.

Mark 7: 14-23 Hear me, all of you and understand: There is nothing out-side a person that by going into him can defile him, but the things that come out of a person are what defile him. {to the disciples questions} Then are you also without understanding? Do you not see that whatever goes into a person from outside cannot defile him, since it enters not his heart but his stomach and is expelled? What comes out of a person is what defiles him. For from within, out of the heart of man, come evil thoughts, sexual immorality, theft, murder, adultery, coveting, wickedness, deceit, sensuality, envy, slander, pride, foolishness. All these evil things come from within and they defile a person.

Luke 16: 15-18 You are those who justify yourselves before men, but God knows your hearts. For what is exalted among men is an abomination in the sight of God. The Law and the Prophets were until John; since then the good news of the kingdom of God is preached and everyone forces his way into it. But it is easier for heaven and earth to pass away than for one dot of the Law to become void. Everyone who divorces his wife and marries another commits adultery and he who marries a woman divorced from her husband commits adultery.

Matt 5: 17-20 Do not think that I have come to abolish the Law of the Prophets; I have not come to abolish them but to fulfill them. For truly, I say to you, until heaven and earth pass away, not an iota, not a dot, will pass from the Law until all is accomplished. Therefore whoever relaxes one of the least of these commandments and teaches others to do the same will be called least in the kingdom of heaven, but whoever does them and teaches them will be called great in the kingdom of heaven. For I tell you, unless your righteousness exceeds that of the scribes and Pharisees, you will never enter the kingdom of heaven.

John 8: 7-11 Let him who is without sin among you be the first to throw a stone at her. Woman, where are they? Has no one condemned you? {Woman: No one, Lord.} Neither do I condemn you; go and from now on sin no more.

Matt 22: 18-21 Why put me to the test, you hypocrites? Show me the coin for the tax. Whose likeness and inscription is this?

{Caesar's.} Therefore render to Caesar the things that are Caesar's and to God the things that are God's.

Luke 20: 24-25 Show me a denarius. Whose likeness and inscription does it have? {Caesar's.} Then render to Caesar the things that are Caesar's and to God the things that are God's.

Mark 12: 15-17 Why put me to the test? Bring me a denarius and let me look at it. Whose likeness and inscription is this? {Caesar's.} Render to Caesar the things that are Caesar's and to God the things that are God's.

Matt 17: 25-27 What do you think, Simon? From whom do kings of the earth take toll or tax? From their sons or from others? {Peter: From others.} Then the sons are free. However, not to give offense to them, go to the sea and cast a hook and take the first fish that comes up and when you open its mouth you will find a shekel. Take that and give it to them for me and for yourself.

CHAPTER 9

PREPAREDNESS

My Overall Message:

Please consider adding to your journal what you determine to be Jesus' overall message on this topic.

Author's Overall Message:

I must open my heart to every insight God sews in me, internalize every teaching Jesus gives me, proactively seek to understand the Word of God and commit to correct each failure to act on it while I still have time on Earth.

Matt 13: 3-9   A sower went out to sow. And as he sowed, some seeds fell along the path and the birds came and devoured them. Other seeds fell on rocky ground where they did not have much soil and immediately they sprang up, since they had no depth of soil, but when the sun rose they were scorched. And since they had no root, they withered away. Other seeds fell among thorns and the thorns grew up and choked them. Other seeds fell on good soil and produced grain, some a hundredfold, some sixty, some thirty. He who has ears, let him hear.

Matt 13: 11-17 To you it has been given to know the secrets of the kingdom of heaven, but to them it has not been given. For to the one who has, more will be given and he will have an abundance, but from the one who has not, even what he has will be taken away. This is why I speak to them in parables, because seeing they do not see and hearing they do not hear, nor do they understand. Indeed, in their case the prophecy of Isaiah is fulfilled that says:

"You will indeed hear but never understand and you will indeed see but never perceive. For this people's heart has grown dull and with their ears they can barely hear and their eyes they have closed, lest they should see with their eyes and hear with their ears and understand with their heart and turn and I would heal them." But blessed are your eyes, for they see and your ears, for they hear. Truly, I say to you, many prophets and righteous people longed to see what you see and did not see it and to hear what you hear and did not hear it.

Matt 13: 18-23 Hear then the parable of the sower: When anyone hears the Word of the kingdom and does not understand it, the evil one comes and snatches away what has been sown in his heart. This is what was sown along the path. As for what was sown on rocky ground, this is the one who hears the Word and immediately receives it with joy, yet he has no root in himself, but endures for a while and when tribulation or persecution arises on account of the Word, immediately he falls away. As for what was sown among thorns, this is the one who hears the Word, but the cares of the world and the deceitfulness of riches choke the Word and it proves unfruitful. As for what was sown on good soil, this is the one who hears the Word and understands it. He indeed bears fruit and yields, in one case a hundredfold, in another sixty and in another thirty.

Mark 4: 3-9 Listen! A sower went out to sow. And as he sowed, some seed fell along the path and the birds came and devoured it. Other seed fell on rocky ground, where it did not have much soil and immediately it sprang up, since it had no depth of soil. And when the sun rose it was scorched and since it had no root, it withered away. Other seed fell among thorns and the thorns grew up and choked it and it yielded no grain. And other seeds fell into good soil and produced grain, growing up and increasing and yielding thirtyfold and sixtyfold and a hundredfold. He who has ears to hear, let him hear.

Mark 4: 11-12   To you has been given the secret of the kingdom of God, but for those outside everything is in parables, so that ". . . they may indeed see but not perceive and may indeed hear but not understand, lest they should turn and be forgiven."

Mark 4: 13-20   Do you not understand this parable? How then will you understand all the parables? The sower sows the Word. And these are the ones along the path, where the Word is sown: when they hear, Satan immediately comes and takes away the Word that is sown in them. And these are the ones sown on rocky ground: the ones who, when they hear the Word, immediately receive it with joy. And they have no root in themselves, but endure for a while; then, when tribulation or persecution arises on account of the Word, immediately they fall away. And others are the ones sown among thorns. They are those who hear the Word, but the cares of the world and the deceitfulness of riches and the desires for other things enter in and choke the Word and it proves unfruitful. But those that were sown on the good soil are ones who hear the Word and accept it and bear fruit, thirtyfold and sixtyfold and a hundredfold.

Luke 8: 5-8   A sower went out to sow his seed. And as he sowed, some fell along the path and was trampled underfoot and the birds of the air devoured it. And some fell on the rock and as it grew up, it withered away, because it had no moisture. And some fell among thorns and the thorns grew up with it and choked it. And some fell into good soil and grew and yielded a hundredfold. He who has ears to hear, let him hear.

Luke 8: 10-15   To you it has been given to know the secrets of the kingdom of God, but for others they are in parables, so that "seeing they may not see and hearing they may not understand." Now the parable is this: The seed is the Word of God. The ones along the path are those who have heard. Then the devil comes and takes away the Word from their hearts, so that they may not believe and be saved. And the ones on the rock are those who, when they hear the Word, receive it with joy. But these have no root; they believe for a while and in time of testing fall away. And as for what fell among the thorns, they are those who hear, but as they go on their way they are choked by the cares and riches and pleasures of life and their fruit does not mature. As for that in the good soil, they are those who, hearing the Word, hold it fast in an honest and good heart and bear fruit with patience.

Mark 4: 21-25 Is a lamp brought in to be put under a basket, or under a bed and not on a stand? For nothing is hidden except to be made manifest; nor is anything secret except to come to light. If anyone has ears to hear, let him hear. Pay attention to what you hear: with the measure you use, it will be measured to you and still more will be added to you. For to the one who has, more will be given and from the one who has not, even what he has will be taken away.

Luke 8: 16-18 No one after lighting a lamp covers it with a jar or puts it under a bed, but puts it on a stand, so that those who enter may see the light. For nothing is hidden that will not be made manifest, nor is anything secret that will not be known and come to light. Take care then how you hear, for to the one who has, more will be given and from the one who has not, even what he thinks that he has will be taken away.

Luke 11: 33-36 No one after lighting a lamp puts it in a cellar or under a basket, but on a stand, so that those who enter may see the light. Your eye is the lamp of your body. When your eye is healthy, your whole body is full of light, but when it is bad, your body is full of darkness. Therefore be careful lest the light in you be darkness. If then your whole body is full of light, having no part dark, it will be wholly bright, as when a lamp with its rays gives you light.

Luke 10: 21-24 I thank You, Father, Lord of heaven and earth, that You have hidden these things from the wise and understanding and revealed them to little children; yes, Father, for such was Your gracious will. All things have been handed over to me by my Father and no one knows who the Son is except the Father, or who the Father is except the Son and anyone to whom the Son chooses to reveal Him. Blessed are the eyes that see what you see! For I tell you that many prophets and kings desired to see what you see and did not see it and to hear what you hear and did not hear it.

Luke 13: 6-9   A man had a fig tree planted in his vineyard and he came seeking fruit on it and found none. And he said to the vinedresser "Look, for three years now I have come seeking fruit on this fig tree and I find none. Cut it down. Why should it use up the ground?" And he answered him "Sir, let it alone this year also, until I dig around it and put on manure. Then if it should bear fruit next year, well and good; but if not, you can cut it down."

Luke 11: 5-13   Which of you who has a friend will go to him at midnight and say to him "Friend, lend me three loaves, for a friend of mine has arrived on a journey and I have nothing to set before him," and he will answer from within "Do not bother me; the door is now shut and my children are with me in bed. I cannot get up and give you anything"? I tell you, though he will not get up and give him anything because he is his friend, yet because of his impudence he will rise and give him whatever he needs. And I tell you, ask and it will be given to you; seek and you will find; knock and it will be opened to you. For everyone who asks receives and the one who seeks finds and to the one who knocks it will be opened. What father among you, if his son asks for a fish, will instead of a fish give him a serpent; or if he asks for an egg, will give him a scorpion? If you then, who are evil, know how to give good gifts to your children, how much more will the heavenly Father give the Holy Spirit to those who ask Him!

Matt 7: 7-11   Ask and it will be given to you; seek and you will find; knock and it will be opened to you. For everyone who asks receives and the one who seeks finds and to the one who knocks it will be opened. Or which one of you, if his

61

son asks him for bread, will give him a stone? Or if he asks for a fish, will give him a serpent? If you then, who are evil, know how to give good gifts to your children, how much more will your Father who is in heaven give good things to those who ask Him!

Luke 13: 2-5   Do you think that these Galileans were worse sinners than all the other Galileans, because they suffered in this way? No, I tell you; but unless you repent, you will all likewise perish. Or those eighteen on whom the tower in Siloam fell and killed them: do you think that they were worse offenders than all the others who lived in Jerusalem? No I tell you; but unless you repent, you will all likewise perish.

CHAPTER 10

PHARISEES ET AL

My Overall Message:

Please consider adding to your journal what you determine to be Jesus' overall message on this topic.

Author's Overall Message:

I am as much a hypocrite as the Jewish leaders. <u>I need to discern what, of what I read and hear, is consistent with what I am taught by Jesus.</u>

Matt 23: 2-7   The scribes and the Pharisees sit on Moses' seat, so practice and observe whatever they tell you - but not what they do. For they preach, but do not practice. They tie up heavy burdens, hard to bear and lay them on people's shoulders, but they themselves are not willing to move them with their finger. They do all their deeds to be seen by others. For they make their phylacteries broad and their fringes long and they love the place of honour at feasts and the best seats in the synagogues and greetings in the marketplaces and being called rabbi by others.

Luke 20: 46-47 Beware of the scribes, who like to walk around in long robes and love greetings in the marketplaces and the best seats in the synagogues and the places of honour at feasts, who devour widows' houses and for a pretense make long prayers. They will receive the greater condemnation.

Mark 12: 38-40 Beware of the scribes, who like to walk around in long robes and like greetings in the marketplaces and the best seats in the synagogues and the places of honour at feasts, who devour widows' houses and for a pretense make long prayers. They will receive the greater condemnation.

Matt 23: 25-28 Woe to you, scribes and Pharisees, hypocrites! For you clean the outside of the cup and the plate, but inside they are full of greed and self-indulgence. You blind Pharisee! First clean the inside of the cup and the plate, that the outside also may be clean. Woe to you, scribes and Pharisees, hypocrites! For you are like whitewashed tombs, which outwardly appear beautiful, but within are full of dead people's bones and all uncleanness. So you also outwardly appear righteous to others, but within you are full of hypocrisy and lawlessness.

Luke 11: 39-44 Now you Pharisees cleanse the outside of the cup and of the dish, but inside you are full of greed and wickedness. You fools! Did not He who made the outside make the inside also? But give as alms those things that are within and behold, everything is clean for you. But woe to you Pharisees! For you tithe mint and rue and every herb and neglect justice and the love of God. These you ought to have done, without neglecting the others. Woe to you Pharisees! For you love the best seat in the synagogues and greetings in the marketplaces. Woe to you! For you are like unmarked graves and people walk over them without knowing it.

Matt 23: 23-24 Woe to you, scribes and Pharisees, hypocrites! For you tithe mint and dill and cumin and have neglected the weightier matters of the law: justice and mercy and faithfulness. These you ought to have done, without neglecting the others. You blind guides, straining out a gnat and swallowing a camel!

Luke 12: 1-3 Beware of the leaven of the Pharisees, which is hypocrisy. Nothing is covered up that will not be revealed, or hidden that will not be known. Therefore whatever you have said in the dark will be heard in the light and what you have whispered in private rooms shall be proclaimed on the housetops.

Mark 8: 15-21 Watch out; beware of the leaven of the Pharisees and the leaven of Herod. {to disciples discussing having only one loaf of bread} Why are you discussing the fact that you have no bread? Do you not yet perceive or under-stand? Are your hearts hardened? Having eyes do you not see and having ears do you not hear? And do you not remember? When I broke the five loaves for the five thousand, how many baskets full of broken pieces did you take up? {Twelve.} And the seven for the four thousand, how many baskets full of broken pieces did you take up? {Seven.} Do you not yet understand?

Matt 16: 6-11 Watch and beware of the leaven of the Pharisees and Sadducees. O you of little faith, why are you discussing among yourselves the fact that you have no bread? Do you not yet perceive? Do you not remember the five loaves for the five thousand and how many baskets you gathered? Or the seven loaves for the four thousand and how many baskets you gathered? How is it that you fail to understand that I did not speak about bread? Beware of the leaven of the Pharisees and Sadducees.

Matt 23: 13-15 But woe to you, scribes and Pharisees, hypocrites! For you shut the kingdom of heaven in people's faces. For you nei-ther enter yourselves nor allow those who would enter to go in. Woe to you scribes and Pharisees, hypocrites! For you travel across sea and land to make a single proselyte and when he becomes a proselyte, you make him twice as much a child of hell as yourselves.

Matt 23: 16-22 Woe to you, blind guides, who say "If anyone swears by the temple, it is nothing, but if anyone swears by the gold of the temple, he is bound by his oath." You blind fools! For which is greater, the gold or the temple that has made the gold sacred? And you say "If anyone swears by the altar, it is nothing, but if anyone swears by the gift that is on the altar, he is bound by his oath." You blind men! For which is greater, the gift or the altar that makes the gift sacred? So whoever swears by the altar swears by it and by everything on it. And whoever swears by the temple swears by it and by Him who dwells in it. And whoever swears by heaven swears by the throne of God and by Him who sits upon it.

Matt 23: 29-36 Woe to you, scribes and Pharisees, hypocrites! For you build the tombs of the prophets and decorate the monuments of the righteous, saying "If we had lived in the days of our fathers, we would not have taken part with them in shedding the blood of the prophets." Thus you witness against yourselves that you are sons of those who murdered the prophets. Fill up, then, the measure of your fathers. You serpents, you brood of vipers, how are you to escape being sentenced to hell? Therefore I send you prophets and wise men and scribes, some of whom you will kill and crucify and some you will flog in your synagogues and persecute from town to town, so that on you may come all the righteous blood shed on earth, from the blood of innocent Avel to the blood of Zechariah the son of Barachiah, whom you murdered between the sanctuary and the altar. Truly, I say to you, all these things will come upon this generation.

Luke 11: 46-52 Woe to you lawyers also! For you load people with burdens hard to bear and you yourselves do not touch the burdens with one of your fingers. Woe to you! For you build the tombs of the prophets whom your fathers killed. So you are witnesses and you consent to the deeds of your fathers, for they killed them and you build their tombs. Therefore also the Wisdom of God said "I will send them prophets and apostles, some of whom they will kill and persecute," so that the blood of all the prophets, shed from the foundation of the world, may be charged against this generation, from the blood of Abel to the blood of Zechariah, who perished between the alter and the sanctuary. Yes I tell you, it will be required of this generation. Woe to you lawyers! For you have taken away the key of knowledge. You did not enter yourselves and you hindered those who were entering.

Matt 23: 8-12 But you are not to be called rabbi, for you have one teacher and you are all brothers. And call no man your father on earth, for you have one Father, who is in heaven. Neither be called instructors, for you have one instructor, the Christ. The greatest among you shall be your servant. Whoever exalts himself will be humbled and whoever humbles himself will be exalted.

CHAPTER 11

REJECTING JESUS

My Overall Message:

Please consider adding to your journal what you determine to be Jesus' overall message on this topic.

Author's Overall Message:

<u>I reject Jesus whenever I put my will ahead of God's will</u>. Because Jesus has left no room for doubt about God's will, the guilt is mine and <u>I will have no excuse</u>.

John 3: 16-21   For God so loved the world, that He gave His only Son, that whoever believes in Him should not perish but have eternal life. For God did not send His Son into the world to condemn the world, but in order that the world might be saved through Him. Whoever believes in Him is not condemned, but whoever does not believe is condemned already, because he has not believed in the name of the only Son of God. And this is the judgement: the light has come into the world and people loved the darkness rather than the light because their deeds were evil. For everyone who does wicked things hates the light and does not come to the light, lest his deeds should be exposed. But whoever does what is true comes to the light, so that it may be clearly seen that his deeds have been carried out in God.

John 5: 37-47   And the Father who sent me has Himself borne witness about me. His voice you have never heard, His form you have never seen and you do not have His Word abiding in you, for you do not believe the one whom He has sent.

You search the Scriptures because you think that in them you have eternal life; and it is they that bear witness about me, yet you refuse to come to me that you may have life. I do not receive glory from people. But I know that you do not have the love of God within you. I have come in my Father's name and you do not receive me. If another comes in his own name, you will receive him. How can you believe, when you receive glory from one another and do not seek the glory that comes from the only God? Do not think that I will accuse you to the Father. There is one who accuses you: Moses, on whom you have set your hope. If you believed Moses, you would believe me; for he wrote of me. But if you do not believe his writings, how will you believe my words?

John 8: 39-47 {Jews: Abraham is our father.} If you were Abraham's children, you would be doing what Abraham did, but now you seek to kill me, a man who has told you the truth that I heard from God. This is not what Abraham did. You are doing what your father did. {We were not born of sexual immorality. We have one Father - even God.} If God were your Father you would love me, for I came from God and I am here. I came not on my own accord, but He sent me. Why do you not understand what I say? It is because you cannot bear to hear my Word. You are of your father the devil and your will is to do your father's desires. He was a murderer from the beginning and has nothing to do with the truth, because there is no truth in him. When he lies, he speaks out of his own character, for he is a liar and the father of lies. But because I tell the truth, you do not believe me. Which one of you convicts me of sin? If I tell the truth, why do you not believe me? Whoever is of God hears the Word of God. The reason why you do not hear them is that you are not of God.

John 15: 18-25 If the world hates you, know that it has hated me before it hated you. If you were of the world, the world would love you as its own; but because you are not of the world, but I chose you out of the world, therefore the world hates you. Remember the Word that I said to you: "A servant is not greater than his master." If they persecuted me, they will also persecute you. If they kept my Word, they will also keep yours. But all these things they will do to you on account of my name, because they do not know Him who sent me. If I had not come and spoken to them, they would not have been guilty of sin, but now they have no excuse for their sin. Whoever hates me hates my Father also. If I had not done among them the works that no one else did, they would not be guilty of sin, but now they have seen and hated both me and my Father. But the Word that is written in their Law must be fulfilled: "They hated me without a cause."

John 9: 39-41 For judgement I came into this world, that those who do not see may see and those who see may become blind. {Pharisees: Are we also blind?} If you were blind, you would have no guilt, but now that you say "We see," your guilt remains.

Matt 21: 33-37 Hear another parable. There was a master of a house who planted a vineyard and put a fence around it and dug a winepress in it and built a tower and leased it to tenants and went into another country. When the season for fruit drew near, he sent his servants to the tenants to get his fruit. And the tenants took his servants and beat one, killed another and stoned another. Again he sent other servants, more than the first. And they did the same to them. Finally he sent his son to them, saying "They will respect my son."

Matt 21: 38-44 But when the tenants saw the son, they said to themselves "This is the heir. Come, let us kill him and have his inheritance." And they took him and threw him out of the vineyard and killed him. When therefore the owner of the vineyard comes, what will he do to those tenants? {He will put those wretches to a miserable death and let out the vineyard to other tenants who will give him the fruits in their seasons.} Have you never read in the Scriptures: "The stone that the builders rejected has become the cornerstone; this was the Lord's doing and it is marvelous in our eyes"? Therefore I tell you, the kingdom of God will be taken away from you and given to a people producing its fruits. And the one who falls on this stone will be broken to pieces; and when it falls on anyone, it will crush him.

Luke 20: 9-18   A man planted a vineyard and let it out to tenants and went into another country for a long while. When the time came, he sent a servant to the tenants, so that they would give him some of the fruit of the vineyard. But the tenants beat him and sent him away empty-handed. And he sent another servant. But they also beat and treated him shamefully and sent him away empty-handed. And he sent yet a third. This one also they wounded and cast out. Then the owner of the vineyard said, "What shall I do? I will send my beloved son; perhaps they will respect him." But when the tenants saw him, they said to themselves "This is the heir. Let us kill him, so that the inheritance may be ours." And they threw him out of the vineyard and killed him. What then will the owner of the vineyard do to them? He will come and destroy those tenants and give the vineyard to others. {Surely not!} What then is this that is written: "The stone that the builders rejected has become the cornerstone"? Everyone who falls on that stone will be broken to pieces and when it falls on anyone, it will crush him.

Mark 12: 1-11   A man planted a vineyard and put a fence around it and dug a pit for the winepress and built a tower and leased it to tenants and went into another country. When the season came, he sent a servant to the tenants to get from them some of the fruit of the vineyard. And they took him and beat him and sent him away empty-handed. Again he sent to them another servant and they struck him on the head and treated him shamefully. And he sent another and him they killed. And so with many others: some they beat and some they killed. He had still one other, a beloved son. Finally, he sent him to them, saying "They will respect my son." But those tenants said to one another "This is the heir. Come, let us kill him and the inheritance will be ours." And they took him and killed him and threw him out of

71

the vineyard. What will the owner of the vineyard do? He will come and destroy the tenants and give the vineyard to others. Have you not read this Scripture: "The stone that the builders rejected has become the corner stone; this was the Lord's doing and it is marvelous in our eyes."?

Mark 6: 2-4   {Synagogue observers: Where did this man get these things? What is the wisdom given to Him? How are such mighty works done by His hands? Is not this the carpenter, the son of Mary and brother of James and Joses and Judas and Simon? And are not His sisters here with us?} A prophet is not without honour, except in his home town and among his relatives and in his own household.

Matt 13: 57   A prophet is not without honour except in his hometown and in his own household.

Luke 4: 23-27   Doubtless you will quote to me this proverb "Physician, heal yourself." What we have heard You did at Capernaum, do here in Your home town as well. Truly, I say to you, no prophet is acceptable in his hometown. But in truth, I tell you, there were many widows in Israel in the days of Elijah, when the heavens were shut up three years and six months and a great famine came over all the land and Elijah was sent to none of them but only to Zarephath, in the land of Sidon, to a woman who was a widow. And there were many lepers in Israel in the time of the prophet Elisha and none of them was cleansed, but only Naaman the Syrian.

CHAPTER 12

SALVATION

My Overall Message:

Please consider adding to your journal what you determine to be Jesus' overall message on this topic.

Author's Overall Message:

Salvation requires putting God's values above worldly values. God continuously offers His help but it is up to me to accept it. *Professing* a love of Jesus is not enough. I must *do* what He insists upon.

John 3: 3-8   {Nicodemus: How can a man be born again when he is old? Can he enter a second time into his mother's womb and be born?} Truly, truly, I say to you, unless one is born again he cannot see the kingdom of God. Truly, truly, I say to you, unless one is born of water and the Spirit, he cannot enter the kingdom of God. That which is born of the flesh is flesh and that which is born of the Spirit is spirit. Do not marvel that I said to you "You must be born again." The wind blows where it wishes and you hear its sound, but you do not know where it comes from or where it goes. So it is with everyone who is born of the Spirit.

John 3: 9-15   {Nicodemus: How can these things be?} Are you the teacher of Israel and yet you do not understand these things? Truly, truly, I say to you, we speak of what we know and bear witness to what we have seen, but you do not receive our testimony. If I have told you earthly things and you do not believe, how can you believe if I tell you heavenly things? No one has ascended into heaven except He who descended from heaven, the Son of Man. And as Moses lifted up the serpent in the wilderness, so must the Son of Man be lifted up, that whoever believes in Him may have eternal life.

John 12: 44-50 Whoever believes in me, believes not in me but in Him who sent me. And whoever sees me sees Him who sent me. I have come into the world as light, so that whoever believes in me may not remain in darkness. If anyone hears my words and does not keep them, I do not judge him; for I did not come to judge the world but to save the world. The one who rejects me and does not receive my words has a judge; the Word that I have spoken will judge him on the last day. For I have not spoken on my own authority, but the Father who sent me has Himself given me a commandment - what to say and what to speak. And I know that His commandment is eternal life. What I say, therefore, I say as the Father has told me.

Luke 15: 3-10 What man of you, having a hundred sheep, if he has lost one of them, does not leave the ninety-nine in the open country and go after the one that is lost, until he finds it? And when he has found it, he lays it on his shoulders, rejoicing. And when he comes home, he calls together his friends and his neighbours, saying to them "Rejoice with me, for I have found my sheep that was lost." Just so I tell you, there will be more joy in heaven over one sinner who repents than over ninety-nine righteous persons who need no repentance. Or what woman, having ten silver coins, if she loses one coin, does not light a lamp and sweep the house and seek diligently until she finds it? And when she has found it, she calls together her friends and neighbours, saying "Rejoice with me, for I have found the coin that I had lost." Just so, I tell you, there is joy before the angels of God over one sinner who repents.

Matt 18: 10-14 See that you do not despise one of these little ones. For I tell you that in heaven their angels always see the face of my Father who is in heaven. What do you think? If a man has a hundred sheep and one of them has gone astray does he not leave the ninety-nine on the mountains and go in search of the one that went astray? And if he finds it, truly, I say to you, he rejoices over it more than over the ninety-nine that never went astray. So it is not the will of my Father who is in heaven that one of these little ones should perish.

Luke 19: 5-10   Zacchaeus, hurry and come down, for I must stay at your house today. Today salvation has come to this house, since he also is a son of Abraham. For the Son of Man came to seek and to save the lost.

John 5: 19-24   Truly, truly, I say to you, the Son can do nothing of His own accord, but only what He sees the Father doing. For whatever the Father does, that the Son does likewise. For the Father loves the Son and shows Him all that He Himself is doing. And greater works than these will He show Him, so that you may marvel. For as the Father raises the dead and gives them life, so also the Son gives life to whom He will. The Father judges no one, but has given all judgement to the Son, that all may honour the Son, just as they honour the Father. Whoever does not honour the Son does not honour the Father who sent Him. Truly, truly, I say to you, whoever hears my Word and believes Him who sent me has eternal life. He does not come into judgement, but has passed from death to life.

Matt 7: 21-27   Not everyone who says to me "Lord, Lord," will enter the kingdom of heaven, but the one who does the will of my Father who is in heaven. On that day many will say to me "Lord, Lord, did we not prophesy in Your name and cast out demons in Your name and do many mighty works in Your name?" And then will I declare to them "I never knew you; depart from me, you workers of lawlessness." Everyone then who hears these words of mine and does them will be like a wise man who built his house on the rock. And the rain fell and the floods came and the winds blew and beat on that house, but it did not fall, because it had been founded on the rock. And everyone who hears these words of mine and does not do them will be like a foolish man who built his house on the sand. And the rain fell and the floods came and the winds blew and beat against that house and it fell and great was the fall of it.

Luke 6: 46-49 Why do you call me "Lord, Lord," and not do what I tell you? Everyone who comes to me and hears my words and does them, I will show you what he is like: he is like a man building a house, who dug deep and laid the foundation on the rock. And when a flood arose, the stream broke against that house and could not shake it, because it had been well built. But the one who hears and does not do them is like a man who built a house on the ground without a foundation. When the stream broke against it, immediately it fell and the ruin of that house was great.

Matt 21: 28-32 What do you think? A man had two sons. And he went to the first and said, "Son, go and work in the vineyard today." And he answered, "I will not," but afterward he changed his mind and went. And he went to the other son and said the same. And he answered, "I go sir" but did not go. Which of the two did the will of his father? {The first.} Truly, I say to you, the tax collectors and the prostitutes go into the kingdom of God before you. For John came to you in the way of righteousness and you did not believe him, but the tax collectors and the prostitutes believed him. And even when you saw it, you did not afterward change your minds and believe him.

CHAPTER 13

MIRACLES

My Overall Message:

Please consider adding to your journal what you determine to be Jesus' overall message on this topic.

Author's Overall Message:

The miracles Jesus performed were real. Because I have sufficiently processed my lifelong doubts, I can finally accept this.

John 2: 3-8   {Mother of Jesus: They have no wine.} Woman, what does this have to do with me? My hour has not yet come. {Mother of Jesus: Do whatever He tells you.} Fill the jars with water. Now draw some out and take it to the master of the feast.

John 11: 3-16   {Sisters of Lazarus: Lord, he whom You love is ill.} This illness does not lead to death. It is for the glory of God, so that the Son of God may be glorified through it. Let us go to Judea again. {Disciples: Rabbi, the Jews were just now seeking to stone You and are You going there again?} Are there not twelve hours in the day? If anyone walks in the day, he does not stumble, because he sees the light of this world. But if anyone walks in the night, he stumbles, because the light is not in him. Our friend Lazarus has fallen asleep, but I go to awaken him. {Disciples: Lord, if he has fallen asleep, he will recover.} Lazarus has died and for your sake I am glad that I was not there, so that you may believe. But let us go to him. {Thomas the Twin: Let us also go, that we may die with him.}

John 11: 21-27   {Martha: Lord, if You had been here, my brother would not have died. But even now I know that whatever You ask from God, God will give You.} Your brother will rise again. {I know that he will rise again in the resurrection on the last day.} I am the resurrection and the life. Whoever believes in me, though he die, yet shall he live and everyone who lives and believes in me shall never die. Do you believe this? {Yes, Lord; I believe that You are the Christ, the Son of God, who is coming into the world.}

John 11: 32-44   {Mary: Lord, if You had been here, my brother would not have died.} Where have you laid him? {Lord, come and see.} {Jews, seeing Jesus weeping: See how He loved him! Could not He who opened the eyes of the blind man also have kept this man from dying?} Take away the stone. {Martha: Lord, by this time there will be an odour, for he has been dead four days.} Did I not tell you that if you believed you would see the glory of God? Father, I thank You that You have heard me. I know that You always hear me, but I said this on account of the people standing around, that they may believe that You sent me. Lazarus, come out. Unbind him and let him go.

John 6: 5-12   Where are we to buy bread, so that these people may eat? {Philip: Two hundred denarii would not buy enough bread for each of them to get a little. Andrew: There is a boy here who has five barley loaves and two fish but what are they for so many?} Have the people sit down. Gather up the leftover fragments, that nothing may be lost.

Mark 6: 37-38   You give them something to eat. How many loaves do you have? Go and see. {Disciples: Five and two fish.}

Matt 14: 16-18   They need not go away; you give them something to eat. {Disciples: We have only five loaves here and two fish.} Bring them here to me.

Luke 9: 13-14   You give them something to eat. Have them sit down in groups of about fifty each.

Mark 8: 2-5   I have compassion on the crowd, because they have been with me now three days and have nothing to eat. And if I send them away hungry to their homes, they will faint on the way. And some of them have come from far away. {Disciples: How can one feed these people with bread here in this desolate place?} How many loaves do you have? {Disciples: Seven.} {leftovers: 7 baskets after 4000 people had eaten}

Matt 15: 32-34 I have compassion on the crowd because they have been with me now three days and have nothing to eat. And I am unwilling to send them away hungry, lest they faint on the way. How many loaves do you have?

Mark 6: 50   {walking on the sea where the disciples were terrified by the storm} Take heart; it is I. Do not be afraid.

John 6: 20   {walking on a rough sea} It is I; do not be afraid.

Matt 14: 27-31 {Disciples: It is a ghost!} Take heart; it is I. Do not be afraid. Come. {Peter, Lord, save me.} O you of little faith, why did you doubt?

CHAPTER 14

RICHES

My Overall Message:

Please consider adding to your journal what you determine to be Jesus' overall message on this topic.

Author's Overall Message:

Jesus' words leave no room for doubt. <u>I must share the gifts of which I am God's steward, not merely more than others do but as much as I am able.</u>

Mark 10: 28-31 {Peter: See, we have left everything and followed You.} Truly I say to you, there is no one who has left house or brothers or sisters or mother or father or children or lands, for my sake and for the gospel, who will not receive a hundredfold now in this time, houses and brothers and sisters and mothers and children and lands, with persecutions and in the age to come eternal life. But many who are first will be last and the last first.

Matt 6: 19-24 Do not lay up for yourselves treasures on earth, where moth and rust destroy and where thieves break in and steal, but lay up for yourselves treasures in heaven, where neither moth nor rust destroys and where thieves do not break in and steal. For where your treasure is there your heart will be also. The eye is the lamp of the body. So, if your eye is healthy, your whole body will be full of light, but if your eye is bad, your whole body will be full of darkness. If then the light in you is darkness, how great is the darkness! No one can serve two masters, for either he will hate the one and love the other, or he will be devoted to the one and despise the other. You cannot serve God and money.

Matt 19: 16-26 {Rich man: Teacher, what good deed must I do to have eternal life?} Why do you ask me about what is good? There is only one who is good. If you would enter life, keep the commandments. {Which ones?} You shall not murder; You shall not commit adultery; You shall not steal; You shall not bear false witness; Honour your father and your mother and You shall love your neighbour as yourself. {All these I have kept. What do I still lack?} If you would be perfect, go, sell what you possess and give to the poor and you will have treasure in heaven; and come, follow me. Truly, I say to you, only with difficulty will a rich person enter the kingdom of heaven. Again I tell you, it is easier for a camel to go through the eye of a needle than for a rich person to enter the kingdom of God. {Disciples: Who, then, can be saved?} With man this is impossible, but with God all things are possible.

Mark 10: 17-27 {Rich man: Good Teacher, what must I do to inherit eternal life?} Why do you call me good? No one is good except God alone. You know the commandments: Do not murder. Do not commit adultery. Do not steal. Do not bear false witness. Do not defraud. Honour your father and mother. {Teacher, all these I have kept from my youth.} You lack one thing: go, sell all that you have and give to the poor and you will have treasure in heaven; and come, follow me. How difficult it will be for those who have wealth to enter the kingdom of God! Children, how difficult it is to enter the kingdom of God. It is easier for a camel to go through the eye of a needle than for a rich person to enter the kingdom of God. {Disciples: Then who can be saved?} With man it is impossible, but not with God. For all things are possible with God.

Luke 18: 18-30 {Rich ruler: Good Teacher, what must I do to inherit eternal life?} Why do you call me good? No one is good except God alone. You know the commandments: "Do not commit adultery. Do not murder. Do not steal. Do not bear false witness. Honour your father and mother."

{All these I have kept from my youth.} One thing you still lack. Sell all that you have and distribute to the poor and you will have treasure in heaven; and come, follow me. How difficult it is for those who have wealth to enter the kingdom of God! For it is easier for a camel to go through the eye of a needle than for a rich person to enter the kingdom of God. What is impossible with men is possible with God. Truly, I say to you, there is no one who has left house or wife or brothers or parents or children, for the sake of the kingdom of God, who will not receive many times more in this time and in the age to come eternal life.

Luke 12: 14-21 {Teacher, tell my brother to divide the inheritance with me.} Man, who made me a judge or arbitrator over you? Take care and be on your guard against all covetousness, for one's life does not consist in the abundance of his possessions. The land of a rich man produced plentifully and he thought to himself "What shall I do, for I have nowhere to store my crops?" And he said, "I will do this: I will tear down my barns and build larger ones and there I will store all my grain and my goods. And I will say to my soul, Soul, you have ample goods laid up for many years; relax, eat, drink, be merry." But God said to him "Fool! This night your soul is required of you and the things you have prepared, whose will they be?" So is the one who lays up treasure for himself and is not rich toward God.

Luke 16: 19-24 There was a rich man who was clothed in purple and fine linen and who feasted sumptuously every day. And at his gate was laid a poor man named Lazarus, covered with sores, who desired to be fed with what fell from the rich man's table. Moreover, even the dogs came and licked his sores. The poor man died and was carried by the angels to Abraham's side. The rich man also died and was buried and in Hades, being in torment, he lifted up his eyes and saw Abraham far off and Lazarus at his side. And he called out "Father Abraham, have mercy on me and send Lazarus to dip the end of his finger in water and cool my tongue, for I am in anguish in this flame."

Luke 16: 25-31 But Abraham said, "Child, remember that you in your lifetime received your good things and Lazarus in like manner bad things; but now he is comforted here and you are in anguish. And besides all this, between us and you a great chasm has been fixed, in order that those who would pass from here to you may not be able and none may cross from there to us." And he said, "Then I beg you, Father, to send him to my father's house – for I have five brothers – so that he may warn them, lest they also come into this place of torment." But Abraham said, "They have Moses and the Prophets; let them hear them." And he said, "No, Father Abraham, but if someone goes to them from the dead, they will repent." He said to him "If they do not hear Moses and the Prophets, neither will they be convinced if someone should rise from the dead."

Mark 12: 43-44 Truly, I say to you, this poor widow has put in more than all those who are contributing to the offering box. For they all contributed out of their abundance, but she out of her poverty has put in everything she had, all she had to live on.

Luke 21: 3-4 Truly, I tell you this poor widow has put in more than all of them. For they all contributed out of their abundance, but she out of her poverty put in all she had to live on.

CHAPTER 15

COMMANDMENTS

My Overall Message:

Please consider adding to your journal what you determine to be Jesus' overall message on this topic.

Author's Overall Message:

I find the overall message of this topic to be self-evident and impossible to misconstrue.

Mark 12: 28-34 {Scribe: Which commandment is the most important of all?} The most important is "Hear, O Israel: The Lord our God, the Lord is one. And you shall love the Lord your God with all your heart and with all your soul and with all your mind and with all your strength." The second is this: "You shall love your neighbour as yourself." There is no other commandment greater than these. {You are right, Teacher. You have truly said that He is one and there is no other besides Him. And to love Him with all the heart and with all the understanding and with all the strength and to love one's neighbour as oneself, is much more than all whole burnt offerings and sacrifices.} You are not far from the kingdom of God.

Matt 22: 36-40 {Lawyer: Teacher, which is the great commandment in the law?} You shall love the Lord your God with all your heart and with all your soul and with all your mind. This is the great and first commandment. And a second is like it: You shall love your neighbour as yourself. On these two commandments depend all the Laws and the Prophets.

Luke 10: 25-37 {Lawyer: Teacher, what shall I do to inherit eternal life?} What is written in the Law? How do you read it? {Lawyer: You shall love the Lord your God with all your heart and with all your soul and with all your strength and with all your mind and your neighbour as yourself.} You have answered correctly; do this and you will live. {And who is my neighbour?} A man was going down from Jerusalem to Jericho and he fell among robbers, who stripped him and beat him and departed, leaving him half dead. Now by chance a priest was going down that road and when he saw him he passed by on the other side. So likewise a Levite, when he came to the place and saw him, passed by on the other side. But a Samaritan, as he journeyed, came to where he was and when he saw him, he had compassion. He went to him and bound up his wounds, pouring on oil and wine. Then he set him on his own animal and brought him to an inn and took care of him. And the next day he took out two denarii and gave them to the innkeeper, saying "Take care of him and whatever more you spend, I will repay you when I come back." Which of these three, do you think, proved to be a neighbour to the man who fell among the robbers? {The one who showed him mercy.} You go and do likewise.

John 13: 31-35 Now is the Son of Man glorified and God is glorified in Him. If God is glorified in Him, God will also glorify Him in Himself and glorify Him at once. Little children, yet a little while I am with you, You will seek me and just as I said to the Jews, so now I also say to you "Where I am going you cannot come." A new commandment I give to you, that you love one another: just as I have loved you, you also are to love one another. By this all people will know that you are my disciples, if you have love for one another.

John 15: 1-6 I am the true vine and my Father is the vinedresser. Every branch of mine that does not bear fruit He takes away and every branch that does bear fruit He prunes, that it may bear more fruit. Already you are clean because of the Word that I have spoken to you. Abide in me and I in you. As the branch cannot bear fruit by itself, unless it abides in the vine, neither can you, unless you abide in me. I am the vine; you are the branches. Whoever abides in me and I in him, he it is that bears much fruit, for apart from me you can do nothing. If anyone does not abide in me he is thrown away like a branch and withers; and the branches are gathered, thrown into the fire and burned.

John 15: 7-11 If you abide in me and my words abide in you, ask whatever you wish and it will be done for you. By this my Father is glorified, that you bear much fruit and so prove to be my disciples. As the Father has loved me, so have I loved you. Abide in my love. If you keep my commandments, you will abide in my love, just as I have kept my Father's commandments and abide in His love. These things I have spoken to you, that my joy may be in you and that your joy may be full.

John 15: 12-17 This is my commandment, that you love one another as I have loved you. Greater love has no one than this, that someone lays down his life for his friends. You are my friends if you do what I command you. No longer do I call you servants, for the servant does not know what his master is doing; but I have called you friends, for all that I have heard from my Father I have made known to you. You did not choose me, but I chose you and appointed you that you should go and bear fruit and that your fruit should abide, so that whatever you ask the Father in my name, He may give to you. These things I command you, so that you will love one another.

Matt 7: 12-14 So whatever you wish that others would do to you, do also to them, for this is the Law and the Prophets. Enter by the narrow gate. For the gate is wide and the way is easy that leads to destruction and those who enter by it are many. For the gate is narrow and the way is hard that leads to life and those who find it are few.

CHAPTER 16

DEATH AND RESURRECTION FORETOLD

My Overall Message:

Please consider adding to your journal what you determine to be Jesus' overall message on this topic.

Author's Overall Message:

I have not yet studied these remaining 40 topics so I have no overall message to share on any of them.

Luke 9: 44   Let these words sink into your ears: The Son of Man is about to be delivered into the hands of men.

Luke 9: 18-22   Who do the crowds say that I am? {Disciples: John the Baptist. But others say, Elijah, and others, that one of the prophets of old has risen.} But who do you say that I am? {Peter: The Christ of God.} The Son of Man must suffer many things and be rejected by the elders and chief priests and scribes and be killed and on the third day be raised.

Mark 9: 31   The Son of Man is going to be delivered into the hands of men and they will kill Him. And when He is killed, after three days He will rise.

Matt 17: 22   The Son of Man is about to be delivered into the hands of men and they will kill Him and He will be raised on the third day.

Matt 26: 2   You know that after two days the Passover is coming and the Son of Man will be delivered up to be crucified.

Mark 10: 33-34 See, we are going up to Jerusalem and the Son of Man will be delivered over to the chief priests and the scribes and they will condemn Him to death and deliver Him over to the Gentiles. And they will mock Him and spit on Him and flog Him and kill Him. And after three days He will rise.

Luke 18: 31-33 See, we are going up to Jerusalem and everything that is written about the Son of Man by the prophets will be accomplished. For He will be delivered over to the Gentiles and will be mocked and shamefully treated and spit upon. And after flogging Him, they will kill Him and on the third day He will rise.

Matt 20: 18-19 See, we are going up to Jerusalem. And the Son of Man will be delivered over to the chief priests and scribes and they will condemn Him to death and deliver Him over to the Gentiles to be mocked and flogged and crucified and He will be raised on the third day.

Mark 8: 33 {after Peter rebuked Him upon learning what He foretold} Get behind me, Satan! For you are not setting your mind on the things of God, but on the things of man.

Matt 16: 23 Get behind me, Satan! You are a hindrance to me. For you are not setting your mind on the things of God, but on the things of man.

John 16: 16-22 A little while and you will see me no longer; and again a little while and you will see me. {Disciples: What is this that He says to us "A little while and you will not see me" and "again a little while and you will see me," and "because I am going to the Father"? What does He mean by "a little while"? We do not know what He is talking about.} Is this what you are asking yourselves, what I meant by saying "A little while and you will not see me and again a little while and you will see me"? Truly, truly, I say to you, you will weep and lament, but the world will rejoice. You will be sorrowful, but your sorrow will turn into joy. When a woman is giving birth, she has sorrow because her hour has come, but when she has delivered the baby, she no longer remembers the anguish, for joy that a human being has been born into the world. So also you have sorrow now, but I will see you again and your hearts will rejoice and no one will take your joy from you.

CHAPTER 17

HEALING

My Overall Message:

Please consider adding to your journal what you determine to be Jesus' overall message on this topic.

John 5: 6-17   Do you want to be healed? {Sir, I have no one to put me into the pool when the water is stirred up and while I am going another steps down before me.} Get up, take up your bed and walk. {later} See, you are well! Sin no more, that nothing worse may happen to you. {on the Sabbath} My Father is working until now and I am working.

Matt 20: 32-33   What do you want me to do for you? {Lord, let our eyes be opened.}

Mark 5: 8-19   {to the man, living among the tombs, bound with chains} Come out of the man, you unclean spirit. What is your name? {My name is Legion, for we are many.} {after the exorcism} Go home to your friends and tell them how much the Lord has done for you and how He has had mercy on you.

Mark 1: 25   {to the man in the synagogue with an unclean spirit} Be silent and come out of him!

Luke 7: 13-14   {to the widow at the death of her only son} Do not weep. Young man, I say to you, arise.

Mark 7: 34   {putting his fingers into the ears and onto the tongue of a deaf mute} Ephphatha. Be opened.

Mark 8: 23-26 {to the blind man after spitting on his eyes and laying his hands on him} Do you see anything? {Blind man: I see men, but they look like trees, walking.} {after laying his hands on his eyes again so that he saw clearly} Do not even enter the village.

John 4: 48-50 {to official seeking son's healing} Unless you see signs and wonders you will not believe. {Official: Sir, come down before my child dies.} Go; your son will live.

Luke 11: 24-26 When the unclean spirit has gone out of a person, it passes through waterless places seeking rest and finding none it says, "I will return to my house from which I came." And when it comes, it finds the house swept and put in order. Then it goes and brings seven other spirits more evil than itself and they enter and dwell there. And the last state of that person is worse than the first.

Matt 12: 43-45 When the unclean spirit has gone out of a person, it passes through waterless places seeking rest, but finds none. Then it says, "I will return to my house from which I came." And when it comes, it finds the house empty, swept and put in order. Then it goes and brings with it seven other spirits more evil than itself and they enter and dwell there and the last state of that person is worse than the first. So also will it be with this evil generation.

Luke 9: 50 {about someone casting out demons} Do not stop him, for the one who is not against you is for you.

Mark 9: 38-41 {John: Teacher, we saw someone casting out demons in Your name and we tried to stop him, because he was not following us.} Do not stop him, for no one who does a mighty work in my name will be able soon afterward to speak evil of me. For the one who is not against us is for us. For truly, I say to you, whoever gives you a cup of water to drink because you belong to Christ will by no means lose his reward.

CHAPTER 18

RESURRECTION

My Overall Message:

Please consider adding to your journal what you determine to be Jesus' overall message on this topic.

Mark 16: 9-14   {Now when He rose early on the first day of the week, He appeared first to Mary Magdalene, from whom He had cast out seven demons. She went and told those who had been with Him, as they mourned and wept. But when they heard that He was alive and had been seen by her, they would not believe it. After these things He appeared in another form to two of them, as they were walking into the country. And they went back and told the rest, but they did not believe them. Afterward He appeared to the eleven themselves as they were reclining at table and He rebuked them for their unbelief and hardness of heart, because they had not believed those who saw Him after He had risen}

John 20: 15-17   {Jesus, appearing unrecognizable to Mary} Woman, why are you weeping? Whom are you seeking? {Mary: Sir, if you have carried Him away, tell me where you have laid Him and I will take Him away.} Mary. {Mary: Rabboni (Teacher)!} Do not cling to me, for I have not yet ascended to the Father, but go to my brothers and say to them "I am ascending to my Father and your Father, to my God and your God."

Matt 28: 9-10   {to Mary and Mary Magdalene on their way back from the empty tomb} Greetings! Do not be afraid; go and tell my brothers to go to Galilee and there they will see me.

John 20: 19-23 {Jesus appearing to disciples in a locked room} Peace be with you. {again} Peace be with you. As the Father has sent me, even so I am sending you. Receive the Holy Spirit. If you forgive the sins of anyone, they are forgiven; if you withhold forgiveness from anyone, it is withheld.

John 20: 26-29 {eight days later, to disciples, in a locked room} Peace be with you. Put your finger here and see my hands; and put out your hand and place it in my side. Do not disbelieve, but believe. {Thomas: My Lord and my God!} Have you believed because you have seen me? Blessed are those who have not seen and yet have believed.

John 21: 3-12 {Peter to Thomas, Nathanael, sons of Zebedee and two other disciples: I am going fishing. We will go with you.} Children, do you have any fish? {No.} Cast the net on the right side of the boat and you will find some. {Disciple to Peter: It is the Lord!} Bring some of the fish that you have just caught. Come and have breakfast.

Luke 24: 36-49 Peace to you! Why are you troubled and why do doubts arise in your hearts? See my hands and my feet, that it is I myself. Touch me and see. For a spirit does not have flesh and bones as you see that I have. Have you anything here to eat? These are my words that I spoke to you while I was still with you, that everything written about me in the Law of Moses and the Prophets and the Psalms must be fulfilled. Thus it is written, that the Christ should suffer and on the third day rise from the dead and that repentance and forgiveness of sins should be proclaimed in His name to all nations, beginning from Jerusalem. You are witnesses of these things. And behold I am sending the promise of my Father upon you. But stay in the city until you are clothed with power from on high.

Luke 24: 17-27 What is this conversation that you are holding with each other as you walk? {Cleopas: Are you the only visitor to Jerusalem who does not know the things that happened there in these days?} What things? O foolish ones and slow of heart to believe all that the prophets have spoken!

Was it not necessary that the Christ should suffer these things and enter into His glory? {And beginning with Moses and all the Prophets, He interpreted to them in all the Scriptures the things concerning Himself.}

CHAPTER 19

HOLY SPIRIT

My Overall Message:

Please consider adding to your journal what you determine to be Jesus' overall message on this topic.

John 14: 15-24   If you love me, you will keep my commandments. And I will ask the Father and He will give you another Helper, to be with you forever, even the Spirit of truth, whom the world cannot receive, because it neither sees Him nor knows Him. You know Him, for He dwells with you and will be in you. I will not leave you as orphans; I will come to you. Yet a little while and the world will see me no more, but you will see me. Because I live, you also will live. In that day you will know that I am in my Father and you in me and I in you. Whoever has my commandments and keeps them, he it is who loves me. And he who loves me will be loved by my Father and I will love him and manifest myself to him. {Judas (not Iscariot): Lord, how is it that You will manifest Yourself to us and not to the world?} If anyone loves me, he will keep my Word and my Father will love him and we will come to him and make our home with him. Whoever does not love me does not keep my words. And the Word that you hear is not mine but the Father's who sent me.

John 14: 25-31   These things I have spoken to you while I am still with you. But the Helper, the Holy Spirit, whom the Father will send in my name, He will teach you all things and bring to your remembrance all that I have said to you. Peace I leave with you; my peace I give to you. Not as the world gives do I give to you. Let not your hearts be troubled, neither let them be afraid. You heard me say to you "I am going away and I will come to you." If you loved me, you would have rejoiced, because I am going to the Father, for the Father is greater than I. And now I have told you before it takes place, so that when it does take place you may believe. I will no longer talk much with you, for the ruler of this world is coming. He has no claim on me, but I do as the Father has commanded me, so that the world may know that I love the Father. Rise, let us go from here.

John 15: 26 -29   But when the Helper comes, whom I will send to you from the Father, the Spirit of truth, who proceeds from the Father, He will bear witness about me. And you also will bear witness, because you have been with me from the beginning. I have said all these things to you to keep you from falling away. They will put you out of the synagogues. Indeed, the hour is coming when whoever kills you will think he is offering service to God. And they will do these things because they have not known the Father nor me. But I have said these things to you, that when their hour comes you may remember that I told them to you. I did not say these things to you from the beginning, because I was with you.

Luke 12: 8-12   And I tell you, everyone who acknowledges me before men, the Son of Man also will acknowledge before the angels of God, but the one who denies me before men will be denied before the angels of God. And everyone who speaks a word against the Son of Man will be forgiven, but the one who blasphemes against the Holy Spirit will not be forgiven. And when they bring you before the synagogues and the rulers and the authorities, do not be anxious about how you should defend yourself or what you should say, for the Holy Spirit will teach you in that very hour what you ought to say.

John 16: 5-15   But now I am going to Him who sent me and none of you asks me "Where are you going?" But because I have said these things to you, sorrow has filled your heart. Nevertheless, I tell you the truth: it is to your advantage that I go away, for if I do not go away, the Helper will not come to you. But if I go, I will send Him to you. And when He comes, He will convict the world concerning sin and righteousness and judgement: concerning sin, because they do not believe in me; concerning righteousness, because I go to the Father and you will see me no longer; concerning judgement, because the ruler of this world is judged. I still have many things to say to you, but you cannot bear them now. When the Spirit of truth comes, He will guide you into all the truth, for He will not speak on His own authority, but whatever He hears He will speak and He will declare to you the things that are to come. He will glorify me, for He will take what is mine and declare it to you. All that the Father has is mine; therefore I said that He will take what is mine and declare it to you.

CHAPTER 20

FASTING

My Overall Message:

Please consider adding to your journal what you determine to be Jesus' overall message on this topic.

Luke 5: 34-35   {Pharisees: The disciples of John fast often and offer prayers, and so do the disciples of the Pharisees, but yours eat and drink.} Can you make wedding guests fast while the bridegroom is with them? The days will come when the bridegroom is taken away from them and they will fast in those days.

Luke 5: 36-39   No one tears a piece from a new garment and puts it on an old garment. If he does, he will tear the new and the piece from the new will not match the old. And no one puts new wine into old wineskins. If he does, the new wine will burst the skins and it will be spilled and the skins will be destroyed. But new wine must be put into fresh wineskins. And no one after drinking old wine desires new, for he says, "The old is good."

Mark 2: 19-22   Can the wedding guests fast while the bridegroom is with them? As long as they have the bridegroom with them they cannot fast. The days will come when the bridegroom is taken away from them and then they will fast in that day. No one sews a piece of unshrunk cloth on an old garment. If he does, the patch tears away from it, the new from the old and a worse tear is made. And no one puts new wine into old wineskins. If he does, the wine will burst the skins - and the wine is destroyed and so are the skins. But new wine is for fresh wineskins.

Matt 9: 15-17 Can the wedding guests mourn as long as the bridegroom is with them? The days will come when the bridegroom is taken away from them and then they will fast. No one puts a piece of unshrunk cloth on an old garment, for the patch tears away from the garment and a worse tear is made. Neither is new wine put into old wineskins. If it is, the skins burst and the wine is spilled and the skins are destroyed. But new wine is put into fresh wineskins and so both are preserved.

Matt 11: 12-19 From the days of John the Baptist until now the kingdom of heaven has suffered violence and the violent take it by force. For all the Prophets and the Law prophesied unto John and if you are willing to accept it, he is Elijah who is to come. He who has ears to hear, let him hear. But to what shall I compare this generation? It is like children sitting in the marketplaces and calling to their playmates "We played the flute for you and you did not dance; we sang a dirge and you did not mourn." For John came neither eating nor drinking and they say, "He has a demon." The Son of Man came eating and drinking and they say, "Look at Him! A glutton and a drunkard, a friend of tax collectors and sinners!" Yet wisdom is justified by her deeds.

Luke 7: 31-35 To what then shall I compare the people of this generation and what are they like? They are like children sitting in the marketplace and calling to one another "We played the flute for you and you did not dance; we sang a dirge and you did not weep." For John the Baptist has come eating no bread and drinking no wine and you say, "He has a demon." The Son of Man has come eating and drinking and you say, "Look at Him! A glutton and a drunkard, a friend of tax collectors and sinners!" Yet wisdom is justified by all her children.

CHAPTER 21

MISSION

My Overall Message:

Please consider adding to your journal what you determine to be Jesus' overall message on this topic.

Mark 1: 38	Let us go on to the next towns that I may preach there also, for that is why I came out.
Luke 4: 43	I must preach the good news of the kingdom of God to the other towns as well; for I was sent for this purpose.
Luke 2: 48-49	{His mother: Son, why have you treated us so? Behold your father and I have been searching for You in great distress.} Why were you looking for me? Did you not know that I must be in my Father's house?
Matt 9: 9-13	{to Matthew} Follow me. {Pharisees: Why does your teacher eat with tax collectors and sinners?} Those who are well have no need of a physician, but those who are sick. Go and learn what this means "I desire mercy and not sacrifice." For I came not to call the righteous, but sinners.
Mark 2: 14-17	{to Levi, son of Alphaeus, the tax collector} Follow me. {to the Pharisees} Those who are well have no need of a physician, but those who are sick. I came not to call the righteous, but sinners.
Luke 5: 27-32	{to Levi, a tax collector} Follow me. {to the Pharisees} Those who are well have no need of a physician, but those who are sick. I have not come to call the righteous but sinners to repentance.

John 4: 31-38   {Disciples: Rabbi, eat.} I have food to eat that you do not know about. My food is to do the will of Him who sent me and to accomplish His work. Do you not say "There are yet four months, then comes the harvest."? Look, I tell you, lift up your eyes and see that the fields are white for harvest. Already the one who reaps is receiving wages and gathering fruit for eternal life, so that sower and reaper may rejoice together. For here the saying holds true "One sows and another reaps." I sent you to reap that for which you did not labour. Others have laboured and you have entered into their labour.

Luke 4: 18-21   {having unrolled the scroll} "The Spirit of the Lord is upon me, because He has anointed me to proclaim good news to the poor. He has sent me to proclaim liberty to the captives and recovering of sight to the blind, to set at liberty those who are oppressed, to proclaim the year of the Lord's favour." Today this Scripture has been fulfilled in your hearing.

Luke 5: 10   {to Simon} Do not be afraid; from now on you will be catching men.

Matt 4: 19   {to the brothers, Simon and Andrew} Follow me and I will make you fishers of men.

CHAPTER 22

GIFTS

My Overall Message:

Please consider adding to your journal what you determine to be Jesus' overall message on this topic.

Luke 19: 12-19 A nobleman went into a far country to receive for himself a kingdom and then return. Calling ten of his servants, he gave them ten minas and said to them "Engage in business until I come." But his citizens hated him and sent a delegation after him, saying "We do not want this man to reign over us." When he returned, having received the kingdom, he ordered these servants to whom he had given the money to be called to him, that he might know what they had gained by doing business. The first came before him, saying "Lord, your mina has made ten minas more." And he said to him "Well done, good servant! Because you have been faithful in a very little, you shall have authority over ten cities." And the second came, saying "Lord, your mina has made five minas." And he said to him "And you are to be over five cities."

Luke 19: 20-27 Then another came, saying "Lord, here is your mina, which I kept laid away in a handkerchief; for I was afraid of you, because you are a severe man. You take what you did not deposit and reap what you did not sow." He said to him "I will condemn you with your own words, you wicked servant! You knew that I was a severe man, taking what I did not deposit and reaping what I did not sow? Why then did you not put my money in the bank and at my coming I might have collected it with interest?" And he said to those who stood by "Take the mina from him and give it to the one who has ten minas." And they said to him "Lord, he has ten minas!" "I tell you that to everyone who has, more will be given, but from the one who has not, even what he has will be taken away. But as for these enemies of mine, who did not want me to reign over them, bring them here and slaughter them before me."

Matt 25: 14-21 For it will be like a man going on a journey, who called his servants and entrusted to them his property. To one he gave five talents, to another two, to another one; to each according to his ability. Then he went away. He who had received the five talents went at once and traded with them and he made five talents more. So also he who had the two talents made two talents more. But he who had received the one talent went and dug in the ground and hid his master's money. Now after a long time the master of those servants came and settled accounts with them. And he who had received the five talents came forward, bringing five talents more, saying "Master, you delivered to me five talents; here I have made five talents more." His master said to him "Well done, good and faithful servant. You have been faithful over a little; I will set you over much. Enter into the joy of your master."

Matt 25: 22-23 And he also who had the two talents came forward, saying "Master, you delivered to me two talents; here I have made two talents more." His master said to him "Well done, good and faithful servant. You have been faithful over a little; I will set you over much. Enter into the joy of your master."

Matt 25: 24-30 He also who had received the one talent came forward, saying "Master, I knew you to be a hard man, reaping where you did not sow and gathering where you scattered no seed, so I was afraid and I went and hid your talent in the ground. Here you have what is yours." But the master answered him "You wicked and slothful servant! You knew that I reap where I have not sowed and gather where I scattered no seed? Then you ought to have invested my money with the bankers and at my coming I should have received what was my own with interest. So take the talent from him and give it to him who has the ten talents. For to everyone who has will more be given and he will have an abundance. But from the one who has not, even what he has will be taken away. And cast the worthless servant into the outer darkness. In that place there will be weeping and gnashing of teeth."

Luke 12: 47-48 And that servant who knew his master's will but did not get ready or act according to his will, will receive a severe beating. But the one who did not know and did what deserved a beating, will receive a light beating. Everyone to whom much was given, of him much will be required and from him to whom they entrusted much, they will demand the more.

CHAPTER 23

FEAR

My Overall Message:

Please consider adding to your journal what you determine to be Jesus' overall message on this topic.

Matt 6: 25-27 Therefore I tell you, do not be anxious about your life, what you will eat or what you will drink, nor about your body, what you will put on. Is not life more than food and the body more than clothing? Look at the birds of the air; they neither sow nor reap nor gather into barns and yet your heavenly Father feeds them. Are you not of more value than they? And which of you by being anxious can add a single hour to his span of life?

Matt 6: 28-34 And why are you anxious about clothing? Consider the lilies of the field, how they grow: they neither toil nor spin, yet I tell you, even Solomon in all his glory was not arrayed like one of these. But if God so clothes the grass of the field, which today is alive and tomorrow is thrown into the oven, will He not much more clothe you, O you of little faith? Therefore do not be anxious, saying "What shall we eat?" or "What shall we drink?" or "What shall we wear?" For the Gentiles seek after all these things and your heavenly Father knows that you need them all. But seek first the kingdom of God and His righteousness and all these things will be added to you. Therefore do not be anxious about tomorrow, for tomorrow will be anxious for itself. Sufficient for the day is its own trouble.

Luke 12: 22-26 Therefore I tell you, do not be anxious about your life, what you will eat, nor about your body, what you will put on. For life is more than food and the body more than clothing. Consider the ravens: they neither sow nor reap, they have neither storehouse nor barn and yet God feeds them. Of how much more value are you than the birds! And which of you by being anxious can add a single hour to his span of life? If then you are not able to do as small a thing as that, why are you anxious about the rest?

Luke 12: 27-31 Consider the lilies, how they grow: they neither toil nor spin, yet I tell you, even Solomon in all his glory was not arrayed like one of these. But if God so clothes the grass, which is alive in the field today and tomorrow is thrown into the oven, how much more will He clothe you, O you of little faith! And do not seek what you are to eat and what you are to drink, nor be worried. For all the nations of the world seek after these things and your Father knows that you need them. Instead, seek His kingdom and these things will be added to you.

Luke 12: 32-34 Fear not, little flock, for it is your Father's good pleasure to give you the kingdom. Sell your possessions and give to the needy. Provide yourselves with money bags that do not grow old, with a treasure in the heavens that does not fail, where no thief approaches and no moth destroys. For where your treasure is, there will your heart be also.

Luke 12: 4-7 I tell you, my friends, do not fear those who kill the body and after that have nothing more that they can do. But I will warn you whom to fear: fear him who, after he has killed, has authority to cast into hell. Yes, I tell you, fear him! Are not five sparrows sold for two pennies? And not one of them is forgotten before God. Why, even the hairs of your head are all numbered. Fear not; you are of more value than many sparrows.

Matt 10: 24-33 A disciple is not above his teacher, nor a servant above his master. It is enough for the disciple to be like his teacher and the servant like his master. If they have called the master of the house Beelzebul, how much more will they malign those of his household? So have no fear of them, for nothing is covered that will not be revealed, or hidden that will not be known. What I tell you in the dark, say in the light and what you hear whispered, proclaim on the housetops. And do not fear those who kill the body but cannot kill the soul. Rather fear him who can destroy both soul and body in hell. Are not two sparrows sold for a penny? And not one of them will fall to the ground apart from your Father. But even the hairs of your head are all numbered. Fear not, therefore; you are of more value than many sparrows. So everyone who acknowledges me before men, I also will acknowledge before my Father who is in heaven, but whoever denies me before men, I also will deny before my Father who is in heaven.

CHAPTER 24

SIGNS

My Overall Message:

Please consider adding to your journal what you determine to be Jesus' overall message on this topic.

Mark 8: 12   {to Pharisees demanding a sign} Why does this generation seek a sign? Truly, I say to you, no sign will be given to this generation.

Luke 11: 29-32   This generation is an evil generation. It seeks for a sign, but no sign will be given to it except the sign of Jonah. For as Jonah became a sign to the people of Nineveh, so will the Son of Man be to this generation. The queen of the South will rise up at the judgement with the men of this generation and condemn them, for she came from the ends of the earth to hear the wisdom of Solomon and behold, something greater than Solomon is here. The men of Nineveh will rise up at the judgement with this generation and condemn it, for they repented at the preaching of Jonah and behold, something greater than Jonah is here.

Matt 12: 39-42   An evil and adulterous generation seeks for a sign, but no sign will be given to it except the sign of the prophet Jonah. For just as Jonah was three days and three nights in the belly of the great fish, so will the Son of Man be three days and three nights in the heart of the earth. The men of Nineveh will rise up at the judgement with this generation and condemn it, for they repented at the preaching of Jonah and behold something greater than Jonah is here. The queen of the South will rise up at the judgement with this generation and condemn it, for she came from the ends of the earth to hear the wisdom of Solomon and behold, something greater than Solomon is here.

Matt 16: 2-4   When it is evening, you say, "It will be fair weather, for the sky is red." And in the morning, "It will be stormy today, for the sky is red and threatening." You know how to interpret the appearance of the sky, but you cannot interpret the signs of the times. An evil and adulterous generation seeks for a sign, but no sign will be given to it except the sign of Jonah.

Luke 12: 54-56   When you see a cloud rising in the west, you say at once "A shower is coming." And so it happens. And when you see the south wind blowing, you say, "There will be scorching heat," and it happens. You hypocrites! You know how to interpret the appearance of earth and sky, but why do you not know how to interpret the present time?

CHAPTER 25

LOVE

My Overall Message:

Please consider adding to your journal what you determine to be Jesus' overall message on this topic.

Mark 14: 6-9   {to the woman who anointed Jesus with expensive oil} Leave her alone. Why do you trouble her? She has done a beautiful thing to me. For you always have the poor with you and whenever you want, you can do good for them. But you will not always have me. She has done what she could; she has anointed my body beforehand for burial. And truly, I say to you, wherever the gospel is proclaimed in the whole world, what she has done will be told in memory of her.

Matt 26: 10-13   Why do you trouble the woman? For she has done a beautiful thing to me. For you always have the poor with you, but you will not always have me. In pouring this ointment on my body, she has done it to prepare me for burial. Truly, I say to you, wherever this gospel is proclaimed in the whole world, what she has done will also be told in memory of her.

John 12: 5-8   {Judas Iscariot: Why was this ointment not sold for three hundred denarii and given to the poor?} Leave her alone, so that she may keep it for the day of my burial. The poor you always have with you, but you do not always have me.

Luke 7: 41-50   A certain moneylender had two debtors. One owed five hundred denarii and the other fifty. When they could not pay, he cancelled the debt of both. Now which of them will love him more? Do you see this woman? I entered your house; you gave me no water for my feet, but she has wet my feet with her tears and wiped them with her hair. You gave me no kiss, but from the time I came in she has not ceased to kiss my feet. You did not anoint my head with oil, but she has anointed my feet with ointment. Therefore I tell you, her sins, which are many, are forgiven for she loved much. But he who is forgiven little, loves little. Your sins are forgiven. Your faith has saved you; go in peace.

Luke 10: 41-42 Martha, Martha, you are anxious and troubled about many things, but one thing is necessary. Mary has chosen the good portion, which will not be taken away from her.

CHAPTER 26

BELIEF

My Overall Message:

Please consider adding to your journal what you determine to be Jesus' overall message on this topic.

John 10: 24-30 {Jews: How long will You keep us in suspense? If You are the Christ, tell us plainly.} I told you and you do not believe. The works that I do in my Father's name bear witness about me, but you do not believe because you are not part of my flock. My sheep hear my voice and I know them and they follow me. I give them eternal life and they will never perish and no one will snatch them out of my hand. My Father who has given them to me is greater than all and no one is able to snatch them out of the Father's hand. I and the Father are one.

John 10: 32-38 I have shown you many good works from the Father; for which of them are you going to stone me? {Jews: It is not for a good work that we are going to stone You but for blasphemy, because You, being a man, make Yourself God.} Is it not written in your Law "I said, you are gods"? If he called them gods to whom the word of God came – and Scriptures cannot be broken – do you say of Him whom the Father consecrated and sent into the world "You are blaspheming," because I said, "I am the Son of God"? If I am not doing the works of my Father, then do not believe me; but if I do them, even though you do not believe me, believe the works, that you may know and understand that the Father is in me and I am in the Father.

John 7: 33-38 I will be with you a little longer and then I am going to Him who sent me. You will seek me and you will not find me. Where I am you cannot come. {Jews: Where does this man intend to go that we will not find Him? Does He intend to go to the Dispersion among the Greeks and teach the Greeks?} If anyone thirsts, let him come to me and drink. Whoever believes in me, as the Scripture has said "Out of his heart will flow rivers of living water."

CHAPTER 27

BREAD FROM HEAVEN

My Overall Message:

Please consider adding to your journal what you determine to be Jesus' overall message on this topic.

John 6: 26-34   Truly, truly, I say to you, you are seeking me, not because you saw signs, but because you ate your fill of the loaves. Do not labour for the food that perishes, but for the food that endures to eternal life, which the Son of Man will give to you. For on Him God the Father has set His seal. {Crowd: What must we do, to be doing the works of God?} This is the work of God that you believe in Him whom He has sent. {Crowd: Then what sign do You do, that we may see and believe You? What work do You perform? Our fathers ate the manna in the wilderness: as it is written, 'He gave them bread from heaven to eat.'} Truly, truly, I say to you, it was not Moses who gave you the bread from heaven, but my Father gives you the true bread from heaven. For the bread of God is He who comes down from heaven and gives life to the world. {Crowd: Sir, give us this bread always.}

John 6: 35-40   I am the bread of life; whoever comes to me shall not hunger and whoever believes in me shall never thirst. But I said to you that you have seen me and yet do not believe. All that the Father gives me will come to me and whoever comes to me I will never cast out. For I have come down from heaven, not to do my own will but the will of Him who sent me. And this is the will of Him who sent me that I should lose nothing of all that He has given me, but raise it up on the last day. For this is the will of my Father, that

114

everyone who looks on the Son and believes in Him should have eternal life and I will raise him up on the last day.

John 6: 42-51 {Jews: Is not this Jesus, the son of Joseph, whose father and mother we know? How does He now say, "I have come down from heaven"?} Do not grumble among yourselves. No one can come to me unless the Father who sent me draws him. And I will raise him up on the last day. It is written in the Prophets "And they will all be taught by God." Everyone who has heard and learned from the Father comes to me - not that anyone has seen the Father except He who is from God; He has seen the Father. Truly, truly, I say to you, whoever believes has eternal life. I am the bread of life. Your fathers ate the manna in the wilderness and they died. This is the bread that comes down from heaven, so that one may eat of it and not die. I am the living bread that came down from heaven. If anyone eats of this bread, he will live forever. And the bread that I will give for the life of the world is my flesh.

John 6: 52-58 {Jews: How can this man give us His flesh to eat?} Truly, truly, I say to you, unless you eat the flesh of the Son of Man and drink His blood, you have no life in you. Whoever feeds on my flesh and drinks my blood has eternal life and I will raise him up on the last day. For my flesh is true food and my blood is true drink. Whoever feeds on my flesh and drinks my blood abides in me and I in him. As the living Father sent me and I live because of the Father, so whoever feeds on me, he also will live because of me. This is the bread that came down from heaven, not as the fathers ate and died. Whoever feeds on this bread will live forever.

John 6: 60-70 {Disciples: This is a hard saying; who can listen to it?} Do you take offense at this? Then what if you were to see the Son of Man ascending to where He was before? It is the Spirit who gives life; the flesh is of no avail. The words that I have spoken to you are spirit and life. But there are some of you who do not believe. This is why I told you that no one can come to me unless it is granted him by

the Father. {after many disciples left Him, to the twelve}
Do you want to go away as well? {Peter: Lord, to whom
shall we go? You have the words of eternal life, and we
have believed, and have come to know, that You are the
Holy One of God.} Did I not choose you, the Twelve? And
yet one of you is a devil.

CHAPTER 28

DIVORCE

My Overall Message:

Please consider adding to your journal what you determine to be Jesus' overall message on this topic.

Mark 10: 3-12   What did Moses command you? {Pharisees: Moses allowed a man to write a certificate of divorce and to send her away.} Because of your hardness of heart he wrote you this commandment. But from the beginning of creation "God made them male and female. Therefore a man shall leave his father and mother and hold fast to his wife and they shall become one flesh." So they are no longer two but one flesh. What therefore God has joined together, let not man separate. Whoever divorces his wife and marries another commits adultery against her and if she divorces her husband and marries another, she commits adultery.

Matt 19: 4-12   Have you not read that He who created them from the beginning made them male and female and said, "Therefore a man shall leave his father and his mother and hold fast to his wife and they shall become one flesh"? So they are no longer two but one flesh. What therefore God has joined together, let not man separate. {Pharisees: Why then did Moses command one to give a certificate of divorce and to send her away?} Because of your hardness of heart Moses allowed you to divorce your wives, but from the beginning it was not so. And I say to you: whoever divorces his wife, except for sexual immorality and marries another, commits adultery. {Disciples: If such is the case of a man with his wife, it is better not to marry.} Not everyone can receive this saying, but only those to whom it is given. For there are eunuchs who have been so from birth and there are eunuchs who have been made eunuchs by men and there are eunuchs who have made themselves eunuchs for the sake of the kingdom of heaven. Let the one who is able to receive this receive it.

Matt 5: 31-32   If was also said "Whoever divorces his wife, let him give her a certificate of divorce." But I say to you that everyone who divorces his wife, except on the ground of sexual immorality, makes her commit adultery. And whoever marries a divorced woman commits adultery.

CHAPTER 29

CHILD-LIKE APPROACH

My Overall Message:

Please consider adding to your journal what you determine to be Jesus' overall message on this topic.

Luke 18: 16-17 Let the children come to me and do not hinder them, for to such belongs the kingdom of God. Truly, I say to you, whoever does not receive the kingdom of God like a child shall not enter it.

Mark 10: 14-16 {to disciples rebuking people bringing children to Jesus} Let the children come to me; do not hinder them, for to such belongs the kingdom of God. Truly, I say to you, whoever does not receive the kingdom of God like a child shall not enter it.

Matt 18: 3-6 Truly, I say to you, unless you turn and become like children, you will never enter the kingdom of heaven. Whoever humbles himself like this child is the greatest in the kingdom of heaven. Whoever receives one such child in my name receives me, but whoever causes one of these little ones who believe in me to sin, it would be better for him to have a great millstone fastened around his neck and to be drowned in the depth of the sea.

Matt 19: 14 Let the little children come to me and do not hinder them, for to such belongs the kingdom of heaven.

CHAPTER 30

RELATIONSHIPS IN HEAVEN

My Overall Message:

Please consider adding to your journal what you determine to be Jesus' overall message on this topic.

Luke 20: 34-38 The sons of this age marry and are given in marriage, but those who are considered worthy to attain to that age and to the resurrection from the dead neither marry nor are given in marriage, for they cannot die anymore, because they are equal to angels and are sons of God, being sons of the resurrection. But that the dead are raised, even Moses showed, in the passage about the bush, where he calls the Lord the God of Abraham and the God of Isaac and the God of Jacob. Now He is not God of the dead, but of the living, for all live to Him.

Matt 22: 29-32 You are wrong, because you know neither the Scriptures nor the power of God. For in the resurrection they neither marry nor are given in marriage, but are like angels in heaven. And as for the resurrection of the dead, have you not read what was said to you by God? "I am the God of Abraham and the God of Isaac and the God of Jacob"? He is not God of the dead, but of the living.

Mark 12: 24-27 Is this not the reason you are wrong, because you know neither the Scriptures nor the power of God? For when they rise from the dead, they neither marry nor are given in marriage, but are like angels in heaven. And as for the dead being raised, have you not read in the book of Moses, in the passage about the bush, how God spoke to him, saying "I am the God of Abraham and the God of Isaac and the God of Jacob."? He is not God of the dead, but of the living. You are quite wrong.

CHAPTER 31

HIGH PRIESTLY PRAYER

My Overall Message:

Please consider adding to your journal what you determine to be Jesus' overall message on this topic.

John 17: 1-10   Father, the hour has come; glorify Your Son that the Son may glorify You, since You have given Him authority over all flesh, to give eternal life to all whom You have given Him. And this is eternal life, that they know You the only true God and Jesus Christ whom You have sent. I glorified You on earth, having accomplished the work that You gave me to do. And now, Father, glorify me in Your own presence with the glory that I had with You before the world existed. I have manifested Your name to the people whom You gave me out of the world. Yours they were and You gave them to me and they have kept Your Word. Now they know that everything that You have given me is from You. For I have given them the words that You gave me and they have received them and have come to know in truth that I came from You; and they believed that You sent me. I am praying for them. I am not praying for the world but for those who You have given me, for they are Yours. All mine are Yours and Yours are mine and I am glorified in them.

John 17: 11-19   And I am no longer in the world, but they are in the world and I am coming to You. Holy Father, keep them in Your name, which You have given me that they may be one, even as we are one. While I was with them, I kept them in Your name, which You have given me. I have guarded them and not one of them has been lost except the son of destruction, that the Scripture might be fulfilled. But now I am coming to You and these things I speak in the world, that they may have my joy fulfilled in themselves. I have given them Your Word and the world has hated them because they are not of the world, just as I am not of the world. I do not ask that You take them out of the world, but that You keep them from the evil one. They are not of the world, just as I am not of the world. Sanctify them in the truth; Your Word is truth. As You sent me into the world, so I have sent them into the world. And for their sake I consecrate myself, that they also may be sanctified in truth.

John 17: 20-26 I do not ask for these only, but also for those who will believe in me through their word, that they may all be one, just as You, Father, are in me and I in You, that they also may be in us, so that the world may believe that You have sent me. The glory that You have given me I have given to them, that they may be one even as we are one, I in them and You in me, that they may become perfectly one, so that the world may know that You sent me and loved them even as You loved me. Father, I desire that they also, whom You have given me, may be with me where I am, to see my glory that You have given me because You loved me before the foundation of the world. O righteous Father, even though the world does not know You, I know You and these know that You have sent me. I made known to them Your name and I will continue to make it known, that the love with which You have loved me may be in them and I in them.

CHAPTER 32

PRODIGAL SON

My Overall Message:

Please consider adding to your journal what you determine to be Jesus' overall message on this topic.

Luke 15: 11-20 There was a man who had two sons. And the younger of them said to his father "Father, give me the share of property that is coming to me." And he divided his property between them. Not many days later, the younger son gathered all he had and took a journey into a far country and there he squandered his property in reckless living. And when he had spent everything, a severe famine arose in that country and he began to be in need. So he went and hired himself out to one of the citizens of that country, who sent him into his fields to feed pigs. And he was longing to be fed with the pods that the pigs ate and no one gave him anything. But when he came to himself, he said, "How many of my father's hired servants have more than enough bread, but I perish here with hunger! I will arise and go to my father and I will say to him, 'Father, I have sinned against heaven and before you. I am no longer worthy to be called your son. Treat me as one of your hired servants.'" And he arose and came to his father. But while he was still a long way off, his father saw him and felt compassion and ran and embraced him and kissed him.

Luke 15: 21-27 And the son said to him "Father, I have sinned against heaven and before you. I am no longer worthy to be called your son." But the father said to his servants "Bring quickly the best robe and put it on him and put a ring on his hand and shoes on his feet. And bring the fattened calf and kill it and let us eat and celebrate. For this my son was dead and is alive again; he was lost and is found." And they began to celebrate. Now his older son was in the field and as he came and drew near to the house, he heard music and dancing. And he called one of the servants and asked what these things meant. And he said to him "Your brother has come and your father has killed the fattened calf, because he has received him back safe and sound."

Luke 15: 28-32 But he was angry and refused to go in. His father came out and entreated him. But he answered his father "Look, these many years I have served you and I never disobeyed your command, yet you never gave me a young goat that I might celebrate with my friends. But when this son of yours came, who has devoured your property with prostitutes, you killed the fattened calf for him!" And he said to him "Son, you are always with me and all that is mine is yours. If was fitting to celebrate and be glad, for this your brother was dead and is alive; he was lost and is found."

CHAPTER 33

JUDGING

My Overall Message:

Please consider adding to your journal what you determine to be Jesus' overall message on this topic.

Luke 6: 37-38   Judge not and you will not be judged; condemn not and you will not be condemned; forgive and you will be forgiven; give and it will be given to you. Good measure, pressed down, shaken together, running over, will be put into your lap. For with the measure you use it will be measured back to you.

Luke 6: 39-42   Can a blind man lead a blind man? Will they not both fall into a pit? A disciple is not above his teacher, but everyone when he is fully trained will be like his teacher. Why do you see the speck that is in your brother's eye, but do not notice the log that is in your own eye? How can you say to your brother "Brother, let me take out the speck that is in your eye," when you yourself do not see the log that is in your own eye? You hypocrite, first take the log out of your own eye and then you will see clearly to take out the speck that is in your brother's eye.

Matt 7: 1-5   Judge not, that you be not judged. For with the judgement you pronounce you will be judged and with the measure you use it will be measured to you. Why do you see the speck that is in your brother's eye, but do not notice the log that is in your own eye? Or how can you say to your brother "Brother, let me take the speck out of your eye, when there is the log in your own eye? You hypocrite, first take the log out of your own eye and then you will see clearly to take the speck out of your brother's eye.

125

CHAPTER 34

CLEANSING THE TEMPLE

My Overall Message:

Please consider adding to your journal what you determine to be Jesus' overall message on this topic.

Luke 19: 46   It is written "My house shall be a house of prayer," but you have made it a den of robbers.

Mark 11: 17   {after driving out sellers, buyers, money changers and pigeon sellers} Is it not written "My house shall be called a house of prayer for all the nations"? But you have made it a den of robbers.

Matt 21: 13-16   It is written "My house shall be called a house of prayer", but you make it a den of robbers. {Children: Hosanna to the Son of David!} {Priests and scribes: Do You hear what these are saying?} Yes, have you never read "Out of the mouth of infants and nursing babies you have prepared praise"?

John 2: 16-19   Take these things away; do not make my Father's house a house of trade. {Jews: What sign do You show us for doing these things?} Destroy this temple and in three days I will raise it up.

CHAPTER 35

BEATITUDES

My Overall Message:

Please consider adding to your journal what you determine to be Jesus' overall message on this topic.

Luke 6: 20-23 Blessed are you who are poor, for yours is the kingdom of God. Blessed are you who are hungry now, for you shall be satisfied. Blessed are you who weep now, for you shall laugh. Blessed are you when people hate you and when they exclude you and revile you and spurn your name as evil, on account of the Son of Man! Rejoice in that day and leap for joy, for behold, your reward is great in heaven; for so their fathers did to the prophets.

Luke 6: 24-26 But woe to you who are rich, for you have received your consolation. Woe to you who are full now, for you shall be hungry. Woe to you who laugh now, for you shall mourn and weep. Woe to you, when all people speak well of you, for so their fathers did to the false prophets.

Matt 5: 3-12 Blessed are the poor in spirit, for theirs is the kingdom of heaven. Blessed are those who mourn for they shall be comforted. Blessed are the meek, for they shall inherit the earth. Blessed are those who hunger and thirst for righteousness, for they shall be satisfied. Blessed are the merciful, for they shall receive mercy. Blessed are the pure in heart, for they shall see God. Blessed are the peacemakers, for they shall be called sons of God. Blessed are those who are persecuted for righteousness' sake, for theirs is the kingdom of heaven. Blessed are you when others revile you and persecute you and utter all kinds of evil against you falsely on my account. Rejoice and be glad, for your reward is great in heaven, for so they persecuted the prophets who were before you.

CHAPTER 36

REMAINING TOPICS

My Notes on the Remaining Topics:

Please consider adding these notes to your journal.

Least and Greatest

Luke 9: 46-48 {to the disciples, arguing over who is the greatest, Jesus takes up a child} Whoever receives this child in my name receives me and whoever receives me receives Him who sent me. For he who is least among you all is the one who is great.

Luke 22: 25-30 The kings of the Gentiles exercise lordship over them and those in authority over them are called benefactors. But not so with you. Rather, let the greatest among you become as the youngest and the leader as one who serves. For who is the greater, one who reclines at table or one who serves? Is it not the one who reclines at table? But I am among you as the one who serves. You are those who have stayed with me in my trials and I assign to you, as my Father assigned to me, a kingdom, that you may eat and drink at my table in my kingdom and sit on thrones judging the twelve tribes of Israel.

Mark 9: 35-37 If anyone would be first, he must be last of all and servant of all. Whoever receives one such child in my name receives me and whoever receives me, receives not me but Him who sent me.

John the Baptist

Luke 7: 24-28   What did you go out into the wilderness to see? A reed shaken by the wind? What then did you go out to see? A man dressed in soft clothing? Behold, those who are dressed in splendid clothing and live in luxury are in king's courts. What then did you go out to see? A prophet? Yes, I tell you and more than a prophet. This is he of whom it is written "Behold, I send my messenger before your face, who will prepare your way before you." I tell you, among those born of women none is greater than John. Yet the one who is least in the kingdom of God is greater than he.

Matt 11: 7-11   What did you go out into the wilderness to see? A reed shaken by the wind? What then did you go out to see? A man dressed in soft clothing? Behold, those who wear soft clothing are in kings' houses. What then did you go out to see? A prophet? Yes I tell you and more than a prophet. This is he of whom it is written "Behold I send my messenger before your face, who will prepare your way before you." Truly, I say to you, among those born of women there has arisen no one greater than John the Baptist. Yet the one who is least in the kingdom of heaven is greater than he.

Good Shepherd

John 10: 1-11   Truly, truly, I say to you, he who does not enter the sheepfold by the door but climbs in by another way, that man is a thief and a robber. But he who enters by the door is the shepherd of the sheep. To him the gatekeeper opens. The sheep hear his voice and he calls his own sheep by name and leads them out. When he has brought out all his own, he goes before them and the sheep follow him, for they know his voice. A stranger they will not follow, but they will flee from him, for they do not know the voice of strangers. Truly, truly, I say to you, I am the door of the sheep. All who came before me are thieves and robbers, but the sheep did not listen to them. I am the door. If anyone enters by me, he will be saved and will go in and out and find pasture. The thief comes only to steal and kill and destroy. I came that they may have life and have it abundantly. I am the good shepherd. The good shepherd lays down his life for the sheep.

John 10: 12-18 He who is a hired hand and not a shepherd, who does not own the sheep, sees the wolf coming and leaves the sheep and flees and the wolf snatches them and scatters them. He flees because he is a hired hand and cares nothing for the sheep. I am the good shepherd. I know my own and my own know me, just as the Father knows me and I know the Father; and I lay down my life for the sheep. And I have other sheep that are not of this fold. I must bring them also and they will listen to my voice. So there will be one flock, one shepherd. For this reason the Father loves me, because I lay down my life that I may take it up again. No one takes it from me, but I lay it down of my own accord. I have authority to lay it down and I have authority to take it up again. This charge I have received from my Father.

Son of God

Luke 20: 41-44 How can they say that the Christ is David's son? For David himself says in the book of Psalms "The Lord said to my Lord, Sit at my right hand, until I make your enemies your footstool." David thus calls Him Lord, so how is He his son?

Mark 12: 35-37 How can the scribes say that the Christ is the son of David? David himself, in the Holy Spirit, declared, "The Lord said to my Lord, Sit at my right hand, until I put your enemies under your feet." David himself calls Him Lord. So how is He his son?

Matt 22: 42-45 What do you think about the Christ? Whose son is He? {Pharisees: The son of David.} How is it then that David, in the Spirit, calls Him Lord, saying "The Lord said to my Lord, Sit at my right hand, until I put your enemies under your feet"? If then David calls Him Lord, how is He his son?

Temptation

Luke 4: 4   {to the devil's temptation} It is written "Man shall not live by bread alone."

Luke 4: 8   {to the devil's temptation} It is written "You shall worship the Lord your God and Him only shall you serve."

Luke 4: 12   {to the devil's temptation} It is said, "You shall not put the Lord your God to the test."

Matt 4: 4-10   {to the devil's temptation} It is written "Man shall not live by bread alone, but by every word that comes from the mouth of God." Again it is written "You shall not put the Lord your God to the test." Be gone, Satan! For it is written "You shall worship the Lord your God and Him only shall you serve."

Forgiveness

Matt 18: 21-27 {Peter: Lord, how often will my brother sin against me and I forgive him? As many as seven times?} I do not say to you seven times, but seventy times seven. Therefore the kingdom of heaven may be compared to a king who wished to settle accounts with his servants. When he began to settle, one was brought to him who owed him ten thousand talents. And since he could not pay, his master ordered him to be sold, with his wife and children and all that he had and payment to be made. So the servant fell on his knees, imploring him "Have patience with me and I will pay you everything." And out of pity for him, the master of that servant released him and forgave him the debt.

Matt 18: 28-35 But when that same servant went out, he found one of his fellow servants who owed him a hundred denarii and seizing him, he began to choke him, saying "Pay what you owe." So his fellow servant fell down and pleaded with him "Have patience with me and I will pay you." He refused and went and put him in prison until he should pay the debt. When his fellow servants saw what had taken place, they were greatly distressed and they went and reported to their master all that had taken place. Then his master summoned him and said to him "You wicked servant! I forgave you all that debt because you pleaded with me. And should not you have had mercy on your fellow servant, as I had mercy on you?" And in anger his master delivered him to the jailers, until he should pay all his debt. So also my heavenly Father will do to every one of you, if you do not forgive your brother from your heart.

False Prophets

Matt 7: 15-20   Beware of the false prophets, who come to you in sheep's clothing but inwardly are ravenous wolves. You will recognize them by their fruits. Are grapes gathered from thorn bushes, or figs from thistles? So, every healthy tree bears good fruit, but the diseased tree bears bad fruit. A healthy tree cannot bear bad fruit, nor can a diseased tree bear good fruit. Every tree that does not bear good fruit is cut down and thrown into the fire. Thus you will recognize them by their fruits.

Luke 6: 43-45   For no good tree bears bad fruit, nor again does a bad tree bear good fruit, for each tree is known by its own fruit. For figs are not gathered from thorn bushes, nor are grapes picked from a bramble bush. The good person out of the good treasure of his heart produces good and the evil person out of his evil treasure produces evil, for out of the abundance of the heart his mouth speaks.

Jesus Calls His Disciples

John 1: 38-42   What are you seeking? {John's disciples: Rabbi, where are You staying?} Come and you will see. {looking at Andrew's brother, Simon Peter} So you are Simon the son of John? You shall be called Cephas (Peter).

133

John 1: 43-51   {finding Philip on the way to Galilee} Follow me. {Nathaniel in reply to Philip: Can anything good come out of Nazareth?} Behold, an Israelite indeed, in whom there is no deceit! {Nathaniel: How do You know me?} Before Philip called you, when you were under the fig tree, I saw you. {Nathaniel: Rabbi, You are the Son of God! You are the King of Israel!} Because I said to you "I saw you under the fig tree," do you believe? You will see greater things than these. Truly, truly, I say to you, you will see heaven opened and the angels of God ascending and descending on the Son of Man.

Matt 4: 19   {to Simon and Andrew} Follow me and I will make you fishers of men.

Washing the Disciples' Feet

John 13: 6-10   {Peter: Lord, do You wash my feet?} What I am doing you do not understand now, but afterward you will understand. {Peter: You shall never wash my feet.} If I do not wash you, you have no share with me. {Peter: Lord, not my feet only but also my hands and my head!} The one who has bathed does not need to wash, except for his feet, but is completely clean. And you are clean, but not every one of you.

John 13: 12-20   Do you understand what I have done to you? You call me Teacher and Lord and you are right, for so I am. If I then, your Lord and your Teacher, have washed your feet, you also ought to wash one another's feet. For I have given you an example, that you also should do just as I have done to you. Truly, truly, I say to you, a servant is not greater than his master, nor is a messenger greater than the one who sent him. If you know these things, blessed are you if you do them. I am not speaking of all of you; I know whom I have chosen. But the Scripture will be fulfilled: "He who ate my bread has lifted his heel against me." I am telling you this now, before it takes place, that when it does take place you may believe that I am He. Truly, truly, I say to you, whoever receives the one I send receives me and whoever receives me receives the one who sent me.

Mother and Brothers

Luke 8: 21   My mother and my brothers are those who hear the Word of God and do it.

Mark 3: 32-35   {Crowd: Your mother and Your brothers are outside, seeking You.} Who are my mother and my brothers? Here are my mother and my brothers! Whoever does the will of God, he is my brother and sister and mother.

Build My Church

Matt 16: 13-19 Who do people say that the Son of Man is? But who do you say that I am? {Peter: You are the Christ, the Son of the living God.} Blessed are you, Simon Bar-Jonah! For flesh and blood has not revealed this to you, but my Father who is in heaven. And I tell you, you are Peter and on this rock I will build my church and the gates of hell shall not prevail against it. I will give you the keys of the kingdom of heaven and whatever you bind on earth shall be bound in heaven and whatever you loose on earth shall be loosed in heaven.

Mark 8: 27-29   Who do people say that I am? {Disciples: John the Baptist; and other say, Elijah; and others, one of the prophets.} But who do you say that I am? {Peter You are the Christ.}

Ministry Beginnings

Matt 4: 17   {at the start of Jesus' ministry} Repent, for the kingdom of heaven is at hand.

Accountability

Matt 12: 33-37 Either make the tree good and its fruit good, or make the tree bad and its fruit bad, for the tree is known by its fruit. You brood of vipers! How can you speak good, when you are evil? For out of the abundance of the heart the mouth speaks. The good person out of his good treasure brings forth good and the evil person out of

135

his evil treasure brings forth evil. I tell you, on the day of judgement people will give account for every careless word they speak, for by your words you will be justified and by your words you will be condemned.

Temptation Avoidance

Matt 18: 7-9   Woe to the world for temptations to sin! For it is necessary that temptations come, but woe to the one by whom the temptation comes! And if your hand or your foot causes you to sin, cut it off and throw it away. It is better for you to enter life crippled or lame than with two hands or two feet to be thrown into the eternal fire. And if your eye causes you to sin, tear it out and throw it away. It is better for you to enter life with one eye than with two eyes to be thrown into the hell of fire.

Oaths

Matt 5: 33-37   Again you have heard that it was said to those of old "You shall not swear falsely, but shall perform to the Lord what you have sworn." But I say to you, Do not take an oath at all, either by heaven, for it is the throne of God, or by the earth, for it is His footstool, or by Jerusalem, for it is the city of the great King. And do not take an oath by your head, for you cannot make one hair white or black. Let what you say be simply "Yes" or "No"; Anything more than this comes from evil.

Division versus Peace

Luke 12: 49-53   I came to cast fire on the earth and would that it were already kindled! I have a baptism to be baptised with and how great is my distress until it is accomplished! Do you think that I have come to give peace on earth? No, I tell you, but rather division. For from now on in one house there will be five divided, three against two and two against three. They will be divided, father against son and son against father, mother against daughter and daughter against mother, mother-in-law against her daughter-in-law and daughter-in-law against mother-in-law.

Feast of Booths

John 7: 3-8   {Jesus' brothers: Leave here and go to Judea that Your disciples also may see the works You are doing. For no one works in secret if he seeks to be known openly. If You do these things, show Yourself to the world. For not even His brothers believed in Him.} My time has not yet come, but your time is always here. The world cannot hate you, but it hates me because I testify about it that its works are evil. You go up to the feast. I am not going up to this feast, for my time has not yet fully come.

Rewards

Matt 10: 40-42 Whoever receives you receives me and whoever receives me receives Him who sent me. The one who receives a prophet because he is a prophet will receive a prophet's reward and the one who receives a righteous person because he is a righteous person will receive a righteous person's reward. And whoever gives one of these little ones even a cup of cold water because he is a disciple, truly, I say to you, he will by no means lose his reward.

Baptism by John

Matt 3: 14-15   {John: I need to be baptized by you and do you come to me?} Let it be so now, for thus it is fitting for us to fulfill all righteousness.

Dogs What Is Holy

Matt 7: 6   Do not give dogs what is holy and do not throw your pearls before pigs, lest they trample them underfoot and turn to attack you.

CONCLUSION

Having completed your study of *THE SAYINGS OF JESUS* you are now very likely ready to discern His overall message. As you read in the Introduction, you have reminders here to try out my process of doing it. Following these reminders you will find my example of my process. As you'll see, I copied the underlined portions of each topic message onto the first of the two pages and assembled them onto the second.

My Highlights of Jesus' Messages by Topic

Please consider listing, on one page of your journal, the underlined parts of each of the topic messages which you have discerned.

My Discernment of Jesus' Overall Message

Please consider combining, on the next page of your journal, the under-lined parts of your topic messages into a few paragraphs that you discern to be Jesus' overall message.

Author's Highlights of Jesus' Message in Each of the Fifteen Most Important Topics

The first step in my discernment of Jesus' overall message was to list, on one page, for each of the fifteen most important topics, the parts of their messages that I had underlined.

- Jesus was a man.
- I must love Jesus more than anyone. I am fully accountable.
- Jesus was God Incarnate.

- I will be judged at the moment of my death as one of the few sheep or one of the many goats.
- I must love my enemies and use my gifts to help those who cannot repay me.
- I must grow my faith in my prayers for God's help in accomplishing whatever Jesus demands of me.
- Eternal life with God is far beyond what I can imagine and to realize it, I must respond to His invitation and adequately prepare for it.
- I must increase *my* righteousness and avoid judgement of others.
- I must proactively seek to understand the Word of God and commit to correct each failure to act on it.
- I need to discern what, of what I read and hear, is consistent with what I am taught by Jesus.
- I reject Jesus whenever I put my will ahead of God's will. I will have no excuse.
- *Professing* a love of Jesus is not enough. I must *do* what He insists upon.
- The miracles Jesus performed were real.
- I must share the gifts of which I am God's steward, not merely more than others do but as much as I am able.

Author's Discernment of Jesus' Overall Message

The second step was to combine the underlined parts into what I felt they showed to be Jesus' overall message.

> Jesus was a man. The miracles Jesus performed were real. Jesus was God Incarnate.
>
> Eternal life with God is far beyond what I can imagine and to realize it, I must respond to His invitation and adequately prepare for it. I need to discern what, of what I read and hear, is consistent with what I am taught by Jesus. *Professing* a love of Jesus is not enough. I must *do* what He insists upon.
>
> I must love my enemies and use my gifts to help those who cannot repay me. I must increase *my* righteousness and avoid judgement of others. I must share the gifts of which I am God's steward, not merely more than others do but as much as I am able.

I must proactively seek to understand the Word of God and commit to correct each failure to act on it. I must grow my faith in my prayers for God's help in accomplishing whatever Jesus demands of me. I reject Jesus whenever I put my will ahead of God's will. I will have no excuse. I must love Jesus more than anyone. I am fully accountable. I will be judged at the moment of my death as one of the few sheep or one of the many goats.

Experiential Learning

THE SAYINGS OF JESUS is the textbook of a process called *Experiential Learning*.

Experiential Learning is a means of re-examining and evaluating your assertions, ideas and beliefs. It is a process for discerning what you can learn from each major interaction that has made up your life on Earth. The interactions you experienced include people, events and readings. Each will have given you the opportunity for considerable reflection. Your reflection on each of them will lead you, in most cases, to one or more learnings. Taken as a whole, these learnings will help you to arrive at sound and supported knowledge of life's purpose.

Experiential Learning is fully described in a sister book entitled *Discovering* LIFE'S PURPOSE – RE-EXAMINING *THE CLUB*. This book – *THE SAYINGS OF JESUS* – is the Appendix of this sister book.

If you ever decide to undertake *Experiential Learning*, I'm sure you will find it a fascinating, challenging and rewarding course of study. Every day, I say a prayer for you that you feel God's call to you to return to *THE SAYINGS OF JESUS* from time to time and to undertake *Experiential Learning*.

The Research that Produced *THE SAYINGS OF JESUS* (for nerds only)

Figure 1, on the final two pages of this book, presents a summary spread-sheet showing the results of the research that produced *THE SAYINGS OF JESUS*. Columns three and four list the *# of words* and *# of quotes* in each topic Jesus is quoted as having addressed. Columns five and six list the *words rank* and the *quotes rank* of each topic (which you may notice are simply sorts by columns three and four respectively). Column seven lists the sum of the *words rank* and *quotes rank*. Finally, column two is the *topic rank* (which is a simple sequencing of the *rank sum* from lowest to highest).

The chapters of THE SAYINGS OF JESUS were sequenced by *topic rank*. Let's look a bit further at how each column of this summary spreadsheet was populated.

To produce columns three and four, it was first necessary to determine the *# of words* each topic contained. Excel had already calculated the *# of words* in each *quote* in the *overall* spreadsheet. Sorting this overall spreadsheet by topic permitted Excel to calculate the *# of words* and *# of quotes* in each *topic* to populate this *summary* spreadsheet.

To produce columns five and six, I then sorted this *summary* spreadsheet by the *# of words* such that the topic with the most *# of words* came first and the topic with the least *# of words* came last. I then assigned a *words rank* to each topic such that the topic with the most *# of words* was assigned a *words rank* of 1 and the topic with the least *# of words* was assigned a rank of 55. With this done, I re-sorted this spreadsheet by the *# of quotes* and assigned a *quotes rank* to each topic in the same way as I had done with the prior sort.

To produce column seven, I then summed these two rankings to produce a *rank sum* for each topic. Summing the *words rank* and the *quotes rank* was my way of combining these two criteria of importance. For example, because *Discipleship* had a *words rank* of 3 and a *quotes rank* of 2, I assigned it a *rank sum* of 5.

To produce column two, I simply sorted the summary spreadsheet by *rank sum*. For example, *Passion and Death's rank sum* and *Discipleship's rank sum* were each 5. Because 5 was the lowest *ranks sum*, I assigned them a *topic rank* of 1 and 2 respectively.

The *topic rank* of the remainder of the 55 topics was similarly assigned. I sequenced the chapters of THE SAYINGS OF JESUS by *topic rank*.

Finally, I did an analysis of the spreadsheet to identify the *focus* of Jesus' message. To accomplish this, Excel calculated *cumulative* sums for each topic. For example, the 2950 words of *Passion and Death* added to the 2981 words of *Discipleship* produced a *cumulative words sum* of 5931 for *Discipleship* (2950+2981). Similarly the 40 quotes of *Passion and Death* added to the 29 quotes of *Discipleship* produced a *cumulative quotes sum* of 69 (40+29) for *Discipleship*.

If you feel like doing the math for the next topic, *Authority*, you'll discover its *cumulative words sum* is 8950 (5931+3019) and its *cumulative quotes sum* is 92 (69+23). If you trust the spreadsheet and don't feel like doing any more math, you can see that continuing this process right through to the lowest ranked topic, *Dogs What is Holy*, produces the last row of the summary spreadsheet which shows an *overall cumulative words sum* of almost 41,000 and an *overall cumulative quotes sum* of almost 400.

The bold-titled rows of the summary spreadsheet show how the cumulative sums determine Jesus' focus.

Calculating the percentages, that the cumulative sums of the first five topics are of the overall cumulative sums of all 55 topics, shows that these first five topics cover over a third of all Jesus is quoted as having said. The percentages of the cumulative sums of the next ten topics show they do as well.

Is it not striking that the percentages of the cumulative sums of the remaining 40 topics cover less than a third of all Jesus is quoted as having said?

Taking the highest ranking fifteen topics as a group, you can see that they represent over two thirds of all Jesus said. To me, this shows that they cover what Jesus considered the most important parts of His message.

Figure 1

The Sayings of Jesus

TOPIC	TOPIC RANK	# OF WORDS	# OF QUOTES	WORDS RANK	QUOTES RANK	RANK SUM
PASSION AND DEATH	1	2950	40	4	1	5
DISCIPLESHIP	2	2981	29	3	2	5
AUTHORITY	3	3019	23	2	4	6
CLOSE OF THE AGE	4	3173	22	1	5	6
GUIDANCE	5	2551	21	5	6	11
1ST THIRD CUMULATIVE SUM		14674	135			
1ST THIRD % OF OVERALL		35.9%	34.4%			
FAITH	6	1308	29	11	3	14
KINGDOM OF GOD	7	1752	14	7	8	15
LAWS	8	1443	19	9	7	16
PREPAREDNESS	9	1925	11	6	12	18
PHARISEES ET AL	10	1313	14	10	9	19
REJECTING JESUS	11	1679	11	8	13	21
SALVATION	12	1287	9	12	15	27
MIRACLES	13	729	13	18	10	28
RICHES	14	1241	9	13	16	29
COMMANDMENTS	15	1051	6	14	19	33
2ND THIRD CUMULATIVE SUM		13728	135			
2ND THIRD % OF OVERALL		33.6%	34.4%			

TOPIC	TOPIC RANK	# OF WORDS	# OF QUOTES	WORDS RANK	QUOTES RANK	RANK SUM
DEATH AND RESURRECTION FORETOLD	16	712	11	20	14	34
HEALING	17	472	12	25	11	36
RESURRECTION	18	729	8	19	18	37
HOLY SPIRIT	19	865	4	15	23	38
FASTING	20	574	5	23	20	43
MISSION	21	360	9	27	17	44
GIFTS	22	805	3	16	28	44
FEAR	23	709	4	21	24	45
SIGNS	24	413	5	26	21	47
LOVE	25	349	5	30	22	52
BELIEF	26	357	3	28	29	57
BREAD FROM HEAVEN	27	783	1	17	41	58
DIVORCE	28	299	3	32	30	62
CHILD-LIKE APPROACH	29	201	4	38	25	63
RELATIONSHIPS IN HEAVEN	30	285	3	33	31	64
HIGH PRIESTLY PRAYER	31	611	1	22	42	64
PRODIGAL SON	32	490	1	24	43	67
JUDGING	33	283	2	34	34	68
CLEANSING THE TEMPLE	34	137	4	43	26	69
BEATITUDES	35	281	2	35	35	70
LEAST AND GREATEST	36	198	3	39	32	71
JOHN THE BAPTIST	37	233	2	37	36	73
GOOD SHEPHERD	38	353	1	29	44	73
SON OF GOD	39	157	3	41	33	74
TEMPTATION	40	96	4	49	27	76
FORGIVENESS	41	303	1	31	45	76
FALSE PROPHETS	42	161	2	40	37	77
JESUS CALLS HIS DISCIPLES	43	153	3	42	38	80
WASHING THE DISCIPLES' FEET	44	257	1	36	46	82
MOTHER AND BROTHERS	45	54	2	52	39	91
BUILD MY CHURCH	46	110	1	44	47	91
MINISTRY BEGINNINGS	47	38	2	53	40	93
ACCOUNTABILITY	48	107	1	45	48	93
TEMPTATION AVOIDANCE	49	106	1	46	49	95
OATHS	50	104	1	47	50	97
DIVISION VS PEACE	51	97	1	48	51	99
FEAST OF BOOTHS	52	95	1	50	52	102
REWARDS	53	82	1	51	53	104
BAPTISM BY JOHN	54	29	1	54	54	108
DOGS WHAT IS HOLY	55	25	1	55	55	110
3RD THIRD CUMULATIVE SUM		12473	123			
3RD THIRD % OF OVERALL		30.5%	31.3%			
OVERALL CUMULATIVE SUM		40875	393			

CPSIA information can be obtained
at www.ICGtesting.com
Printed in the USA
BVHW091312061022
648825BV00013B/293